Willie Maley
THE MAN WHO MADE
CELTIC

Willie Maley
THE MAN WHO MADE
CELTIC

DAVID W. POTTER

TEMPUS

First published 2003
This edition published 2004

Tempus Publishing Limited
The Mill, Brimscombe Port,
Stroud, Gloucestershire, GL5 2QG

British Library Cataloguing in Publication Data.
A catalogue record for this book is available from the British Library.

ISBN 0 7524 3229 X

Typesetting and origination by Tempus Publishing Limited
Printed in Great Britain by Midway Colour Print, Wiltshire

CONTENTS

To anyone who ever has, or ever intends to, wear the green, or who has any kind of interest in Scottish football.

ACKNOWLEDGEMENTS

This book owes absolutely everything to the research done by two great Celtic historians – Pat Woods, who lent me his magnificent scrapbook of Willie Maley, and Eugene MacBride, who with meticulous scholarship has amassed a collection of detail on every game ever played by Celtic Football Club. In addition, I have been encouraged and supported by Tom Campbell and George Sheridan, and I also owe a great deal to the librarians in the Wellgate Library in Dundee with its massive collection of newspapers. Willy Maley (no relation) of Glasgow University was also very supportive.

THE AUTHOR

David Potter is a teacher of Classics and Spanish, and lives happily in Kirkcaldy with his wife. He has three children, all of whom have now grown up and left the nest. His hobbies are football, cricket, drama, the poetry of Burns and walking his beloved dog. He is an unashamed lover of Glasgow Celtic and Forfar Athletic. He writes in *The Alternative View* and Forfar Athletic's programme.

PREVIOUS WORKS
Our Bhoys Have Won The Cup
Jock Stein – The Celtic Years (in collaboration with Tom Campbell)
The Encyclopedia of Scottish Cricket
The Mighty Atom – The Life and Times of Patsy Gallacher
Wee Troupie – The Life and Times of Alec Troup
Celtic in The League Cup

INTRODUCTION

Why, man, he doth bestride the narrow world
Like a Colossus; and we petty men
Walk under his huge legs, and peep about
To find ourselves dishonourable graves

So says Cassius of Julius Caesar, according to William Shakespeare. In such a way we must consider Willie Maley in the context of the early years of Celtic Football Club and indeed of Scottish football.

How much Maley contributed to Celtic can probably be summed up in the phrase 'Willie Maley – he is Celtic'. There could certainly have been no Celtic without him, and a glance at today's magnificent stadium – an awesome sight when full – will show how much Celtic means to so many people in Glasgow, Scotland and beyond. None of this would have happened had it not been for the vision and energy of Willie Maley.

Let us step into the imaginary world of what would have happened if there had been no Willie Maley at Celtic, if he had said that fateful night 'No, I'm going to stick to athletics' or 'No, I'll play football for Third Lanark instead.' We would in 2003 see Scottish football as a minority sport, played on a part-time semi-professional basis with such good players as there were being enticed away to play for some English or European team. Occasionally an able Scotsman like Murdoch, Baxter or Dalglish might make his way into the Great Britain team.

Thankfully, there would have been no sectarian chants from the small crowds at football games, but something far worse than that might have occurred. The British Government would have been compelled to spend an inordinate amount of money to deal with the 'ethnic Irish' problem of Scotland, brought to the fore by the many reports which highlighted the amount of 'shiftless young men of Irish extraction in Glasgow and the surrounding area' with little to do to amuse them. 'A disaffected, disillusioned cultural minority have convinced themselves of their own inferiority' would read one report and another would have said 'The Irish in Scotland have little to rally them or to inspire them.'

Violence would flare from time to time. The Rebellion of 1943, for example, remains a blot on the Irish in Scotland, giving as it did so much encouragement to Hitler. The George Square Bombings of 1967 saw many deaths and brutal repression by the British Army. Thankfully, this seemed by the early years of the twenty-first century to have eased. Yet the problem remained. If there was only some way in which the Irish could be culturally assimilated into Scottish society…

This is what Scotland might have been like without Willie Maley. Any argument about who the greatest Celt of all time was is totally pointless. Had it not been for Willie Maley, there would have been no Celtic (and therefore no Rangers either). Jimmy Quinn, Patsy Gallacher, Jimmy McGrory, Jock Stein and even today's Martin O'Neill and Henrik Larsson owe absolutely everything to this man – Willie Maley, the man who made Celtic.

One

BIRTH AND ORIGINS

William Patrick Maley was born on 25 April 1868 at army barracks in Newry in what is now Northern Ireland. In those days, of course, it was all called Ireland and the whole of the Emerald Isle was seen as a much loved but occasionally wayward scion of the British Empire. It was, indeed, this waywardness which necessitated an occupational force: trouble had never been far away throughout the eighteenth century and there had been a major rebellion in 1797 and 1798. 1828 had seen Catholic Emancipation but no end to the troubles. A major rebellion had been threatened in 1848, following the Great Famine – hence the presence of the British Army.

William was the third son of Thomas Maley (sometimes called O'Maley, O'Malley or Malley), who was a sergeant in the Royal North British Fusiliers. Thus although Willie (as he was almost always called) Maley was born in Ireland, his origins were anything but Fenian – quite the opposite in fact. Thomas Maley was himself an Irishman from Ennis in County Clare. He was from farming stock, born the son of Charles O'Malley, a farmer, and Susan McNamara in 1830, but had joined the British Army because he saw it as a good career opportunity. He was possibly quite ambivalent about the Irish problem. He was in no doubt about what the British had done to his country – he had been alive in Ireland at the time of the Great Famine, although it had not affected him or his family personally. He also knew all about the evils of the absentee landlords, the high rents and the sheer naked exploitation of the resources of his land.

On the other hand, he did not see the violence of the Fenians or the other wild men of his country as any sort of answer. He probably did believe that the solution to Ireland's problems lay in some sort of separation from Britain, but this would have to come gradually and with consent and agreement, taking into account the feelings of the Protestant Orangemen of the North who were also, after all, Irishmen. In the meantime, joining the Army – although occasionally attracting the unwelcome accusations of being 'disloyal' and even 'a traitor' to the Irish cause – was a good career.

His career in the British Army did on occasion conflict with his conscience. He was quite happy to serve Queen Victoria in the Crimea, the West Indies, Malta, Canada, India or any other place that they put him, but when it came to his own country, he was not quite so sure. Once or twice he knew he had been less than totally enthusiastic in his pursuit of Fenian terrorists. So far he had managed to avoid any great clash between job and conscience – except once – but these were not easy times for Ireland, nor for Irishmen serving in the British Army.

Ireland itself was forever, it was believed, on the cusp of another rebellion and in 1867, the year before Willie's birth, violence had spread to the mainland of Great Britain. March of that year had seen what became known as the Manchester Martyrs incident when an attempt had been made to release two Fenians from a prison van in Manchester, and blood had been spilt. Worse than that occurred at Clerkenwell Prison on 13 December 1867 when thirteen people were killed in a bomb outrage.

Sergeant Maley's clash with his conscience came one day in 1867 when he caught a suspected Fenian terrorist on the quay at Dublin about to embark on a ship for Scotland. Thomas knew who he was, for they had been hunting him for weeks. His name was Patrick Welsh. Fortunately there was no one else around at the time, no superior officer, nor even privates who might have told the tale. Welsh was in tears, begging to be let off, promising there would be no terrorist activities in Glasgow or Edinburgh if only the Sergeant would let him go. Maley considered. He knew full well that Welsh faced imprisonment at best, the gallows at worst.

It was a moral decision. Maley did not list cowardice, either moral or physical, among his vices. His wife, the gentle Mary, had often felt the Army and the British in general were too hard on these poor Irish lads, whose only fault was an excessive, albeit misguided, love of their country. He thought ... and then without a word, turned his back as the grateful Welsh jumped on board the waiting ship. This particular incident would have significant repercussions.

The barracks at Newry where the Maleys lived in 1868 were as always on high alert, although since 1848 there had been surprisingly little terrorist activity in that part of Ireland. Beneath all the British cant about 'John Bull's other island', Ireland was now a desolate, poor country, its population having been drastically reduced since the famine, its resources relentlessly pillaged by the British Empire and those who collaborated with them. The Roman Catholic Church did attempt to provide some sort of comfort or spiritual leadership, but it was all too aware that it had lost so much of its credibility by its inability or refusal to provide much help during the time of the Famine.

Thomas Maley, being an Irishman but a British soldier as well, sometimes found it difficult to analyse his own feelings. His fellow soldiers would talk about 'Fenian bastards', and his fellow Irishmen would refer to the Army as 'the felons of our land'. At least that young Welsh would not cause any trouble in Ireland, he thought. Nor would the British hang him, as they had done rather too often with young Fenians. He wished there was something more positive that the authorities could offer him.

Army life had many advantages. Thomas Maley enjoyed his job and was recognised as being good at it. He enjoyed seeing just how much good could be done in such a short time with recruits once they enjoyed the Army regime of good regular food, plenty of exercise and a little discipline. He also had a good family life with a lovely wife of Scottish extraction. He had met her when on duty in Canada, where she was born, and persuaded her to become a soldier's wife. Not that she needed much persuasion, for she was herself the daughter of a soldier, Alexander Montgomery, who had been a sergeant major in the Royal Engineers.

Mary Ann Montgomery became a good wife to the soldier and they had two sons. When the third was born in 1868, he was even more delighted but very soon after that, he was delighted to take his 'honourable discharge' from the Army in 1869 and go, like so many other Irishmen, to Scotland, the land where his wife's family had come from.

It may have been that it was the incident with Welsh that played upon his conscience, for he was well aware that he could have been court-martialled for such behaviour. But he was a good Catholic and felt that it was his duty to God that had to come first. Leaving Ireland and the Army meant that he could live his life in a peaceful country and bring up his family without the threat of terrorism or any problems with their conscience. So to Scotland they went with a military pension, and a friend in the ex-Fenian Mr Welsh – who owed them a few favours. Welsh, now settled in Glasgow, had already written to Sergeant Maley expressing his gratitude for what he had done.

The Maleys were a class above most of the other Irish immigrants. The Irish had begun to trickle into Scotland since the defeat of the 1798 rebellion and its repressive aftermath. They had at that time tended to go to Edinburgh, but the trickle became a flood after the famine of 1846 and 1847 and these luckless folk had been tempted by the prospect of some kind of work to settle in Glasgow, the Central Belt and Dundee. They were poor, ill-clad, ill-fed and ruthlessly exploited by both employers who saw the possibilities of sweated labour and by the landlords of slum dwellings who saw nothing wrong in leasing hovels to them.

The Maleys however, had a little money and prosperity behind them and – blessed with an abstemious father and providential mother in the household – settled in about 1870 in Cathcart, a comparatively prosperous village to the south of Glasgow, some distance away from the teeming horrors of the metropolis (which was even then being called the 'second city of the Empire'). The neighbours in Argyll Place were decent and friendly, being tolerant of the Maleys, their nationality and their religion.

Next door, for example, lived the Matthews family with whom they were on very good terms. The father of the household, Peter Matthews, was a police sergeant and an elder in the Presbyterian Church of Scotland. He also spent some time at a Masonic Lodge, where it was rumoured that the Pope was frequently cursed as being the son of Satan. This was absolute rubbish, Thomas decided, and the Matthews and the Maley families would do all sorts of things together like meet on New Year's Day for a noggin or a dram.

Thomas Maley had not been long in Glasgow before he met an old 'friend'. It was none other than the young Fenian Patrick Welsh, who had now opened a tailor and drapery business in the city centre. The grateful Welsh offered Maley a job, but Maley had other ideas and very soon got a real break in his attempt to supplement his Army pension. He had thought of going back to his old trade as a cobbler, which he had learned in the army, but a job came his way that could hardly have suited him more. It was as a drill instructor in the 3rd Renfrewshire Batallion of the Argyll and Sutherland Highlanders.

Maley was now a contented man. He was wise enough to realise that the real problem in Scottish society was not about religion or ethnic origin, but about poverty. The expansion of the British Empire over the past 100 years and the triumph of the Industrial Revolution with its railways and factories had brought great wealth, but it had not been equally shared. Nor had education (compulsory in Scotland since 1872, although already well embedded in Scottish culture for centuries before that) as yet brought any great tangible benefits to the urban poor, who seemed to be sunk irrevocably in their own mire of filth and ignorance. Therein perhaps lay the difference between Scotland and Ireland, Maley mused. The deprivation and poverty lay in the cities and large towns of Scotland, whereas the Scottish agricultural population were marginally better off in comparative terms. In Ireland the poverty had been rural, but was now shifting to the cities of Dublin, Belfast and Cork – it was now all-encompassing.

By nature, Thomas tended towards the Liberal party of William Gladstone. Gladstone was quite clearly a man of vision and who now seemed in his old age to be perpetually involved in nothing other than the problems of Ireland. But the problem was that social change was not coming quickly enough. The time would soon be at hand when the poor might demand (and none too politely) some advancement. He had read a book recently about the French Revolution of 100 years ago. It worried him, but he had to smile when he thought that Queen Victoria, for all her pomposity and sulking about her dead husband, was hardly Marie Antoinette! Change would have to come some day, though. Perhaps the generation of his sons might provide some answer.

Thomas, being a good (although hardly saintly) Catholic, often counted his blessings. Since arriving in Scotland, Charles, the eldest boy had studied for the priesthood, having resumed the old family name of O'Maley. Tom had become a teacher but was more interested in being a footballer, Willie a fine, handsome, young man was training to be an accountant while spending his weekends playing some kind of sport and young Alec, the darling of his mother's eye and a pleasant surprise after they had arrived in Scotland, was still at school.

Young Tom was the one who caused the most problems for his father. He seemed to have quite a lot of money, more than a young teacher should earn in fact. He was never short of money to take that young woman of his to the music hall or the theatre. Thomas of course knew where it came from, and being a military man and a firm supporter of the law, was a little perturbed about his son earning illegal money. It came, of course, from the coffers of Third Lanark Football Club and was euphemistically described as 'expenses'.

Thomas senior knew little about football, the current Scottish obsession, but was slowly learning. He had once or twice gone to watch 'Thirds' play recently and had been impressed by them and been rightly proud of the play of young Tom. Tom had of course played several years previously for the great Hibernian Football Club of Edinburgh, a team exclusively for Irish Catholics. His father had disapproved of this, for he felt that the Irish in Scotland should now make every effort to integrate with the Scots, and he was happier when Tom started to play for Third Lanark or the 'Sodgers' as they were called. Thomas was even more delighted when he was told that they were in fact the 3rd Lanark Rifle Volunteers. Not only that, but one of the committee men was known to Thomas from his army days! Thomas would pretend not to know that his son was being paid illegally.

Willie and Alec were also both keen sportsmen, Willie in particular being a runner with a fine physique. Both also cycled, played a little cricket in the summer, and of course football in the winter. There seemed to be no stopping this sport called football. Every place seemed to have a team, and Thomas had to admit that he would have enjoyed it in his youth as well. It was good exercise, needed no expensive equipment once you had a ball and it kept young men away from the horrors of drink, prostitution and crime – the presence and sheer amount of which had shocked Thomas since his arrival in Glasgow.

Young Willie had gone to school in Cathcart, but having no real inclination for study, had left school at the age of thirteen. He was, however, a very sharp boy and had picked up the rudiments of reading, writing and arithmetic sufficiently well to get him a job in the office of the calico printworks of Miller, Higginbotham & Co. It was a good start and from then on he moved to The Telephone Company of Glasgow before the firm of chartered accountants called Smith and Wilson recognised the potential of the young man and offered him the opportunity to train as an accountant. He would work five and a half days, but it was also necessary to pass exams and some study was therefore necessary at night. But Saturday afternoon was free – and therefore he could cycle, run or even play football. His mother was delighted with all this.

Mary Maley was a lovely, gentle, intelligent person, totally dedicated to the welfare of her boys. Being a Victorian lady, no thought of a career ever entered her head, although she could think of no reason why women could not for example be doctors some day. She had not always been a Roman Catholic but had accepted the faith of her husband without any great problem. It was after all the same God, she thought. When she said these sort of things at Church, she was aware that she received quizzical glances from some, although the wiser elements would nod sagely.

She kept a good house but despaired occasionally at the tea table when the conversation seemed to be about very little other than sport. Tom junior, wild and energetic, Willie more thoughtful and idealistic and young Alec drinking in every word that his elder brothers would say. Even Thomas senior was affected by the football bug which dominated everything. Mary would occasionally surprise herself by remarking just how much about this game that she had picked up from the men in her life. Willie Groves, for example, played for the Hibernians and the best two teams in England at this time, came from Birmingham and were called Aston Villa and West Bromwich Albion. Also, across on the east coast of Scotland in 1885, some team from Arbroath had beaten an Aberdeen team 36-0!

Scotland's most famous team was Queen's Park, who played not all that far from where the Maleys lived. They had the reputation of being very strict and very snobby, but seemed to be consistently the best team, although Dumbartonshire teams like Renton, Vale of Leven and Dumbarton themselves were also good. In Glasgow there was of course Third Lanark, Clyde, Cowlairs, Partick Thistle and Rangers. Edinburgh, as well as the Hibernians, had a team whose name, the Heart of Midlothian, was culled from the novels of Sir Walter Scott.

It was a dark December night in 1887, when a knock came to the door. Willie laid down his accountancy books and answered it. Three men stood there in what would have been a menacing fashion if Willie had not recognised that one was a priest. They asked to talk to Tom Maley Senior or Junior. Willie brought them in. Thomas immediately recognised his old friend Pat Welsh — and for a horrible moment the thought crossed his mind that they were planning some Fenian rising in Scotland and were here to enlist his support!

They were indeed there to enlist the support of the Maleys, but their purpose was much more peaceful and in the long run far more beneficial to the Irish in Scotland and the rest of the world. Welsh introduced the others as John Glass and Brother Walfrid. They explained their errand. They were wishing to speak to young Tom, to see if he would be interested in joining their football team. They were by no means the first delegation from a football team to approach Tom, but this team, said Brother Walfrid with an Irish accent less diluted than that of the Maley family, would be different. They had not yet played a game, but the idea was to provide funds for poor Irish children in the east end of Glasgow. There would be no profits, the team would consist primarily, but not exclusively, of Irishmen and they thought that Tom Maley, having already played for the Edinburgh Hibernians, would be an excellent adjunct to the team.

Mary Maley, with traditional Irish (and Scottish) hospitality, provided tea and scones for the visitors and listened. She understood little about the intricacies of football, but thought that the charitable purposes of this club seemed a good idea. She also recognised Brother Walfrid as a good man, as the kindly cleric praised her baking. Thomas explained that Tom junior was not at home, as he was out with his young lady, but that he would pass on the message.

Thomas said that he liked the idea that the club was not to be exclusively Catholic — that was what he did not like about the Edinburgh Hibernians — and this gave Brother Walfrid the opportunity to say that the decision had now been taken to call the club the Glasgow Celtic, because 'Celtic' was a word that could encapsulate both Scotland and Ireland. There was still a little doubt about whether it would be pronounced the 'Keltic' or the 'Seltic', but balance of opinion favoured the soft 's'. He expressed the hope that this football team would be a bridge between the Irish immigrants and the Scottish Presbyterians, not all of whom were as welcoming to the Irish as he would have liked.

Time was passing. Willie told the visitors that he had played football (including a game or two for Third Lanark's reserves) as well, but preferred athletics and cycling. Young Alec had school the next day (he had at one point cheekily asked Brother Walfrid for some help with his Latin, and the gentle cleric had been only too keen to help) and retired to bed. The three men took the hint and prepared to go, thanking Mary Maley for her excellent hospitality and leaving an address in Glasgow for Tom to get in touch with them. As an afterthought, Brother Walfrid then looked at the slim and athletic Willie and said 'Why don't you come along with him?'

Two

MALEY THE PLAYER

Willie took up the invitation of Brother Walfrid and did indeed come along with brother Tom when Tom later expressed an interest. The Maleys were very impressed with what was happening there. A piece of land on the eastern outskirts of the city had been leased, but much work was required in the early months of 1888 to have the ground ready for football. This was being done by volunteer labour, and the 'navvy' skills of road-making were being put to good use, under the watchful eye of the likes of John Glass, Pat Welsh and Brother Walfrid. The idea was that the club would play its first game in about May, and then play properly in the following season.

Quite clearly Brother Walfrid had hit upon a good idea. There was a vast number of young Irish men in Glasgow with an interest in football who hitherto had lacked a club with whom they might identify. Hibernian of Edinburgh were quite simply in the wrong city, Queen's Park well established but forbiddingly middle class, Rangers not a great team although already building up a large support, Third Lanark too much associated with the Army, and the other great teams, like Vale of Leven and Renton, out of town in the Dumbartonshire countryside. The Irish had hitherto lacked a focus, and as the intention was charitable as well, then it had to be a good idea.

For Willie, this new club immediately infected him with enthusiasm, so much so that he decided to take football more seriously. He had hitherto played a few games for Third Lanark's 'ham and eggers' – a quaint expression for the reserve team who presumably were not awarded 'expenses' in this nominally amateur game, but received a free tea of ham and eggs instead.

But now he trained hard with his brother and the rest of the lads, went to see the likes of Queen's Park, Heart of Midlothian and Hibernians and read more about the great English teams like Aston Villa and Everton. On 17 March 1888 he took the short trip to Hampden Park to see the big game of Scotland *v.* England, which had been the talk of all Glasgow and attracted 10,000 people to watch it. Willie must have regretted doing so, for Scotland, in spite of having great players like James Kelly, Walter Arnott and James McCall, lost 5-0 to the Englishmen.

Meanwhile, life was progressing at Celtic Park. The ground was opened in early May with a game between Edinburgh Hibernians and Glasgow Cowlairs, and on Monday 28 May, the famous Rangers had been invited to play the first game against Celtic. The Celtic committee had already heard of Willie's studying of accountancy and approached him with a view to his becoming secretary or treasurer of the new club. Willie agreed to be the match secretary and would soon become the secretary but, for the meantime, was more interested in playing.

In his book, *The Story Of The Celtic*, Willie would immodestly say, 'I was young, strong, with plenty of speed and had a happy knack of quickly absorbing advice and tuition'. Working very hard to impress everyone, Willie thoroughly deserved his selection as right half for the first game and was not in the slightest overawed to discover that alongside him, James Kelly of Renton and Scotland had been secured to join the team. In the forward line there would also be men like Neil McCallum of Renton and John Madden of Dumbarton, who were current stars of the game at that time.

In what would now be called 'squad rotation', Rangers fielded only some of their regulars, the rest being made up of their 'swifts', another Victorian name for reserves. A crowd of 2,000 appeared to see the first game of the Celtic club who were already famous even before they played a game. The ground was neat and pleasant, the pitch was smooth and Neil McCallum scored the first goal for the club, James Kelly delighting all who idolised him by scoring another, a header from a corner kick just before half-time. Tom Maley scored a hat-trick, according to some reports – although others say that McCallum scored the fifth.

Both Maleys played well, Willie at right-half and Tom at inside right and the team won 5-2. It was a thoroughly sporting occasion and both teams went off for a 'social evening' afterwards. The health of the new club was toasted by Rangers, food was served, much ale was drunk and impromptu songs and recitations were performed, Tom Maley impressing everyone by his rendition of the famous Victorian story of the sinking ship:

'Twas a dirty night, and a dirty trick
When a ship went down in the Atlantic...'

Everyone expressed the wish that this would be the first of many encounters between these two Glasgow teams. Their wish would of course be granted. Celtic applied for membership of the Glasgow Football Association and the Scottish Football Association for the following season, and their applications were accepted.

Willie was now smitten with this game of football, spending all of the summer of 1888 practising either at the Celtic Park or on any piece of ground along with Tom and Alec. There were indeed several other friendlies played over the summer against Dundee Harp (another avowedly Irish team), Mossend Swifts and Clyde. The new season would start in September and Willie was determined to be there and to play for the team as often as he could. His parents smiled tolerantly.

Willie was also becoming more socially aware. He had been told that the Celtic club had been formed for charitable purposes, and he saw as he looked about him that there were reasons for all this. The summer of 1888 was a good one and Willie noticed the number of children who went around without shoes. He was a lot more perturbed when autumn and winter came and these same children still did not have shoes. On the other hand, there were some incredibly rich people in Glasgow as well in Bearsden, Partick and his own town of Cathcart. Something was wrong about all that. Willie saw quite clearly the reasons for which the new club had been formed.

The 1888/89 season saw the new team involved in many competitions, although the Scottish League would not be formed for a couple of years yet. Maley played sporadically, occasionally affected by injury and sometimes prevented by other commitments, such as his athletics. He also impressed everyone by his administrative ability in his role as match secretary. The team started off its honourable tradition of doing well in the Scottish Cup, beating Shettleston, Cowlairs, Albion Rovers, St Bernard's, Clyde, East Stirling and the great Dumbarton team to reach the 1889 final against Third Lanark.

Thus, the two Maleys found themselves playing in the Scottish Cup Final in the first year of the club's existence. Nothing of course succeeds like success, and the club's meteoric rise was accompanied by huge crowds of supporters. It is easy to understand the mindset of their supporters in the early days. The club was a rallying call, a standard, a flag bearer for the hitherto underprivileged tribe called the 'Glasgow Irish'. Such immediate success did of course bring with it its counterblast. Some Scottish Presbyterians resented the success of the 'Irishmen' as the newspapers frequently referred to them, but from now on, Maley realised, the name 'Celtic' was going to mean a great deal in Scottish football and Scottish society.

Celtic's first Scottish Cup Final was a farce. Scheduled for the ridiculous date of 2 February, the organisers received their due reward when Glasgow was covered in a blizzard on that date. The game was played, in the interests of preventing a riot among the large crowd who had assembled at Hampden Park, but declared a 'friendly', although this news was not leaked to the public until after the game. Third Lanark won the friendly 3-0, a ludicrous game of football with players sliding all over the field and the goalkeepers and referee continually pelted with snowballs. The Cup Final was re-scheduled for the following week. Then on a drier but harder pitch, Thirds delighted their fans by winning 2-1.

Maley was naturally disappointed with this. It would have been a marvellous achievement for the side to have won the Scottish Cup in their first full year, but there was a certain amount of consolation when the club won the Glasgow North Eastern Cup at the end of the season. Maley felt that he had had a good season as far as playing was concerned, but it was in his capacity as match secretary that he showed his vision.

On 16 February 1889, for example, the week after the defeat in the Scottish Cup Final, he arranged a trip to London to play the famous Corinthians. (This was in fact a return fixture for the crack London team had played at Celtic Park on New Year's Day.) A month later the team went to Newcastle to play Newcastle West End, one of the teams who would, a few years later, amalgamate to become Newcastle United. Then in April, a tour was organised to Lancashire first to play Bolton and Burnley, then across the Irish Sea to play Distillery and United Belfast.

The Irish tour in particular was a great success. Both games were won and phenomenal crowds of 8,000 were attracted to see the mighty Glasgow Celtic. Maley played in both games, but it was his ability to make sure that everything ran smoothly that ensured the success of the visit. Maley may have worried about the effect that this avowedly Catholic team might have had on the Protestant half of Belfast, but he need not have. A couple of thousand assembled at the quayside to see them depart back to Scotland and they all sang 'Will Ye No' Come Back Again?'

This was the origin of another great Celtic tradition, namely the willingness to play football all over the world, not merely in the parochial environment of Glasgow. Maley (with the backing of the committee) realised that if there was any justification for the cause of Celtic in humanitarian or other terms, then their football had to evangelise and publicise the cause over the whole world, and not just in their own back yard.

Yet another great Celtic tradition was initiated in the first year, (and one in which Maley was very much involved) and that was the playing of good football with the emphasis on attack, passing, team-work and work rate. The idea was the simple, perhaps naïve one that people had to be attracted to see the game, and the way to do it was to play the game in an attractive way. Maley as wing-half was the first of many great passers of a ball (one thinks of Peter Wilson, Pat Crerand and Bobby Murdoch in later years) and his part in the Celtic team was beginning to be noticed. Maley's ambition, like that of most players, was to play for Scotland.

There was of course another dimension to this in Maley's case. Maley had inherited from his father a desire for integration of the Irish community into Scotland. The Maley family were proudly Irish, but no less in love with Scotland into whose society they craved admission. Not for them was the narrow bigotry of some of their contemporaries, the paranoia which saw discrimination (not always without cause) and victimization at every turn. Maley's vision was of a thriving Scotland in which the Catholic Irish would be an integral part, and also a recognisable unit, accepted as being both Irish and Scottish and embodying the best of both cultures.

Maley would argue for example at a very early stage of the club's existence for the deployment of Scottish Protestants. In theory, this was one of the principles of the club, but the first game, for example, was played by eleven men who were, seemingly, all Catholic. Clearly a balance would have to be struck, for the club's support was over-whelmingly Irish, but Maley hoped that in time the distinction between Scots and Irish would become blurred, and that nobody would even know or give a twopenny damn whether a given player was a Protestant or a Catholic.

He was particularly anxious that Celtic would not begin to strug-gle like the Edinburgh Hibernians. Founded in 1875 for Catholic young men, the club, Maley felt had made a mistake in not broaden-ing its horizons. In thus allowing all Protestant young men to go to Hearts or St Bernard's, Hibernians were now struggling (not least because the new Glasgow Celtic team had also taken some players from them!). The new Celtic team (with whom Maley had already embarked on his lifelong love affair) was such a good idea that it must not be allowed to fester and die.

In what was only Celtic's first year, men like Kelly, McLaren, McKeown and Groves were already playing for Scotland, but they were men who had established their reputation elsewhere. Willie wanted to be one of the first 'real' Celts to play for Scotland. He realised too that being technically an Irishman, in that he was born in Ireland, he might have problems convincing them that he was legally entitled to play for Scotland, but he could argue for his Scottish connections (on his mother's side) and that he had lived virtually all his life in Scotland.

The first two seasons in Celtic's life saw only Cup games and friendlies played. The Scottish League would be formed in 1890 and Celtic were invited to join along with Rangers, Hearts, St Mirren, Dumbarton, Third Lanark, Cambuslang, Cowlairs, Abercorn and Vale of Leven. Until the League was formed, there was little to stop any player playing for whoever he wanted to, and of course everything was still totally amateur, at least in theory.

All this begged the question of how much players actually received for playing football. It was no secret that James Kelly had been enticed away from Renton to join Glasgow Celtic. It would have been nice to think that this was for reasons of idealism, rather than money, but one suspects that it wasn't. It was the same case with Maley. In the 1889/90 season he didn't play every week, but he was involved in the one and only Scottish Cup tie they played that year, against Queen's Park. The Saturdays that he was not involved at Celtic Park may have seen him playing for someone else, perhaps Third Lanark or his local team Cathcart, or indulging in one of his other pursuits of cycling or athletics. He obviously considered himself to be good enough to be in a position to pick and choose, but he relished his administrative role at Parkhead.

Celtic did not win the League in its first season of 1890/91, finishing third, but Maley did win his first major medal when Celtic won the Glasgow Cup Final on 14 February 1891 by beating Third Lanark 4-0. Maley was at left half for this game, having temporarily surrendered his right-half spot to Paddy Gallagher (not to be confused with Patsy Gallacher who came onto the scene some twenty years later). It was a good move by Maley to agree to this idea because it proved his versatility, and that he could use his left foot as well as his right.

10,000 fans thronged Hampden Park to see this game, proof once again – if anyone had ever doubted it – of the drawing power of the Celtic, and this time the Celtic supporters went home happy. An own goal, two goals from Johnny Campbell and one from Peter Dowds saw Celtic win the day in what was an outstanding performance. Maley had every reason to be proud of his own performance, and the club were delighted with him.

But far better was to come for Celtic the following year – and not only on the field of play. A problem concerned their ground, and Maley himself highlights it when he says 'trouble came when 1892 brought an old affliction to Irishmen "The Landlord".' Landlords were of course the curse of Ireland, usually absentee landlords who, with official backing and connivance, charged whatever they wished from their tenants and evicted them on a whim or if ever the tenant showed any sign of being troublesome. The owners of the original Celtic Park ground, seeing the phenomenal success of the Celtic and seeing for example that the ground was considered good enough to host an International between Scotland and Ireland, tried to cash in on it and raised the rent ten fold from £50 to £500.

In late 1891, the Celtic committee decided that this was not a feasible proposition and decided to buy a new ground, feeling that they had the capital with which to do so. They contemplated moving to other parts of Glasgow, particularly Possilpark, but decided to settle for staying in the East End where most of their supporters lived. A piece of waste ground which consisted of a quarry hole and other derelictions lay some 200 yards to the south-west of their ground on the other side of Janefield Cemetery. It was owned by Lord Newlands, but Celtic decided to go for a ten-year lease in the first instance with a view to eventual purchase.

Maley, being an accountant was one of the driving forces behind all this. He did all the costing and the necessary work. It was a great risk, for the site looked totally unsuitable, although it was large enough. Volunteer labour was used to fill in the quarry hole, and by 19 March 1892, the ground was not yet completely ready for football but it was ready for the Irish patriot Michael Davitt to plant a shamrock on the centre spot.

Very soon the ground earned the nickname 'Paradise'. This was allegedly because someone had said that the old ground was so bad that the new one was like 'Paradise' in comparison. It may also have something to do with the vicinity of the Janefield Cemetery and the Roman Catholic teachings about Purgatory. The graveyard was where one's sins would be purged for many centuries or millennia (depending on their severity) but after that your soul could leave the cemetery and the first thing you would see would be ... Paradise.

The invitation to Michael Davitt was a clear indication of the unashamed Irish connections of the club. One wonders in passing what Maley's father, old Thomas, thought of this. Davitt was now a respectable politician and since the death of Charles Stuart Parnell the previous autumn, was the leading light in the non-violent wing of Irish republicanism, but he had in the past been a convicted Fenian and had served time for gun-running. Here was Willie Maley, son of a British soldier, inviting this man to plant shamrocks on a football pitch!

In a few years time, the ground would be big enough to house many Scotland internationals, with facilities for athletics and cycling events as well, and it says a great deal for the vision of the founding fathers that they were prepared to take a risk on this project. Maley was shrewd enough to realise that the success of the Celtic club would grow and grow and that very soon a very large ground (far larger than seemed suitable for the 1890s) would be needed for their supporters. The site of the ground has remained the home of Celtic until the present day, surviving an idiotic attempt in the 1990s by the board (ironically run by the grandsons of the James Kelly who was well to the forefront of this idea a hundred years earlier) to move to Cambuslang.

That 1892 was the 'year of the Celtic', as a contemporary source described it, was proved when the team won three Cups – the Glasgow, the Glasgow Charity and the most prestigious trophy of them all in those days, the Scottish Cup. It was the victory of the Scottish Cup (at the second attempt following crowd encroachment trouble) on 9 April 1892 which proved to Scotland that Celtic were here to stay. Not a huge number of Celtic fans actually attended the game, (for prices had been raised to deter them!) but thousands gathered outside Ibrox to listen to the shouts of the crowd. Following the full time whistle which ended the game Celtic 5 Queen's Park 1, news spread like wildfire and the East End went delirious, as bugles and flutes (!) brought the news. Banners were hung out of windows saying 'Our Bhoys Have Won The Cup'.

The normally moderate Maley might well have permitted himself a little something to celebrate what had happened. He himself had had a great game, and the half-back line of Maley, Kelly and Dowds had established a stranglehold over the midfield of Queen's Park, constantly feeding the forwards. Johnny Campbell and Sandy McMahon had scored two goals each and were much fêted by the crowd but the more perspicacious of the supporters would not undervalue the contribution of Willie Maley. On Monday he would enjoy reading what the newspapers said about him. His 'blocking and feeding simply perfect…' '…checking, returning, general engineering was immense'.

Willie was very happy with life as he approached his twenty-fourth birthday that spring. He was now an accountant and was dabbling with the idea of opening a gents' outfitters shop some place in the centre of Glasgow, but most importantly he had discovered that his true métier in life was that of a football player. Once his playing days were over, he could very easily move over entirely to the business side. But most importantly of all, he loved this new club. It had been in existence for less than four years, but they had already won four major trophies, especially important being this year's major trophy, the Scottish Cup. There was definitely a future here, thought Willie.

As the charabanc moved back to the East End that night, the horses were frequently stopped and patted by the adoring crowds as people put green favours on their bridles. The Celtic players would have realised that night what Celtic were all about. This was no football team like Third Lanark or St Mirren. It was the expression of identity of an ethnic minority. The urchins, shoeless and with ragged trousers, running noses and facial sores were cheering, laughing and smiling. They were the risen people. It was as if someone had brought in extra helpings to Oliver Twist and his paupers, thought Willie. The racket of the cheering and the singing and the dancing to the sound of the bugles and the flutes was phenomenal.

A thought struck Willie. If the people can find their identity through football, there will be no need for them to plant bombs, nor assassinate politicians. Celtic must follow the lead given by Charles Stuart Parnell and others. Violence is not the answer for the Irish in Scotland. The appalling problems of poverty must be addressed in other ways. Among other ideas, we must keep this football club going, he thought. Not that there was any chance of the idea breaking down now!

Indeed one of the Celtic committee, Ned McGinn was so delighted with the team's success that year that he sent a telegram to His Holiness The Pope in the Vatican in order to apprise Pope Leo XIII of what a good football team he had in the East End of Glasgow. It is of course a well-known fact that the Vatican was so delighted by the news in 1690 that King William had defeated King James at the Battle of the Boyne, thereby discomfiting the Vatican's inveterate enemy Louis XIV, that candles were lit throughout the Vatican City, but there is no record of whether Pope Leo XIII was in any way impressed by success on the football field!

Yet the new club had learned that in the sometimes unpleasant climate of the 1890s, one had to be tough and even ruthless to survive. Stories are told about crowd problems, in particular the time when supporters of Abercorn, a now-defunct Paisley club, invaded the field at full-time to attack Celtic players. The Celtic committee also had to live on its wits to capture and retain their star players. Stories are told about how players like Reynolds and McMahon were 'captured' and 'rescued' from other clubs, and, as we have discovered, poor Hibernians of Edinburgh were forced into abeyance for a spell, for they lost their star players to Celtic!

The 1892/93 season was something of an anti-climax after the heady season of the 'three Cups'. Three Cup finals were reached, but Celtic went down to Queen's Park in the Scottish and Rangers in the Glasgow Cup Final. But there was adequate recompense in the other Cup. That was the Glasgow Charity Cup played at the end of the season and Celtic beat Rangers 5-0. Maley played at left half that day and was outstanding, feeding left-winger Johnny Campbell for his hat-trick.

The defeat in the 1893 Scottish Cup Final was a hard one to take, both for the club and for Maley personally. After a comparatively trouble-free passage to the final, Celtic actually beat Queen's Park in the first game, but the game had already been declared a 'friendly' because the pitch was too hard. The replay of the game on 11 March was characterised by some robust Queen's Park play, delicately described in the newspapers as 'the excellence of their charging'. Several Celtic players were injured, including Maley, who sustained a kick in the face (an accident, presumably). He was carried off and required a visit to a dentist and the eventual loss of several teeth. Substitutes were not permitted in 1893 and Celtic lost 2-1.

Even more controversial was Queen's Park's second goal. No goal nets were used, and the referee Mr Harrison adjudged correctly that the ball had gone past the post, until convinced to the contrary by the 'scorer' of the so-called 'goal'. Clearly Mr Harrison was of the persuasion that Queen's Park players did not tell lies! It would be some time before Queen's Park and Celtic repaired damaged relationships after this unfortunate encounter.

Maley himself in his account of the game does not dwell too much on the injuries or the robust Queen's Park play, although he admits that they were a factor as well as 'tremendous anxiety'. He is more interested in revealing an early example of what is now called the Celtic Paranoia:

> Then, of course, Celtic, to put it very plainly, were looked upon as interlopers and not too welcome at that, but although they were regarded with feelings amounting almost to hatred in many quarters, their success and unquestioned talent were responsible for an increasing respect for their prowess.

Such feelings of insecurity would affect Maley frequently in later life, even when manifestly not justified by actual events, and establish a precedent followed by Bob Kelly, Jock Stein and others to the effect that everyone has a spite against Celtic for all sorts of reasons – Catholicism, Ireland and success. There is of course a certain amount of truth in this, but there exist similar feelings against Rangers, Manchester United, Real Madrid and other successful football teams.

Celtic, however, won the League Championship for the first time in 1893, a competition not yet held in as high regard as it is today. They had to fight off a determined challenge from Rangers, but Celtic won the League by one point. The Championship was clinched on 9 May when Celtic, with Maley on song, beat Leith Athletic 3-1. Maley missed a few games towards the end of that campaign, but already he had achieved his ambition of playing for Scotland.

However, his selection for Scotland was – perhaps unsurprisingly – a little contentious. In the first place, he was undeniably an Irishman, as indeed was his father. His mother had been born in Canada, but her parents were Scottish, and this heritage was considered sufficient to allow him to play for Scotland. The criticism of his selection seems to centre on the fact that he was an Irishman playing 'for an Irish team', yet he was being chosen to play for Scotland *against* Ireland.

Politics was involved here, and in his administrative capacity with the Celtic club, Maley himself had been instrumental in getting the game to be played at the new Celtic Park, now sufficiently well developed to sustain the expected crowd of about 15,000 on 25 March. It did indeed seem a logical place to play the fixture (the 1891 International between the same two teams had been played at the old Celtic Park) but some of the journalists were a little suspicious when four Celtic men were chosen for the Scottish team. The previous week, Scotland had thrashed a dismally weak Welsh team 8-0 and there did not seem to be any logical or tactical reason to change the team. Yet Celtic men Kelly, Maley, McMahon and Campbell all found themselves in the Scottish team, no doubt with the intention of boosting the gate at the very impressive new Celtic Park.

One member of the press wrote complaining about the selection, saying that 'the halves are weak. Mitchell [of Rangers] is acceptable, but Maley and Kelly are simply no good'. Clearly not a man to mince words is this sententious writer of the *Dundee Courier*, but he then goes on to make the bizarre statement that 'Maley had retired'. This is frankly rubbish for Willie Maley had missed only three games that season, and played well enough along with Kelly to see Celtic at the top of the League and to reach two Cup Finals! The writer is presumably mixing Willie up with Tom Maley, who by 1893 had indeed retired.

The anonymous writer is closer to the mark when he berates Kelly for his poor performance against England last year, but his teeth are drawn somewhat by actual events. Scotland beat Ireland by 6-1, with McMahon and Kelly both scoring a goal in a fairly easy victory for the Scots. Maley (given the absence of any adverse criticism) seems to have played a good game, but it would have been interesting to have heard the views of old Thomas Maley as he watched his son playing for the new country against the old. Perhaps he would have preferred his son to have been wearing the green of Ireland rather than the 'thistle' of Scotland, but perhaps he also saw the strength of his son's cogent arguments that the Maley family was now Scottish.

Maley was now, along with the other three Celtic men, retained in the team for the big game against England on 'the classic sward of Richmond' on 1 April. Some accounts give the attendance on a fine, warm day as being 25,000. Certainly the Richmond Athletic ground could not cope with the crowd who kept encroaching and more than once deprived the gentlemen of the press of a good view.

Royalty was there in the shape of the Duke and Duchess of Teck and their daughter Mary who would of course marry the future George V and then become Queen in 1910. James Kelly the captain was introduced to them, but the rest of the team did not have that privilege, something that may have rankled with Maley, for in later years his weakness for royalty was well known. On certain occasions in later life, both in speech and writing, Maley implied that he did indeed shake hands with the future Queen Mary! On other occasions, his bitterness at not being allowed to do so is apparent.

The game as it was, was a good one: 1-1 at half-time and then Scotland went ahead through Sellar of Queen's Park. England equalised half-way through the second half, and the game was level pegging until the last quarter of an hour when England 'went rampant' and scored three times to give a slightly misleading 5-2 scoreline. Maley admits that two of the English goals were scored from his wing, but he insists that they were offside. The referee was an Englishman called Mr J. Clegg, and he was subsequently knighted! One press report sums up Maley's performance thus: 'Maley was very good in the first half, but not so good in the second.'

The Scots were disappointed, but Maley did at least enjoy the experience and his trip to London. He was never again invited to play for the full Scotland team, although he would play for the Scottish League against the Irish League in 1894. This was a 6-0 thrashing of a woefully weak Irish team. Maley had already played against the English League in 1892 (a 2-2 draw at Bolton) and in an unofficial International at Ibrox Park against Canada in 1891 (a comfortable 5-1 victory).

The end of the season saw something that Maley and Celtic had been campaigning for during the short time of the existence of the club. This was the decision on 2 May that professionalism should be legalised. It had been legalised in England since 1885 and the result was that many Scottish youngsters were being enticed away from Scotland, unless clubs were willing to offer illegal wages.

Now the very rich Celtic team, whose coffers had swollen visibly in each of the five years of their existence, could compete on equal terms and legally with Everton, Aston Villa and Woolwich Arsenal. Not everyone in Scotland was happy about this change to professionalism, though. As would happen a century later when Rugby Union was recognised as professional, the changes would be profound. Professionalism accelerated the decline of the small village teams like Renton and Vale of Leven. Queen's Park remain to this day obdurate in their refusal to countenance professionalism, and they pay the penalty for this by their consistently low status in the Scottish League.

Celtic were thus the Scottish League Champions, the winners of the Charity Cup and unlucky losers of two other Cups in 1893. Maley was aware that his playing days were one day to come to an end, but with the arrival of professionalism, he saw that the future of this club would be an awesome one. He wished to be around in an administrative capacity. The 'feel good' factor was still there, and although there was not yet any great or obvious amelioration in the living conditions of the Glasgow Irish, something had clearly happened in the last five years to give them hope and to put a few smiles on the wizened and anxious faces.

The pattern was repeated in the following year, 1894, for although the League Championship and the Glasgow Charity Cup were won again, the club sustained another disappointment in the loss of the Scottish Cup final to Rangers, remarkably this team's first success in the Scottish Cup after twenty-one years of existence. In front of a massive crowd at Hampden, believed to be in excess of 25,000, on a wet day in the middle of February, Rangers triumphed with a 3–1 scoreline. Maley played well, although he had been ill the previous day and had to be given some sort of medication or 'dope' by the doctor. He scored Celtic's only goal in the game from a corner kick. It was generally agreed that Celtic's forward line, especially the great Sandy McMahon, did not do themselves justice.

Maley played all season, apart from a short spell being out through injury at the start, and it is noticeable that the form of the team picked up when he returned. The half-back line was unbalanced with Maley consistently good at right half and worthy of another Scottish cap in the opinion of supporters, but left half was a problem – so much so that Maley was frequently deployed there. There could be little doubt however that the Championship-winning team of 1894 was built around the twin rocks of Maley and Kelly.

Occasionally, the supporters might have been a little perplexed when the team as listed contained a man called 'Montgomery' who looked and played more than a little like Willie Maley. Such 'alias' nomenclature was not uncommon in Victorian football, and it appears that perhaps Maley's employers in his accountancy firm may have disapproved of one of their employees playing professional football so blatantly now that it had been legalised. Therefore Maley had recourse to the use of his mother's maiden name to throw them off the scent.

As always when a player plays well, there is no lack of offers from other teams. England on several occasions tried to snare him. In January 1894, for example, he had the opportunity to move away from Glasgow, for Sheffield United offered him the opportunity to join them, with the added bonus of the guarantee of a job as an accountant in the Duke of Norfolk's estate. Willie thought it over, but decided that he liked Glasgow and Celtic too much to leave.

Summer 1894 saw Maley in a difficult position. The committee were re-elected en masse on 15 May, but Maley was accused by some of rigging the election, by not sending out ballot papers to some members and giving two to others! A special meeting was called by Maley for mid-June, and there the election was declared null and void, but it was held again that very night by open acclamation and show of hands. The committee were re-elected, an hour after they had been deposed.

This incident perhaps shows Maley in a poor light, although he always claimed that he was scrupulously honest in his dealings. Yet nothing was proved against him, and no attempt was ever made to depose Maley himself from his position as secretary. It did, however, show that not all was harmonious at the new Celtic Park. In a few years' time, things would happen which would bring matters to a head.

1894/95 was a difficult season for the club, although both Glasgow Cups were annexed. There was a great deal of internal bickering, particularly when things went wrong on the field, and Maley struggled with injury and loss of form. He was hardly too old for the game at the age of twenty-seven, but he was aware that there were younger and fitter men than he on the opposition. In particular, he was aware that he had a shocker in the game when Celtic went down 1-0 in the Scottish Cup at Carolina Port, Dundee. It was a game that would give a tremendous boost to the development of football on Tayside, but it was a disaster for Celtic.

He would have loved to retire at the end of that season to concentrate on the administrative side of the club and his own business interests, but he still trained with the club and kept himself fit. In fact, two consecutive heavy defeats to Edinburgh teams (Hearts and St Bernard's) in September 1895 compelled his further participation as a player and he played sporadically throughout the rest of the season, as the team played spectacularly with Sandy McMahon in full flow in the forward line to win the 1896 Championship.

Maley thus played in the club's record victory, the 11-0 demolition of Dundee on 26 October 1895, a game played in the aftermath of a rather early fall of snow. This club had, of course, put Celtic out of the Scottish Cup the previous year, this defeat rankled, and it was a tremendous Celtic effort that so humiliated the Dundonians. Two of them were injured and had to leave the park, but there remains the suspicion that they were only too glad to depart the scene and thus avoid being part of this pasting. Maley himself actually claims that there were times in this game when men like McMahon and Blessington 'refused to score' lest they be deemed guilty of 'rubbing it in'! A few weeks later he won another Glasgow Cup medal, when Celtic beat Queen's Park at a muddy Ibrox.

1896 was a remarkable year for Maley. On 6 February he married Helen Pye, whom he had been courting for some time. She was a pretty girl, only nineteen and several years younger than Maley. When he met her, she was training to be a maternity nurse. They would have children, two boys, but sadly it was not destined to be the happiest of marriages. She remains a shadowy, nebulous figure in Maley's life, clearly taking second place to football, but for a while all was well as they moved into a nice house at 38 Whitevale Street, Glasgow.

It was perhaps financial considerations which compelled the newly wed Maley to think of the possibility of moving to England, where money would be in more plentiful supply. Manchester City were interested in him and on 24 February 1896, he joined City on a month's trial. It does not seem to have been a success. Perhaps he was missing Glasgow, his beloved Celtic and his new wife, but in any case a month later he returned to Celtic, having played only one game for Manchester City. City won that game 5-1 against Loughborough Town, but there were no further games for Maley in England.

Just as the season was ending, Maley received the sad news of the death of his father, Thomas Maley senior. He had been ill with pneumonia for some time, since attending his son's wedding in February, but his wife had thought that he was making progress and was hoping that the better weather would bring about a permanent recuperation. Sadly, he passed away on 7 May 1896. He was sixty-six. Maley, of course, was devoted to his father, and this was a bad blow. His father had always encouraged him in a game that he (Thomas) had not grown up with. He had been very proud to see his sons Willie and Tom taking part in the formation of the Celtic organization, and also to see Willie play for Scotland.

Celtic won the Charity Cup that year, playing the semi-final against Rangers only a couple of days after Thomas's death. 6-1 was the scoreline, and Maley's mother insisted that he attend the game (although he was injured and was not actually scheduled to play), for it would show more respect for his father if he did that. A week later when the Charity Cup was won in extra time against Queen's Park, the goalscorer Sandy McMahon said that this was the most fitting tribute to that friend of the Celts, old Thomas Maley.

Perhaps this reminder of mortality persuaded Maley to address himself even more urgently to his future. At the end of the 1896 season Maley, without making any formal announcement, was making it clear to his fellow committee members that his playing days were over. He was quite happy to work in his administrative capacity (in which he excelled) and he also enjoyed other sports. He was soon to make them sit up and take notice in athletics.

It was on 26 June 1896 at Hampden Park that he became the 100-yards champion of Scotland. He had run for the Clydesdale Harriers in the 1880s, but had given up the sport in favour of football. With his football career now over, he returned to athletics and had been 'pacing' his old friend Harry Bell for the 220 yards. In the course of this, one of the trainers remarked on what a good turn of speed Maley had and that it might be an idea to enter the 100 yards.

The Scottish Amateur Athletic Union were very lucky in that they landed ideal summer weather, although with a slight breeze, for the Championships which attracted a crowd of over 10,000 to Hampden Park. The 100 yards was divided into three heats instead of the normal two and Maley 'a strong, well-built fellow', according to *Scottish Sport* won the third heat. Interestingly enough, he is described as 'Maley of the Celtic'. The final then saw the three winners of the heats – W. Wilson of Glasgow, J.B. Auld of Ayrshire and W. Maley 'of the Celtic'. After two false starts, Maley started well, but at 70 yards, Wilson had an 'infinitesimal' lead until Maley, with a 'final thrust carried the day' and beat Auld into second place. The time was given as 11 seconds which was a very good one, but *Scottish Sport* thinks that Maley's strength was the key factor as the wind was blowing in their faces.

Maley also tried his hand at the 220 yards although with less success and he still did a great deal of cycling, although mainly for recreation and pleasure. He did, however, bring many cyclists to Celtic Park and the cycle track was a feature of the ground for many years. In athletics, he served on the committee of the Scottish Amateur Athletic Association for thirty years, becoming in time their president.

But it was football that had become Maley's obsession and passion. He had won two Scottish caps, won the Scottish Cup for Celtic in 1892, and the League Championship on three occasions, as well as the two Glasgow Cups several times. He probably could have gone on playing for a year or so after 1896, but he was well aware of the adage that the time to retire is when people are still saying 'Why', and before they begin to say 'Why not'. After a distinguished, although not necessarily brilliant career, it was time to hang up his boots.

Or so he thought. Kick-off time was approaching on 28 November 1896 at Parkhead. A good crowd had assembled to see a Scottish League game between Celtic and Hibernians and the weather, although dull, was dry enough. Maley was talking away happily to a few spectators and some of the Hibs men when a fellow committeeman asked for a quick word with him. 'Can it wait until half time?' asked the slightly irritated Maley. 'No, I'm afraid it can't' was the reply.

It transpired that three Celtic players – Divers, Battles and Meehan – were refusing to play. They were unhappy about the presence in the press box of a journalist from the *Scottish Referee*. This journalist had been highly critical of Celtic's rough play in a few recent games and had been particularly sarcastic about Barney Battles, whom he had called 'gentle Barney'. The three players were demanding that this journalist be excluded, otherwise they would refuse to don the jersey.

Maley was being asked for his opinion about what should be done. He had never had any great sympathies with organizations like trade unions and their methods of striking and withdrawing their labour, and there was an added dimension to this in that giving in to the rebels' demands would infringe the great Victorian concept of 'freedom of the press'. Maley realised that Celtic needed the press to be on their side, and he therefore agreed with the rest of the committee that there would be no giving in to the troublemakers, even if it meant taking the field with only eight men.

In fact, there were nine, for reserve Barney Crossan was on hand, and a message was sent to get Tom Dunbar who was playing for the reserves at Hampden Park to join the first team and bring them up to 10. This left one place, and the suggestion was made that Willie was still fit enough to turn out. Somewhat reluctantly he did so (although in later years he would never fail to boast about it), and the makeshift team did well enough to contain Hibs to a 1–1 draw.

Maley was possibly still recovering from the aches and pains of this occasion when something momentous happened in his life. On 7 December 1896, his wife Helen gave birth to Charles Thomas Stormonth Maley. Maley was delighted about this and named the baby after his brother Charles (currently a priest in Ayrshire) and his late father. Interestingly, Maley's occupation on the birth certificate is given as Master Draper, for by this time he had opened a gentleman's outfitter shop in the centre of Glasgow. Clearly football and Celtic at this time were a mere interest, albeit a passionate and all-embracing one. The draper's business was what put the bread on the table at this point.

The troublemakers at the Hibs game seldom played again for Celtic, but there was more trouble to come with disastrous consequences for the club in the Scottish Cup at Arthurlie in early January 1897. Twice in their history have Celtic been 'giant-killed' in the Scottish Cup – Arthurlie in 1897 and Inverness Caledonian Thistle in 2000. The common factor on both occasions was player unrest. A more pleasant long-term consequence was the appointment of a good manager.

This time, the great Dan Doyle did not turn up, and the Celtic team, already weakened by injuries and the loss of the three men who refused to play against Hibs in November, went down 4–2 to the incredulous Arthurlie. The pitch was terrible, but this does not excuse Celtic's awful performance. Maley, apparently, did not play in this game, although he was pressed into service the following week, in spite of being 'retired'. No answer seems available as to why he didn't perform on this occasion. Perhaps he himself was injured, or more likely he was too busy charging round Glasgow trying to persuade other players to play for Celtic that day.

In any case, Celtic were humiliated, but this reverse would stir the club into making the necessary long-term changes in their structure and organization, something that would have a particular effect on Willie Maley.

Three

EARLY MISTAKES AND INGATHERING OF TALENT

The disasters of the 1896/97 season meant that changes at the club were inevitable. Maley was convinced that the Players' Strike of November 1896 and the fiasco at Arthurlie could have been avoided if the club had been run on a proper professional footing, by which he meant that the club had to be run like a business with paid officials and a board of directors rather than the current structure of a few volunteer committeemen.

He was, of course, already a businessman. He was now a trained accountant and had opened a shop (the first of several) which sold gentlemen's clothes. Indeed, he described himself as a 'Hosier, Hatter and Glover' – something that was clearly aimed at the Glasgow middle class, and which would seem to have little real relevance to the needs of the people who supported Celtic, who remained by and large Irish and poor.

In February 1896 he had married Helen Pye in the Gorbals in Glasgow, and by the end of that year his son Charles had been born. He was now settled, as he thought. He was clearly determined to see that his own family would rise above the sometimes all embracing poverty of Glasgow. He possibly, by extension, wished to see the Celtic responsible for a general rise in the welfare, material, emotional and spiritual of all those who supported them. He had come, like many others, to realise that the best way to achieve this lay in the treating of Celtic as a business concern rather than a well-meaning but essentially amateurish attempt to run a professional football club. In this way, he felt that more profits could be used to provide food for poor Irish children.

The dealings to set up the club as a business are labyrinthine, but by spring 1897 Maley emerged as the secretary/manager on a salary of £150 per year. On his second son's birth certificate of November 1898 he describes his occupation in the curious term of a 'mercantile clerk'. Effectively Maley had carte blanche to run the club in any way that he saw fit as regards the signing of players and other administrative matters. Although he would always be answerable to his board, they would in practice seldom fail to back him up for the next forty years, even on occasion when they might have and indeed should have acted decisively against him. Mr Maley was indeed Mr Celtic.

Not yet thirty, Maley must have felt that he had landed on his feet. His family life was at the moment happy, he had begun in business and he now had the opportunity to do what he really wanted to do – run a football club. He had a reasonable amount of money with which to do so, for the club's power to generate money was phenomenal. At their excellent stadium in the East End of Glasgow (to some observers perhaps an obscene example of opulence in the middle of so much grotesque poverty), Scottish Internationals were regularly held and other sports like cycling and athletics (in both of which Maley himself occasionally still participated) took place in the summer.

On one occasion, his cycling very nearly proved his and his brother's undoing. This was in May 1898, when he came very close to killing his brother Tom. He and Tom were practising at Celtic Park on the old racing track on a tandem. Willie's foot slipped, the bike skidded into the spikes of the railing that ran round the ground.

Poor Tom was stabbed in the neck on a spike (uncomfortably close to his jugular vein) and his arm was badly damaged on another. It was possibly an incident like that persuaded the Maleys that football was a better participant sport. Indeed Willie, although definitely retired, still played a few friendly games.

But his playing career now became subsidiary to his management skills. Football, the sport that had more or less taken over the hearts and minds of all Scotland over the past twenty years, remained the raison d'etre of the Celtic club, and Maley was painfully aware that all that Celtic had achieved in their less than ten years of existence would come to naught if there was not to be a good team on the park ... permanently. There must be no more Arthurlies or player strikes.

To prevent this happening, Maley determined on two things. One was that players should be adequately paid – and given more if necessary. Men like McMahon, Campbell and Doyle would recompense the club if they could be secured on contracts and kept happy. No effort nor expense need be spared (and there was already plenty of money in the kitty) to put Celtic to the forefront of the game. Allied to that, Maley determined that there must be iron discipline. Maley was basically a kind, philanthropical Victorian gentleman who became genuinely distressed at any severe cases of illness or poverty that he saw, but he did present a tough exterior. He was not easily deceived and he had the same sort of imposing presence that Jock Stein would have seventy years later. As happened with Stein, the atmosphere changed in any given room if Maley entered, and this was obvious even if you had your back to the door from the change in the demeanour of others in the room.

He would not tolerate any sloppiness nor laziness. Well-paid professionals had to train hard. More importantly, they had to think football and to think Celtic. They had to be committed to the club and to know what the club was about in terms of its supporters and ideals and to be determined to work for them. They were to be told how lucky they were to be professional footballers and particularly lucky that they were playing for what Maley himself clearly believed to be the greatest team on earth.

It's an honour and a privilege to wear those green and white jerseys. [This was one of his catchphrases.] These people out there [indicating the crowd] have given a lot to see you wearing those stripes [Celtic still wore green and white vertical stripes until 1903]. What are you going to give back to them?

Players did not need to be Roman Catholics. Even before the establishment of the Limited Company, this had been agreed and Maley would certainly never have gone along with any policy of narrow sectarianism. 'It is not his creed nor his nationality which counts – it's the man himself,' he said frequently and he boasted about the amount of Jews, Hindus and Muslims who found employment at Parkhead, even though most people who worked at Parkhead were Catholic and second or even third generation Irishmen.

Maley thus found himself in an enviable position. Scotland's large and burgeoning Irish population were more or less entirely lovers of Celtic and there was thus a steady and perpetual pool from which to cream off talent. He was also empowered to go round the British Isles to supplement this reservoir with the occasional established player, who could be of any religion. And he possessed the money with which to do this. He also possessed the football brain and discernment to spot a good player. This was an unbeatable combination of advantages.

1897/98 saw Celtic win the Scottish League by some distance, going through the programme undefeated, but they came a cropper in the Scottish Cup at the ground of Third Lanark, although not before they had gained revenge over Arthurlie. The highlight of the League campaign was a 4-0 win at Ibrox, a great goal being scored by Johnny Campbell, who had been brought back from Aston Villa by Maley, who was convinced that he should never have been allowed to leave in the first place.

Campbell had left in 1895 'through the stupid action of a prominent committeeman' according to Maley. But the star of the Celtic team in the 1890s was Sandy McMahon. Born in Selkirk (although some said Dundee), Sandy was the darling of the Parkhead faithful. A great goalscorer and play-maker (although Maley makes the curious comment 'Of speed he had little'), Sandy earned the title 'The Duke' from a French political character of a similar name and he was the first in a long line of personality goal scorers which are the *sine qua non* of a great Celtic team – one thinks of Quinn, McGrory, McPhail, Deans and Larsson in more recent times. Maley's traditional feelings about attacking, entertaining football demanded a prolific goalscorer. Sandy was the first of many.

Maley was also famous for his ability to spot a good goalkeeper. Davie Adams, Charlie Shaw, John Thomson and Joe Kennaway would come along in later years, but the prototype for these was Dan McArthur. A feature of McArthur was his sheer courage. Football was a much more physical game then and with shoulder charging and other forms of thuggery legally sanctioned, a goalkeeper had to be tough. Dan for his 5ft 7in and 10st was anything but a burly character, but he made up for this in courage and speed. Disturbingly, he was 'kicked unconscious' on several occasions, but kept coming back for more, fully justifying his nickname 'the little demon'.

John Reynolds and James Welford were also brought from Aston Villa. Welford was a particularly interesting character as he had played county cricket for Warwickshire. Everton yielded Jack Bell and Davie Storrier, an Arbroath man who had gone south to try his luck, and at long last 1899 saw Celtic win the Scottish Cup for the second time. It was a convincing victory, but a surprise one. Their opponents were Rangers who had won the League that season with a 100 per cent record, and had twice put four goals past Celtic.

On 28 November 1898, William Patrick Maley junior had entered the world. Maley now had two boys and may well have nurtured the hope that they too would play for Celtic and perhaps Scotland. In this he would be disappointed, for neither of them had the slightest ability to play the game, although they did help their father in 'The Bank' restaurant in later years. Very soon in any case, domestic problems would see Maley leave his wife and two sons in Whitevale Street and move to a house in Partick. There is no evidence, however, to support the idea that Maley was a womaniser. It was merely a fact that he and his wife decided that it would be better for all concerned if they parted. Certainly by the 1901 census, Helen Maley is described as the head of the house in Whitevale Street and Willie Maley is elsewhere.

The pattern of the 1898/99 season was repeated in 1899/1900 with Rangers winning the League and Celtic the Cup. The Scottish Cup Final was at Ibrox on the very windy day of 14 April. Celtic were 3-1 up at half-time, but had to face the wind and Queen's Park's famous R.S. McColl in the second half. They actually went further ahead before Queen's pulled two back, but Celtic held out to win the Scottish Cup for the third time.

This was good enough, but it took the disastrous season of 1901 to convince Maley that a radical change to the club was required. The League was won yet again by Rangers and the Scottish Cup Final was lost to Hearts. In Celtic's defence it could be said that Dan McArthur had an off day in goal with the slippery ball, but Maley was now more and more convinced that the way to sustained success for Celtic (which he craved) was to take time and build up a coterie of youngsters who would mature together rather than buy a few established stars.

The team had come far in its thirteen years, but Maley was aware that it could not stand still. It had to develop and go for success. Maley had his network of spies and used them to build the greatest team that Scotland had ever seen, and perhaps who have not yet been bettered a century later. Maley had been depressed that Rangers were winning four Championships in a row around the turn of the century and perceptively realised that although the Scottish Cup brought more prestige and glory, it was the winner of the Scottish League who could be considered to have played the best and most consistent football.

Maley states in *The Story of The Celtic*:

> But our Directors were by no means idle. They included men who knew football, and would not be satisfied until they had built up a side which was capable of producing and maintaining the standard of their great predecessors.

In this respect, Maley is perhaps too modest. The man who built up the side was indeed himself. His directors would certainly back him, but it was his judgement that was crucial. By way of example, throughout 1900, he had heard stories about a forward called James Quinn who played for a team called Smithston Albion, near Croy. The name was pronounced 'Smeethston' locally, but Maley knew that support for Celtic was particularly strong in that area.

One day when Smithston Albion were playing at Stenhousemuir, Maley decided to go and watch the young Quinn. By chance on the train to Stenhousemuir that day he met his good friend William Wilton, the manager of Rangers, and another man whom he knew to be a Rangers director, on their way to watch a game at Falkirk. Rather than blow his own cover about Quinn, Maley said he was going to the same game in Falkirk. By sheer chance, Maley spied an old cycling friend of his at Falkirk station. This man James McLaren now had a horse and cab. Pretending merely to be exchanging greetings with his old friend in order to deceive the Rangers men, Maley also arranged for McLaren to come and collect him at half-time.

The three men watched the game intently, then at half-time Maley feigned boredom with the game and told Wilton that he was off to 'look up a friend' as long as he was in the area. He was then driven by McLaren at full speed to Stenhousemuir to see James Quinn. He arrived just in time to see the huge bison of a man limping off injured! But he watched Quinn several more times, and had him watched by others as well. He decided to try to sign him, but several times in 1900, Quinn said no. He was not interested, he said, in becoming a professional football player. It was a such a precarious and dangerous way of earning a living. This was strange talk from a miner in an era when pit collapses were very common and the real reason was, Maley suspected, that he did not want to live in Glasgow. Maley pointed out that he needn't live in Glasgow, for the rail links between Croy and Glasgow were now very good. Quinn still expressed reluctance.

But Maley, admiring the strength and courage of the youngster and considering him worth the extra effort, persevered and eventually on Hogmanay 1900 signed him provisionally. A few days into the New Year, Maley persuaded Quinn to join Celtic on a trip to Rothesay. There he signed the full forms. Interestingly enough, Quinn was considered and considered himself as a left-winger in those days. It would be Maley who decided that the mighty shoulders of the man would be handy if he changed position to be a centre forward, although this was by no means his original intention.

Maley had already signed another strong, young man in Willie Loney the previous summer. Loney played for Denny Athletic and Maley was impressed by his no-nonsense approach to the centre half position where he was prepared to attack the ball. He also had a surprising turn of pace for a big man and in time, he would become a centre half who knew how to join the forward line.

The two strong, young men would fill the centre of the field in the great Celtic days at the end of the decade. They became firm friends as well, and rumour had it that the pair of them did on occasion like a drink. One summer Saturday in the middle of the close season, they had been drinking somewhat excessively and arrived at the Celtic Sports apparently intoxicated. Maley tore into Quinn, telling him he was a disgrace to the club. Quinn smiled back and said 'OK Mr Maley, I'm sorry – but wait until you see Loney!' Maley apparently could not repress a smile.

In 1902, another two talented young men, David Hamilton and James McMenemy, both Glaswegians, joined the club. Hamilton was a speedy left-winger and McMenemy was a craftier player, a talented dribbler and passer. He had had a trial for Dundee and Everton, but had not impressed either of them. Maley, however, kept watching him, gave him a few trials in benefit and friendly games under pseudonyms like 'Smith' and eventually in June 1902 signed him 'up a close in Union Street'. McMenemy was probably Maley's greatest-ever acquisition, given the length of time that he played for the club and that he served as trainer in later years. But he might have ended up playing merely amateur football and working in a glass factory, had Maley not kept an eye on him. He was small, slightly built and easily knocked off the ball, but his ball-playing ability more than compensated for these deficiencies.

McMenemy had a friend called Alec Bennett. Maley kept viewing him as well, but seemed to have lost him to Hearts. Unaccountably, Hearts who had given him a trial, failed to sign him and Maley, on the strong recommendation of McMenemy, stepped in and signed Bennett. Bennett was not of Irish or Catholic extraction, and the same was true of yet another great Maley acquisition. This was James Young, soon to be called Sunny Jim, after a famous food advertisement of the time. Maley was not directly involved in the signing, but the man who organised the transfer did so with Maley's blessing. Young was big and strong and a good centre half for Bristol Rovers. But he was homesick for his native Ayrshire, and when Mick Dunbar was sent to Bristol in 1903 by Maley to sign a right-winger called Bobby Muir, Maley added as an afterthought 'They've got a centre half too called Young'.

Dunbar duly signed Muir, and Young, who was in the background, said in a stage whisper: 'I wish I was getting back to Scotland too!' Dunbar overheard as he was meant to do and offered Young terms as well. Young agreed instantly and the three men were on the next train north. It was Maley, however, who realised that the reason why Young was a less than total success at Bristol was that he was being played out of position, and in his first season moved him to right half.

By this time, another good wing half from Ayrshire called James Hay had drifted into Celtic via Ayr United and Glossop, and Maley was also keeping tabs on a youngster whom he had given a trial to, but then farmed out to Stenhousemuir. This was a quietly spoken, phlegmatic, unobtrusive but highly intelligent player called Alec

McNair. He would join the club in due course and become the man with the most appearances for the club – 548 in the League and 56 in the Cup.

Another of Maley's great players was the impish Peter Somers. Born in Avondale in 1878, Peter was with Celtic as early as 1897, but Maley couldn't make up his mind about him, as well as having a certain distrust of his sense of humour. Somers was allowed to go on loan to Clyde and Blackburn Rovers before returning permanently in 1902 to become a great inside left. Maley would call him 'the powder monkey', the name given to those who supplied the ammunition for cannons on board ships. Somers became the 'fetch and carry man' for Jimmy Quinn, as well as fulfilling the sometimes vital role of being the 'court jester' when morale was low. He was also a fine pianist and had a rich baritone voice for the soirées on distant away trips to places like Dundee and Aberdeen.

As the saying goes, Rome, of course, was not built in a day and neither was Maley's great Celtic team which won virtually everything from 1904 to 1910. Although 1901 had seen little return, 1902 saw Celtic move closer to Rangers in the Scottish League, and they were now lying in second place.

The Scottish Cup in 1902 was lost to Hibs, even though Celtic had the apparent advantage of having the final played at Parkhead. A couple of weeks earlier had occurred the first Ibrox disaster, where twenty-six people had met their deaths when a rickety wooden stand behind a goal had collapsed at the Scotland *v.* England international.

Ibrox was thus out of action for the Scottish Cup Final, Hampden was in the throes of reconstruction and not yet ready for a big game, and so it had to be Celtic Park. Hibs reluctantly agreed with this idea, for it was the only large ground available. Celtic, perhaps lulled into a false sense of security, played very badly, and lost to a back-heeler (the only goal of the game)! This remains, more than a hundred years on, the last time that Hibs have won the Scottish Cup.

For Celtic there was some sort of consolation in the Glasgow Exhibition/Ibrox Disaster Trophy, which was played for by Celtic, Rangers, Sunderland and Everton. It was played at the end of the season and indeed it was almost midsummer when Celtic beat Rangers 3-2 in the final. All the goals were scored by young Quinn, who was played in the centre instead of his normal position of outside left.

Maley, and Celtic's directors, showed a stubborn streak here. The Trophy was put up by Rangers and proceeds were to go to victims of the Ibrox disaster. Maley was quite willing to go along with that, but Rangers assumed that the trophy would be given back at the end of the competition, as they themselves had won it in a one-off competition in 1901. Celtic refused to cooperate with this. They had won the competition and consequently intended to keep the cup. They rubbed salt into the Ibrox wound when Rangers and Celtic played there again in August 1902 in another game for the Ibrox Disaster Fund. This time Celtic won 7-2, and Quinn scored another hat-trick!

1902/03 was another disastrous season, however, as the old guard of McMahon and Campbell struggled against injury and old age in the forward line and young Quinn looked out of his depth on the left wing. Form generally was poor, although Maley certainly believed that Rangers had the aid of the referee in enabling them to draw the New Year game. He described the refereeing as 'vile'.

Rangers won the Scottish Cup (beating Celtic comfortably in the quarter-final) and Hibs the League. Yet there was a straw in the wind when the Charity Cup was won in May, and the side included new signings Young and Bennett. Neither played in the position in which they were to become famous, but they both looked as if they had something to offer.

Maley realised that 1903/04 might be an important season for the club. The last big honour had been the Scottish Cup of 1900, and even in the early days of the club, supporters did not like to go too long without having something to celebrate. Such had been the expectations raised in their large and committed support by Celtic's whirlwind start to their existence.

However, the first half of the season was disappointing with three defeats at the hands of the Third Lanark team who would win the

League that season. The Glasgow Cup Final between the two of them had been close, but Maley felt that Celtic should have polished them off in the first game before the replay was necessary.

In the forward line, McMenemy was impressing, as to a lesser extent was Peter Somers, and in the half-back line there were two strong challengers for the centre-half spot – Jim Young and Willie Loney. Both were big, strong and uncompromising defenders, but they had attacking capabilities as well. It was a pity that playing two centre halves was not really a possibility, giving Celtic's commitment to attack and entertain the public.

And yet, why not? The problem with the defence seemed to lie with Barney Battles. Maley had never completely forgiven Battles for his part in the mutiny of 1896, even after Barney had returned from his exile in Liverpool and even after Barney was lauded in the press with titles like 'St Bernard of Parkhead'. McArthur, Storrier and Battles had formed a mighty defence in 1900, but Battles was prone to indiscipline, on and off the field. In addition he was now not so fast as he once was, and Maley wondered about his health. Rumour had it that he liked a drink as well.

Maley bit the bullet one day in February 1904. He told Battles that he was dropped, moved Donnie McLeod to right-back, Willie Orr to left-back and then inserted Sunny Jim into the right half position alongside Willie Loney. This formation would now be called a 'flat back four', but Sunny Jim was now encouraged to attack as well as defend, in the same way as Jimmy Hay did on the left, the only proviso being that if one went forward, the other stayed back.

Maley, under pressure from injuries, had made this switch once before. This was in January, in a game which had been lost to Airdrie. Therefore, 9 January 1904, must technically be the birth of Young, Loney and Hay as the greatest half-back line of all time, arguably in world football. But Maley's hand had been forced that day and the mighty threesome really only came together at a Scottish Cup quarter-final replay at Dens Park, Dundee in February 1904. The game finished goalless, but was considered to be such a success that the move was continued for the next replay which ended up 5-0 for Celtic at Parkhead.

Then, revenge was extracted from Third Lanark in the semi-final for earlier defeats that season. It was a tough game, but Celtic edged through 2-1 with goals from Quinn and Muir. Rangers had beaten Morton in the other semi-final and thus awaited Celtic in the final on 16 April.

Before that, Maley had one of the occasions that he really enjoyed. Celtic Park had been chosen for the 1904 Scotland *v.* England international, perhaps surprisingly getting the nod over the newly built Hampden Park, which was deemed to be not quite completely ready. Ibrox was still out of contention after the disaster of 1902. Maley was perhaps unhappy that no Celtic players were in the Scotland team, although he reckoned that they were all young and that their time would come. He may also have been none too pleased to watch England win 1-0, but nevertheless he acted the genial host. He shook hands with the official parties, greeted everyone, dispensed tea and drinks in the pavilion, joked with the Englishmen and was utterly charming to all, winning praise from the English press for 'the hospitality of the Celtic club and their personable manager'.

It was not, of course, the first time that Celtic Park had been chosen for the 'big' International against England. For crowd reasons, Celtic Park was the almost automatic choice for Ireland games, but Maley sensed that it might be the last time that Parkhead would be chosen for England games. Hampden was now looking mightily impressive. It would be a suitable arena for next week's Scottish Cup Final, which he felt might just be a turning point in the history of the club.

Four

THE GREAT DAYS
1904–10

The pay-off for all Maley's hard work began on 16 April 1904. It was
to be the start of an epoch. It was the first Scottish Cup Final at the
new enlarged Hampden Park (which had been opened the previous
Hallowe'en when Celtic visited Queen's Park), it was the first
Scottish Cup Final which saw Celtic wearing their green and white
hoops that they had worn sporadically throughout that season (alter-
nating them with the green and white vertical stripes), and most
importantly, it saw the emergence of the new Celtic team.

Maley had had no compunction about dropping Alec Bennett
when stories reached his ears that Rangers were interested in him,
and he in them. Such stories were hardly earth shattering, for they
had been common knowledge all over Glasgow, particularly after
Alec's brilliant goal on New Year's Day at Celtic Park, which had
excited the interest of the Ibrox establishment. Nevertheless, Maley
felt compelled to tell the press that Bennett was ill with flu' and
would be unavailable for the final.

Alec had been playing off and on in the centre forward position in
the second half of the season. This move seemed to be to keep

Bobby Muir on the right wing, and apparently one of the many carrots that Rangers dangled before Bennett was a return to his right wing position, for which he was temperamentally better suited. In the circumstances, although Maley had played Bennett throughout the Scottish Cup campaign, he felt that in a final against Rangers, it might be a better idea to drop Alec and bring in Jimmy Quinn, who was hitherto a rather disappointing left-winger, into the centre.

In fact, it turned out to be one of Maley's many brainwaves, and produced arguably one of Celtic's most famous Scottish Cup victories. Rangers were 2-0 up, but Celtic, inspired by Young and McMenemy, fought back and Jimmy Quinn, the hitherto shy, under-performer on the big occasion, scored a hat-trick which would remain until 1972 as the only hat-trick scored in a Scottish Cup Final.

Rangers' two goals were defensive disasters. They were scored early on in the game before many of the 64,000 crowd had settled into Hampden Park, which was having teething problems at the turnstiles in staging its first-ever, big Scottish Cup Final. Goalkeeper Davie Adams collided with a post as he went for the first goal, then while the defence were still trying to regroup, Finlay Speedie scored his second.

Enter Quinn. Head down, he charged through the Rangers defence to score his first, then before half-time picked up a Bobby Muir cross to score his second. Half-time thus arrived with all square at 2-2. Maley had a brief word with his men during the break, telling Davie Adams to forget about it, encouraging his new and comparatively untried left wing of Peter Somers and Davy Hamilton not to be afraid to run at the Rangers defence and giving a smile of encouragement to the miner boy from Croy, who had restored the possibility of a Celtic triumph.

In the second half, Celtic had the benefit of the breeze and were able to take command. Quinn scored late in the game with another great individual run, using his strength to ward off challenges. Celtic might have scored more. The aftermath of Celtic's goal was significant. All the players crowded round Quinn, slapping his shoulders and embracing him. 'The Croy Express was nearly dismembered by the wild embraces of his mates' said the *Courier* but Quinn, stoically showing no emotion, merely walked back to the centre line, as if to say, 'That is my job, scoring goals.'

It was the beginning of the great Celtic team and the beginning of the Quinn legend. Maley smiled and congratulated himself on his perseverance, remembering all the problems that he had had to get Jimmy to sign from Smithston Albion, and his apparent lack of self-confidence, something that seemed bizarre in a man of such a mighty physique. But there was also a small matter to be sorted out regarding Alec Bennett.

Maley went to see Bennett the day after the Cup Final. He told him that he wanted to keep him. He could not guarantee him the right-wing spot, but he had had an offer from Notts County for Bobby Muir. Bobby wanted to return to England, and Maley was prepared to let him go. He saw a future for Bennett at Parkhead, probably on the right wing, for yesterday's events seemed to have solved the centre forward problem. The forward line would, of course, always need to be shuffled around to cover for injuries, but if Muir went south, then Alec looked like the best right-winger. There might be a slight pay increase for Bennett if he stayed, but there must be no more of this nonsense about liking Rangers as a club. His friend Jimmy McMenemy wanted Alec to stay, but one way or other Alec had to decide soon and abide by his decision.

Bennett considered. He did like playing for Celtic, had many friends there and had been heartbroken not to be part of the Scottish Cup Final. But (and here he shuffled edgily), he was a non-Catholic and often felt out of place at Parkhead. Maley nodded sympathetically, but then stated his much repeated dictum that there would never be any religious preferment at Parkhead, for the future of the Irish in Scotland was to integrate, not to oppose. He wanted a multi-denominational team at Celtic Park. 'It is not a man's creed nor his nationality that counts. It's the man himself.' Alec nodded. He had heard it all before, but there was a certain sincerity about it all. He agreed to stay with Celtic, at least for the time being. It was one of Maley's many shrewd moves at this time.

Further triumphs came the way of the Maley family the following week. Willie Maley gave Celtic's game against Kilmarnock a miss to go down with brother Alec to the Crystal Palace ground in London. This was to see his brother Tom's Manchester City team win the FA Cup by beating Bolton Wanderers 1-0, the goal being scored by the great Billy Meredith. In so doing, Maley missed seeing Jimmy Quinn scoring five against Killie, but it was a fine feeling that the Maleys were the Cup-winning managers in both Scotland and England. Their widowed mother loved that, and it was a shame that old Thomas had not lived to see it.

Rangers got some sort of bitter revenge over Quinn in the Charity Cup Final, when a vicious tackle by Nick Smith split open his thigh muscle, but this did not prevent Quinn and Celtic going on tour to Austria. In one of these games in Vienna, Maley actually played for Celtic in his old position at right half after Sunny Jim Young got lost in Frankfurt! Maley was now thirty-six and still fit, but he insisted, since it was a baking hot day, in playing each half in the shaded area of the pitch. Celtic won 4-2 in any case, and their veteran player did not let them down.

Jimmy Quinn was at the centre of a major controversy the follow-ing year, 1904/05. More fruits of Maley's hard work were plucked when the League title was won (in a play-off against Rangers at Hampden in May), by a team who played together with real self-belief and cohesion, every one of them moulded together by Maley, but left by and large to work out tactics for themselves. Rangers had been soundly beaten in the League on 18 February as well as in the Glasgow Cup Final, and were clearly thirsting for revenge when the two teams were drawn together at Parkhead in the semi-final of the Scottish Cup on 25 March. (In those days, the semi-finals were not yet held at neutral venues.)

It was a foul day with driving wind and rain, and a young Rangers team seemed to have adapted better to the conditions. They were two ahead, but the Celtic crowd and Maley himself were by no means discouraged for they remembered what had happened in the final of the previous year. But time was beginning to disappear when

Quinn was held by Rangers defender Craig when Craig was on the ground. Quinn tried to struggle free, but in so doing he kicked Craig in the face. The referee Mr Robertson ordered Quinn off, and the Parkhead crowd immediately invaded the field to protest.

Players had to retreat into the old pavilion for safety, and they never returned. Celtic, whether with the blessing of Maley or not is uncertain, made the sporting gesture of conceding the game. Rather to everyone's surprise, Rangers accepted it, when the normal practice of the time was to have a replay with a view to another huge gate, and Quinn received a lengthy suspension.

It was hardly the end of the matter however. Quinn and Celtic contested the suspension, newspapers were sued for their reporting of the affair, testimonial dinners were held for Jimmy Quinn by his adoring public, and future games between Celtic and Rangers would be affected. It was a constant talking point in Edwardian Scotland, and everybody knew who Quinn was. Maley did nothing to dampen down this uproar, for he realised that there is no such thing as bad publicity. People would throng to see the mighty Quinn.

Maley may have been upset at losing the Scottish Cup (Third Lanark would beat Rangers in the final), but he had begun to realise that the League was the major challenge for the club. Luck could play a part in the destination of the Scottish Cup. It was less easy to claim 'luck' as a factor over a League campaign which lasted (in 1905) over 26 games and was played in all weathers. Maley was about to embark on a love affair with the Scottish League.

1905/06 saw a repeat of 1904/05 in terms of competitions won, apart from the Charity Cup in which they lost to Rangers in the first round. Celtic annexed the Glasgow Cup, but lost in the quarter-final of the Scottish Cup to the eventual winners, the excellent Hearts team on a very hard and sanded Parkhead pitch. But the League was won for the second time in a row without a great deal of bother and in spite of several defeats, notably and notoriously to Port Glasgow in November. Quite a few players saw the unpleasant side of Maley that day as he fulminated against them for their shocking lack of effort and application. Some supporters, indeed, took an even worse deduction from these events, suspecting bribery and corruption – a by no means uncommon charge in those days.

However, by New Year in 1906, Celtic had settled into better form and the League Championship was won at Hampden Park on 10 March when Celtic beat Queen's Park 6-0, Quinn scoring four goals. It was now clear that Maley had built up a fine Celtic team, but in addition to being the best team in Scotland, Maley was always keen to continue his 'missionary' work, taking Celtic on tours of the Highlands and the Borders, and in 1906 they went on another tour of central Europe to play games in Vienna, Prague, Berlin and Budapest.

Celtic and Maley suffered a major blow early in season 1906/07 when Willie Loney broke his arm in a game against Hearts on 15 September. Loney's value to the club had been stressed by the fact that the team had played five competitive games that season without conceding a goal. The mighty half-back line of Young, Loney and Hay had already begun to be the foundation of a truly great team. Loney was the most unspectacular of the trio, but had the nickname of being the 'Obliterator' or 'No Road This Way', such was his almost total command of the middle of the field.

He was, Maley felt, the true successor to James Kelly, and Kelly himself shared that opinion. But now he was likely to be out for a considerable part of the season. Maley experimented for a spell with a youngster called Wilson, but eventually hit upon the expedient of bringing Alec McNair to centre half and giving the right-back slot to Donnie McLeod. This was good enough to win the Glasgow Cup in October, and to bring 1906 to a close with the loss of only three points, all draws to Dundee, Clyde and Kilmarnock.

New Year's Day 1907, saw Celtic's first defeat of the season when they went down 2-1 to Rangers. The defeat, however, was not what upset Maley so much as the sending off once again of Jimmy Quinn. There seemed to have been a certain amount of bad blood between Quinn and Hendry, the left-back of Rangers, but what actually happened is a little obscure. Hendry had body-checked Alec Bennett when Bennett was in full flow, having meted out similar treatment to Jimmy McMenemy earlier. Quinn ran forward to remonstrate with Hendry and in so doing knocked him over without any apparent violent intent.

That is the Celtic version. The other version was that Quinn did indeed punch Hendry and then even kicked him in the face after he had been knocked down. Certainly Mr Kirkham of Burslem (English referees were often used for important Scottish games) had no doubts and off went Quinn.

Quinn was suspended until the beginning of March, and Maley knew that this would be a serious blow to his ambition of becoming the first team to win the Scottish League and the Scottish Cup in the same season. But he deployed Alec Bennett (now temporarily disabused of his Rangers sympathies) in the centre, played the colourful Bobby Templeton on the right wing with Davy Hamilton on the left, and by the time that Quinn returned, the team was still in contention for both trophies, although they had taken an unconscionably long time to dispose of Morton in the Scottish Cup.

The crucial game in the League was against Dundee at Parkhead on 23 March. Dundee were a fine side, and actually ahead of Celtic in the League race, although Celtic had games in hand and could overtake Dundee if they won them all. The game attracted a crowd of 35,000 to Parkhead, and the crowd saw a great game. Dundee would claim that they had the ball over the line, but the referee Mr Kirkham of Preston rejected this. Yet Celtic undeniably had the bulk of the pressure. Quinn almost scored, but in the act of drawing back his foot, Dundee's defender Lee collided with him, thereby sustaining an injury. For the rest of the game, Dundee's centre half Herbert Dainty 'kept Jimmie quiet', in the opinion of the *Dundee Courier*, and a 0-0 draw was the outcome.

This result of course suited Celtic, and the League was eventually secured at Meadowside, the home of Partick Thistle on the evening of Wednesday 24 April, when goals by Quinn and Bennett saw Celtic home. Sadly, it being a midweek game, only 4,000 were there to see the victory, but Celtic's claim to be the best team in Britain and therefore the world was given some credence by what happened at Ibrox the same night. Rangers, third in the Scottish league and lying some ten points behind Celtic, managed to beat Newcastle United 3-0 – and Newcastle were the Champions of the English League!

The Celtic crowd did not turn up in force at Meadowside for several reasons, even though Maley insisted on bringing the Scottish Cup to show it off. One was that it was a midweek fixture and difficult for people outside Glasgow to attend; in any case, the Scottish League was more or less a foregone conclusion as Celtic still had another five games to play and the crowd had presumably spent all their money the previous Saturday celebrating the winning of the Scottish Cup against Hearts.

The Hearts Cup Final was fairly one-sided. Hearts had a few injuries, notably to their star performer Charlie Thomson. A fairly soft penalty was converted by Willie Orr, and then Peter Somers scored a couple of easy goals as the Celtic inside trio of McMenemy, Quinn and Somers 'carried all before them' and gladdened the heart of Mr Maley. A crowd of 50,000 was present, further proof of the drawing power of the Celts.

There had actually been a bigger crowd at Ibrox to see the quarter-final on 9 March against Rangers, and it was round about now that cartoons appeared with Maley and the Rangers management with their hands on money bags, and being referred to as the 'Old Firm'. The press were astonished at the vastness of the crowd, but after Celtic went into a 3-0 lead, they 'began to skail', presumably meaning they went away, either upset at the defeat or elated at the victory. In any case, a heavy snowfall may well have encouraged them to depart.

It was Quinn's first game back after his suspension and it was the first time that the teams had met since Quinn's dismissal at New Year. Both of these factors presumably played a part in attracting the large crowd. Quinn is much praised for his restraint when he was 'kicked in the stomach' by Hendry. He then had a goal disallowed by Mr Lewis of Blackburn for a reason not apparent to the press.

But Celtic were in any case a goal up, a tap-in scored by the 'powder monkey' Peter Somers. Hay with a 'drooping shot' and Hamilton with a header, added to Celtic's lead on either side of half-time. Quinn did not score that day, but he did, nevertheless, justify Maley's faith in him, for he 'drew three men to him' to give room for the rest of the forward line to attack the shaky Rangers defence.

With the Glasgow Cup having been won earlier in the season, Celtic could have won all four available trophies, but played very badly in the final of the Glasgow Charity Cup at Cathkin Park and lost 1–0 to Rangers. Maley was apparently furious and berated his players for letting the side down. He had wanted to win all four trophies, but he would not have all that long to wait.

In the meantime, however, Maley took his team on another tour, this time to Denmark. Two remarkable things happened on this trip abroad. One was that as goalkeeper Davie Adams' mother was ill, they had no recognised goalkeeper with them, leaving John Mitchell and Bobby Templeton to do the honours. The other was that although it was rumoured that Maley himself, still several months short of his fortieth birthday, might perform in the goal, he surprised them all by appearing as a referee, reputedly in one game being hard on Celtic and restricting them to a 4–2 victory over a Danish XI.

1908 is rightly regarded by Celtic historians as being one of the greatest years in the history of the club. As would occur again in 1967, the team won every competition that they entered. The Glasgow Cup was won in October 1907 after three attempts to beat Rangers. There was a perception that the first two finals were drawn deliberately in order to engender more money. One presumes and hopes that this was not true, but it was hardly helped by Maley's boasting about the amount of money that could be earned. In 1909, there would be serious consequences of all this.

It was a superb Celtic team, but they had to work hard for their successes and they fought off determined challenges from Rangers, Dundee and Falkirk. They lost three times in away fixtures at Aberdeen, Hearts and Dundee, but some of the play was absolutely inspirational. Where Maley had done his homework was in the signing of good reserves like McLean, Semple and Kivlichan who were always able to step into the breach where required.

But Maley found himself in trouble on two occasions. In his role as club linesman (neutral linesman were still a generation away), Maley still occasionally got carried away. On 15 February at Port Glasgow, he ran onto the field to remonstrate with referee Jock Bell after McMenemy had been bowled over by a robust challenge. He was then removed from his job as linesman and later suspended for three matches. Similarly, at the end of March at Dens Park, he saw fit to protest to the referee, a Mr J. Fraser about ill treatment meted out to the already injured Peter Somers by the grotesquely misnamed Herbert Dainty of Dundee.

The League was won at Ibrox on 25 April (Maley's fortieth birthday) when Celtic beat Rangers 1-0, 'a scoreline which in no way represents the run of the game', and that was with both McMenemy and Quinn injured early on! Man of the Match was Alec Bennett. Alec completely overran right-back Sharp (whom Rangers had recently signed from Woolwich Arsenal) and scored the only goal of the game. Jimmy Hay (who had recently recovered from a potentially life-threatening appendicitis operation) was tremendous that day and the reporter of the *Dundee Courier* says 'I have never seen the Celtic so fleet of foot'.

This was of course the second week in a row that the Celtic fans had had cause to celebrate, for the previous week the hapless St Mirren had been dumped 5-1 in a very one-sided Scottish Cup Final. That is not to say that there hadn't been problems in the earlier stages of the Scottish Cup, however, for in the semi-final at Pittodrie, Celtic had needed a last-minute McMenemy strike to get the better of Aberdeen, and in February at Ibrox, they had edged Rangers 2-1.

The reporters enjoyed this game against Rangers. 'There was no Quinn, nor anything Quinn-like in Celtic', yet his deputy Kivlichan scored the two goals, one of them 'he was not shooting, but letting out [sic] at a drooping ball from Bennett'. The game was summed up very rhetorically and enigmatically when the *Glasgow Herald* says that Celtic were 'lucky, but not lucky winners'.

To see if Celtic would win the Scottish quadruple, supporters had to wait patiently for 30 May for the final of the Glasgow Charity Cup against Queen's Park. It was worth waiting for, because Celtic won 3-0 in sweltering heat with two goals from McMenemy and one, predictably, from Quinn. As Celtic had also done consistently well against English and Continental opposition, Maley could claim with justice that his side were the best team in the world.

Maley, the undisputed creator of this team, deliberately kept a high profile for himself, being constantly available to the press and the general public with his well-informed, urbane geniality. On train trips to Aberdeen, for example, he would sit with supporters and other passengers talking about football, politics, the King's various illnesses and indispositions, the Liberal government with its changes to society, the rising Labour movement, South Africa and other subjects, impressing everyone with his knowledge and affability. When the subject of Ireland was mentioned, he would tactfully change the subject, but not before expressing his hopes for permanent peace for the land of his birth.

There was one problem however, which Maley did not solve at Parkhead, and that concerned the prodigiously talented right-winger Alec Bennett. Alec had been kept out of the 1904 Scottish Cup Final against Rangers because Maley thought he was being 'tapped' by the Ibrox club and that Alec was indeed a Rangers admirer. Nevertheless, he had been kept at Parkhead by Maley's powers of persuasion. Alec kept playing brilliantly for Celtic (by no means the last Rangers supporter to do so) for the next four great years until he eventually signed for Rangers in early May 1908.

It was a curious business, and one wonders why Maley did not do more to retain Alec in 1908 when he had certainly gone more than the extra mile in 1904. Perhaps Alec was finding it more and more difficult to deal with the Irish Catholic associations at the Celtic club which had perhaps become more prevalent with the recent success, perhaps he and Maley fell out, perhaps Maley felt that with men like McLean, Moran and Kivlichan around, Bennett was now expendable. But whatever happened, in 1908/09, Bennett was wearing the blue of Rangers.

Perhaps the kindly and gentle Alec found Maley too intractable. Perhaps the reason why Bennett loved the blue of Rangers more than the green of Celtic was nothing to do with any inbuilt love of the Ibrox men as a genuine dislike of Maley, who could on occasion be a bully. Even Sunny Jim Young and Jimmy McMenemy would avoid Maley after a defeat, particularly if it was a defeat that cost the club a great deal of money. Certainly David McLean, who went on to play for Scotland in 1912, cited Maley's bullying tactics as one of the reasons why he was glad to leave Parkhead in 1909.

Man-management was a still science in its infancy. The Victorian school of thought (in which Maley was thoroughly immersed) did not need it. An employee should know his place and be glad of it. There is a certain amount of evidence to indicate that although Maley was a favourite uncle to his best players, he was not always so to fringe players or to players who crossed him. This of course shows a distinct similarity to Celtic's other great manager, Jock Stein – and indeed to quite a few other successful ones of other clubs.

The 1908/09 season was the one that was made notorious by the riot at the Scottish Cup Final between Rangers and Celtic, which led to the withholding of the Cup. Indeed, but for the prompt action of Willie Maley's brother Alec, the cup itself might have been burned or stolen. The brave Alec was quick off his mark to save the trophy when what started as a protest degenerated into a mass riot.

To a certain extent, Willie Maley himself might have been inad-vertently responsible for this catastrophe. The first game of the Scottish Cup final had ended in a 2-2 draw on 10 April, Rangers earning a draw thanks in no small measure to Alec Bennett. A replay was scheduled for the following Saturday. Maley was worried about the backlog of fixtures, for Celtic, in the running for their fifth con-secutive Championship, still had eight League fixtures to play after the replay on 17 April. Maley suggested both to his players and to the press that in the event of another draw (a likely result between two well-balanced teams) extra time might be played to produce a winner, for as it was, the season was due to end on the last day of April, and the Scottish Cup Final could not be dragged out much longer. Celtic were behind Dundee in the League, but would, he presumed, catch them up when the outstanding games were played … but time was running out.

Maley's suggestion on 13 April to Rangers and the SFA for extra time fell on deaf ears, and the cynics suspected (not without cause) that another draw would suit Celtic, Rangers and the SFA for even more money would be generated by such an event. The replay was a good one and Celtic were indebted once again to Jimmy Quinn for their second-half equaliser. The referee blew for full-time and the players (apart from a few Celtic ones who perhaps believed that Maley's suggestion had won the day) made their way off. Eventually, they too were called in by a disappointed Maley, but by this time, a few of the bored crowd (there had by now been a lengthy delay) had invaded the playing area.

At this stage, there was no suggestion of violence, merely an opportunity perhaps to shake hands with Quinn or even Maley. Nor was the invasion confined to the fans of either team, who mingled around the playing area exchanging banter and insults. But prompt action from the police was not forthcoming until there were hundreds on the field. Perhaps there was a little heavy-handed stuff from the belated Glasgow constabulary, perhaps someone had argued too vociferously with them, but very soon, to the horror of Maley and William Wilton of Rangers, violence erupted.

Young men burned pay boxes, lit a bonfire and threw stones at the pavilion. Fortunately, the players on both sides were escorted to safety, but the riot continued for several hours. The interesting thing was that, although the riot involved the supporters of Celtic and Rangers, it was not a sectarian riot. As no one (or only a very few) wore supporters colours in 1909, one could not have in any case been able to say who was who. Moreover, although Celtic were very definitely the Catholic and Irish team of Glasgow (and proud of it), Rangers had not yet involved themselves with the extreme Protestant cause. Their supporters, like those of Celtic, were merely upset and feeling cheated of a chance to see the end of an enthralling Cup Final.

One could sympathise with that point of view (Maley certainly did) but the riot could not be excused. It was in some ways a rather civilised riot, in that at least nobody was killed and very few were injured, but the authorities withheld the Scottish Cup, thereby depriving Celtic of their opportunity to win the trophy three years in a row (something that, almost a century later, they still have not done).

On the night of Monday 19 April, when the SFA were making that decision and wondering whether Hampden could or should be rebuilt, Celtic were playing the first of their eight League games to be played Monday, Wednesday, Thursday, Saturday, Monday, Wednesday, Thursday and Friday. 5 were won, 2 drawn and 1 lost, and that was enough to beat the luckless Dundee, who could do nothing but watch their lead being whittled away and finally overtaken.

The genius of Maley was seen in his adaptability. Fringe players like McLean, Kivlichan, Mitchell, and Craig were deployed to cover for the inevitable injuries and exhaustion, and he even outrageously played a man called John Atkinson. Atkinson had played for Hamilton Accies against Celtic in the game on Wednesday 21 April. In this game, Celtic's left-winger Davie Hamilton had had to limp off injured in a disappointing 1-1 draw. Maley, however, had been so impressed by the play of young Atkinson (a medical student at Glasgow University) that he approached him and invited him to play the following day for Celtic against Morton.

As Atkinson was an amateur, there was no legal problem about this and the young John ran out for Celtic on Thursday 22 April and scored twice in a 5-1 victory. John then departed from the Celtic scene, having played a small but by no means negligible part in the 1909 League Championship triumph. No doubt he enjoyed telling his patients in later years how he had worn the green and white jersey and played alongside the mighty Jimmy Quinn!

Thus came to an end the bizarre month of April 1909. Nothing could hide or diminish the fact that Maley had now won five League Championships in a row, and but for riotous spectators might have won the Scottish Cup for the third year running. He was now forty-one years old and at the very height of his powers – there seemed to be no limit to what Celtic and Maley could do. He richly deserved the name 'Mr Celtic', for it was he who had made this club in only twenty-one years!

The following season, 1909/10, was the last of Celtic's six-in-a-row League Championship-winning run. Somehow, it was fitting that the monarch Edward VII should die on 6 May 1910, a matter of days after Celtic won the Championship. Maley's great team have been called the 'Edwardian Celts' and it seemed to personify that era. It was an era, too, in which a limited amount of progress was being made in other respects for the supporters.

The Liberals were in power and were vigorously setting about tackling at least some of the problems that had beset Britain since the Industrial Revolution of a century previously. There was clearly a long way to go, however, as any visitor to a game at Parkhead would have noticed in the gross poverty of those who supported the club. But there was at least something to cheer them up, and that was in the inspired play of the team.

As well as being successful, the team were also entertaining the crowds with the wiles of McMenemy, the fast runs of Hamilton and the goal-scoring exploits of the 'bison' Jimmy Quinn, a man whose fame spread deep into the heart of every Englishman, especially when he and McMenemy scored the goals at Hampden in the 1910 international.

For the start of the 1909/10 season, however, Celtic were two men short from the great team of 1908. Alec Bennett of course, had now been with Rangers for one season, and for reasons never satisfactorily explained, the brilliant inside left Peter Somers disappeared from the scene and reappeared playing for Hamilton Accies. This may be due to a personality clash with Maley. Somers was a great entertainer, as a pianist, a singer and a comedian. He had given, for example, a great rendition on the piano the night of Jimmy Quinn's presentation in 1907 – the presentation being organised by fans to pay for any fines or legal costs Quinn might have to face following his suspensions. Maley of course would encourage musical and dramatic activities, for he always believed that if the team were on tour during the summer, or staying overnight in a hotel at Dundee or Aberdeen for example, the team should entertain the fellow guests with their wide repertoire of tricks. In this respect too, Somers was almost indispensable and a much valued member of the team.

But Somers' cheeky personality could occasionally manifest itself in other respects as well, not least in his lack of fear for Maley. As we have said, Maley was a difficult man to face in the aftermath of a defeat, with even mighty men like Jimmy Quinn and Jimmy Young not keen to meet him. Peter was not like that however, and it may be that he got under the skin of Maley once or twice too often and found himself moving elsewhere. It would certainly have been difficult to believe that Somers left Celtic for football-playing reasons, for Peter was a great player. He was fated to die young in November 1914.

Rangers may have benefited from Alec Bennett but Alec was missing when Celtic beat them 1-0 in the Glasgow Cup Final in October, the goal scored predictably by the ubiquitous Quinn. Rangers finished only a distant third in the League Championship. The League Championship had once again seen Quinn at his best. For example, on Christmas Day 1909 at Kilmarnock, the only goal of the game was scored by Jimmy and it was 'a rampage of a goal, right down the middle, with the whole Kilmarnock defence in pursuit'. Celtic's closest challengers were Falkirk who actually beat Celtic on 23 April to maintain their unbeaten home record, but crucially had gone down the week before to Hearts at Tynecastle.

Celtic thus had to get one point from their two remaining games after the Falkirk defeat, and did so in a way that was distinctly anti-climactic. Once again (as in 1908) it was Maley's birthday (25 April) which saw the League flag won. It was a dull 0-0 draw against Hibs at Parkhead on a Monday before a poor crowd of 2,000, but it did mean that the Championship had now been won for six years in a row. On the following Saturday, the League Champions Celtic went to Dens Park to play the Scottish Cup winners Dundee, but the game finished in another 0-0 draw in front of 12,000 disappointed spectators.

However, things were about to change for the six-in-a-row League Champions. A significant straw in the wind was the defeat in the semi-final of the Scottish Cup at the hands of Clyde in March. The goalkeeper Adams was ill, and injury ruled out Dodds, Young and McMenemy. It was hardly surprising that Celtic should lose in these circumstances, but it was certainly a warning signal to the effect that Celtic's reserve cover was not as comprehensive as it might have been. It was also a sign that the great side were beginning to age simultaneously. Maley would have to rebuild and evolve.

For the moment though, Maley was delighted that six League Championships in a row had been won – a record that would last for sixty years and it would take another great Celtic team to beat it. Praise poured in from every direction, even from the English press, in those days comparatively free of the patronising attitude to Scottish football that afflicts them today. 'Malley's (sic) team are prodigious', 'The Celtic men are quite clearly the leading light of the North' and 'Newcastle must be delighted that Glasgow is to the north of the Wall, otherwise Celtic might be frequent and predatory visitors', were just some of the comments made in the English newspapers.

Maley had every reason to be happy. In 1910, he was more or less a total success in football. Relationships with his board of directors appear to have been excellent, with very few indications of any serious discord at Celtic Park. His relationship with fans was always pleasant, familiar and genial. On a Sunday, the old pavilion at Celtic Park was open to the public and those who wished to could come and have a shower or a bath (facilities that in 1910 were not yet necessarily readily available elsewhere in Glasgow). Maley himself would frequently be on hand, holding court to whoever wanted to listen, and talking about football or indeed anything else, calling people by their first names and generally providing the Glasgow public with the acceptable face of Celtic.

His sociability would always be visible when the team were on a trip. He would be courteous to the other guests and always invite them to a soirée which he would organise around the piano in the hotel drawing room. He would sing Robbie Burns songs and other favourites of the music hall, and encourage his players to do likewise.

Many of them showed their versatility, and in left-back Jamie Weir, they had a real artiste in his recitation of Tam O'Shanter.

With his players, Maley had a Jekyll and Hyde sort of relationship. He could be stern and strict, and he certainly tolerated no nonsense, insisting on fitness and like Stein some sixty years later, he even employed a network of spies to check up on his players if he thought that any of them were overstepping the mark as far as alcohol consumption was concerned. Yet Maley was also a father figure, always polite and charming to wives and extremely concerned for their welfare. The introverted, depressed, brooding side of him had yet to emerge. This would come later.

In himself, he was happy. He regretted the collapse of his marriage and that he had been estranged from his wife for the last decade. His two sons were being brought up by their mother, but he did his best to remain on friendly terms and to see his sons regularly. He realised that any repair to the marriage was unlikely, but that being a Catholic, divorce was impossible. He was a religious man, attending Mass regularly, and was totally convinced that he was doing a good job with Celtic, to the extent of thinking (and even saying) that God had chosen him for this job. If this were so, there could be little doubt in 1910 that the Almighty had chosen well.

Five

PARTIAL FALL
AND TOTAL RECOVERY

All good things must come to an end sooner or later, and by 1911, Celtic were no longer the champions of Scotland. This honour passed to Rangers and Celtic ended up fifth – a severe decline. It is difficult to put a finger on what exactly happened to Celtic that year, other than to say that a few hints of it had been obvious the season before. It was a classic case of great players ageing simultaneously and fresh blood being required. The mighty, even legendary half-back line, for example, of Young, Loney and Hay played together for the last time on 3 September 1910.

The only change in personnel at the start of the season was that of Peter Somers, whose presence on the field was missed more than Maley appreciated. Certainly the inside-left spot was a difficult one to fill. For a spell Peter Johnstone was tried there but it soon became obvious that he was a better defender than an attacker, and John Hastie who had recently joined the club from the quaintly named Glenbuck Cherrypickers was given the nod. John was one of the many players for whom the term 'honest journeyman' would apply. He was certainly no more than that.

Key men like Willie Loney and Jimmy Quinn picked up injuries, as of course was always liable to happen in the rough and tough of the centre of the field, especially as old age (for a footballer!) was beginning to tell. Both men played when half fit, for there was no obvious understudy. In the case of Loney, Tommy McAteer came in at centre half towards the end of the season. He was no Willie Loney, although for that season the defence was not really the problem.

Maley also transposed Dodds and Hay on the left-hand side of the park. Joe Dodds had always been an attacking full-back, and Jimmy Hay a defensive-minded midfielder and the switch seemed logical although for one reason or another, it did not seem to work.

In the forward line, a newcomer to the team was Andy McAtee. What immediately impressed supporters about Andy was his speed, his ability to shoot and his brawny legs in contrast to the rest of him. Andy was wiry, but by no means muscular. He had a few games in the centre covering for Quinn, but his best position would turn out to be on the right wing, something that had been a problem position since the departure of Alec Bennett to Rangers in 1908.

The team got off to an uncharacteristically bad start in the 1910 /11 season by losing 3 games out of 4, and they never really recovered to challenge for the League. Crucially, in October they lost twice to Rangers, once in the League and another time in the Glasgow Cup Final, proof that hegemony had passed, at least temporarily, to the other side of the city. The press were delighted at all this, but for no other reason than that it opened up the League. Indeed, the contest was more interesting than it had been over the past six years. Maley however, saw this press approval as some kind of gloating over the misfortunes of Celtic when all it really indicated was a sense of relief that someone else would win the Championship.

The other side of Maley was apparent, however, in his fulsome congratulations to the Ibrox side for their deserved success. He possibly did welcome a challenge and sensed in his heart of hearts that his fine team which had triumphed from 1904 until 1910 was beginning not necessarily to fall apart, but to need some shoring up.

But 1911 was by no means a failure either, for the Scottish Cup, still the most prestigious tournament in the land, in some peoples' eyes, was won by a Celtic team who did not even concede a goal. Their passage to the final was quiet and uneventful, their best result being a 1-0 win over a strong Aberdeen side in the semi-final, but they certainly enjoyed a little luck with the way that the other results went. First of all, the strong Dundee side (the holders of the Cup) defeated Rangers in a thriller, then Dundee themselves lost to Hamilton Accies in the semi-final through sheer complacency and lack of concentration.

The final was thus between Hamilton and Celtic and the first game was generally agreed to be one of the dullest cup finals ever. The game ended 0-0 on a dry, bumpy pitch and the players thoroughly deserved the boos of the Ibrox crowd, most of whom had departed early, convinced that this game, which ended in a draw like the cup finals of 1909 and 1910, was a fix, one of the recurring charges made about Scottish football in the days before the First World War.

For the replay, Maley made a change in his forward line and, as often with Maley, he got it right. John Hastie, who had played at inside left was dropped, his place taken by the earnest Willie Kivlichan, a former Rangers player (but devout Catholic) who had played on the right wing; the right-wing position was given to young Andy McAtee who had impressed in the games he had played this season.

Something else happened which helped Celtic, and that was a heavy downfall of rain about an hour before the start, bringing to an end an unusually long dry spell. Maley felt this would help young McAtee, who was a tremendous ball player with enormous potential but who needed the ball to come to him fairly low. Once again, Maley's judgement was vindicated by events.

There was an immediate and obvious improvement in the play, and as is often the case, the smaller team, having shot its bolt in the first game, was subdued as Celtic gradually took control. McAtee and McAteer were outstanding, and Celtic's 2-0 win (Quinn and

McAteer being the scorers) should indeed have been much more substantial than that.

Maley's joy at the landing of the Scottish Cup must have been tempered by the knowledge that this was indeed a fairly poor Celtic team, and the fact that they never defeated Rangers in four encounters tended to prove that the League Championship had gone to the best team. But there were still some fine players around – McMenemy had a few years left, Maley felt, as did Sunny Jim Young and Alec McNair, although Quinn was clearly nearing the end of his career.

But Maley fell out with his captain (who was also the captain of the Scotland side) Jimmy Hay. Hay had been none too happy with some of Maley's tactical and positional changes that season, and there is a certain indication that Hay had had as much as he could take of some of Maley's more autocratic methods of man-management. But Hay was a fine player and captain and was much loved by the fans. On Tuesday 25 April, he was given a benefit – a friendly against Partick Thistle – but very soon after that, Hay approached Maley asking for better terms or a transfer.

Maley would very seldom give in to blackmail like that and Hay was conspicuously absent from the summer tour of Europe, having told Maley, after a Charity Cup semi-final against Third Lanark from which he had been dropped, that he was through with the club. Celtic then lost the Charity Cup final to Rangers and no settlement seemed possible. Maley clearly could not force Hay to play, but Celtic still held Hay's registration.

With this dispute still unresolved, Celtic went on their now customary tour of central Europe in late May. Maley had entertained hopes of moving further afield, for as early as January 1910 he and director Tom Colgan had sailed on the SS *California* to investigate the possibilities of a tour of the USA in 1911. Sadly, conditions were so desperately primitive that the possibility of a tour there had to be postponed for a few years. It would, in fact, be twenty years before this happened, but it shows once again Maley's conception of Celtic as a missionary club. He was particularly keen on the USA because he knew that the many Irish and Scottish people who had settled there would be delighted to see Celtic.

The European tour was its usual success with games played in Dresden, Prague, Vienna, Budapest, Basle and Paris, and Maley had the additional pleasure of meeting Brother Walfrid once again. He had clearly aged considerably, but was delighted to see Maley, the players and the team which he, Walfrid, had conceived but Maley had produced. On his return, Maley transferred Hay to Newcastle United on 27 July 1911 for £1,250, having seen that it would be better to cut his losses. The two men were unhappy about the departure, for they had worked well together in the past to produce the six Leagues in a row, and for a while did not speak to each other. But the ice was eventually broken, and after his career was over, Hay was a welcome visitor at Celtic Park.

Clearly, however, in 1911 fresh talent was required, something that Maley had tended to neglect the past six years when it was obvious that what was at Parkhead was good enough to beat anything in Scotland and indeed the world. But now with the League Championship gone, it was perhaps once again time to tap the information of his spies.

Consistent reports had reached Maley's desk from his network of informants about a young man called Patrick Gallacher who came from the Clydebank area. In fact, he was an Irishman from Donegal, which interested Maley a little for he was aware of how few Irishmen actually played for Celtic nowadays. The previous summer, a few days after the death of King Edward VII, Maley had gone to Fir Park, Motherwell to see this young fellow play for Renfrew Juveniles against the Rest of Scotland.

To a certain extent, he was impressed by his trickery and ball play, but the overwhelming impression was that he was just far too frail and thin for the hurly-burly of the game. In any case, Gallacher was an inside right, and if there was one position that was not a problem for Celtic, it was inside right where Jimmy McMenemy continued to ply his trade and was considered to be as good as any. Still, it was worthwhile keeping an eye on the youngster. Maley made a point of seeking him out after the game, introducing himself as 'one Irishman to another' and talked amiably about football, Ireland and how his family had settled in Clydebank.

Gallacher apparently was now playing for Clydebank Juniors in the season 1910/11, and repeatedly Maley would receive a letter from his contacts singing the praises of this youngster. In particular, his respected friend John Dunlop (who in later years would become 'Waverley' of the *Daily Record*) kept telling Maley how good Gallacher was.

The beginning of the 1911/12 season was far from encouraging. Under the captaincy of Sunny Jim Young, the defence continued to play well enough, but there were major problems in the forward line. Quinn was injured yet again (Maley would often reflect on just how much he owed to Jimmy) and youngsters like Andy Donaldson, John Brown and Paddy Travers were hard-working but unproductive. Andy McAtee on the right wing was impressive but would need time, and even Jimmy McMenemy was now beginning to struggle not because of any inability of his own, but because he lacked men of sufficient experience and talent around him.

In the space of four days in September, there were two bad results. On the Wednesday afternoon of 13 September 1911, a lacklustre Celtic team went down 3-0 to Partick Thistle in the Glasgow Cup, and then the team travelled to Dens Park and lost 3-1 to Dundee on the Saturday. Maley was depressed about all this, even finding it difficult to be his usual cheery self to the newspaper reporters and followers of the club who were hanging around the Players and Officials Entrance at the old Dens Park ground. 'We were defeated and Dundee played well' was his curt reply.

For the first time for many years, Maley now had to contend with the realisation that his team were simply not good enough. Criticism of his team in newspapers hurt him, but that was nothing to the boos and catcalls that came from his own supporters. Sometimes he was angry with them, calling them 'ungrateful' and 'unable to realise that you can't win them all', other times he looked at their faces and shared their sense of disappointment. He would always say in public,

'It is our proud boast that we can taste the fruits of victory in the same way as the bitterness of defeat'. That was for public consumption. In private, his feelings were quite different.

He realised that more players were required, and his mind returned to that half-fed looking Irishman called Gallacher. An approach was made and Gallacher was offered a trial on the Holiday Monday 2 October 1911 at Dumfries. This was for the reserve team, for the big team were playing (and struggling to beat) Raith Rovers at Kirkcaldy. Celtic's second string ('the stiffs', 'the swifts' or 'the ham and eggers') beat the Dumfries side 6-1 and Gallacher (under the pseudonym of 'Smith') was mightily impressive, scoring twice.

A few weeks later, Maley himself saw Gallacher in a Celtic jersey for the first time in a friendly against the 'British Army' the pompous name given to the Maryhill Barracks XI. Once again, it was an easy victory and Maley, after seeing him on another few occasions, offered Gallacher part-time terms in November in the wake of a drubbing at the hands of Rangers in October and a feckless 1-1 draw at Falkirk. Gallacher accepted almost immediately, for he had liked the magnetic charm and persuasive powers of the avuncular Maley.

Early December saw Gallacher's debut, but the inconsistent form continued, as did the carping criticism of the spectators, some of whom were simply spoiled and sated by too much success. Significantly, when Quinn played and was fit, Celtic did better and they certainly silenced a few doubters on New Year's Day when they beat Rangers 3-0 at Celtic Park, Quinn scoring a hat-trick. But too many games were drawn and a challenge for the League Championship seldom looked like a realistic possibility.

However, Maley proved himself to be a master tactician in one decision. Young Gallacher was playing too well in the reserves to be left out of the side. In addition to his tricky play, he was an instant success with the fans who loved his comic way of walking, his cheekiness and of course his ability to do things with a football, although they were concerned about his apparent lack of strength to shoot. But this meant that Celtic had two good inside rights, when only one was required. McMenemy or Gallacher could hardly be asked to move to right half for that would have involved displacing Sunny Jim Young, the captain and inspirational driving force.

Apparently, it was McMenemy himself, as wise a man off the field as he was on it, who approached Maley in the middle of March 1912 and suggested that he (McMenemy) should try the inside left position to allow Gallacher to develop as inside right. Maley had been thinking along these lines as well and agreed. It was as well that it had been the much trusted and loved McMenemy who had suggested this, for Maley was never too keen to be seen to do things under pressure, however well intentioned.

This move would win the Scottish Cup for Celtic yet again and salvage an otherwise depressing season. Loney and Quinn were both fit and well, and the team beat the strong Hearts side by an impressive 3-0 scoreline in the semi-final and then Clyde in a final which was spoiled somewhat by a strong gale. Maley may well have permitted himself a chuckle as he reflected that the two goalscorers were McMenemy and Gallacher!

He was presumably as magnanimous and generous to the opposition as he always was because on this occasion the opposition manager was well known to him. It was none other than his younger brother Alec Maley! Alec may well have hoped that Willie would find some place for him at Celtic, but when that did not happen, he struck off on his own. In a similar way, Tom Maley had now no official connection with Celtic, being manager of Bradford Park Avenue, although he remained on friendly terms with this brother and indeed the Celtic club, writing, sometimes under a *nom de plume*, other times openly for the blatantly pro-Celtic *Glasgow Observer*. Clyde's trainer, incidentally, that day was a man called William Struth, a man with whom Maley would clash frequently in the future.

On the following Saturday, Maley staged a great piece of theatre. Kilmarnock were at Parkhead, and the 7,000 crowd saw the Scottish Cup decked in green and white paraded before the start of the game. Instead of asking some of the players to do the job, Maley, believing as always that the triumph of Celtic was the triumph of the downtrodden, picked a few supporters including a small boy with no shoes to walk round the track showing off the trophy.

Celtic also won the Glasgow Charity Cup that season, beating Clyde (who had now sacked Alec Maley after the Scottish Cup defeat) on the device of 'counting corners' after a 0–0 draw. This was the precursor of a penalty shoot-out and in some ways was fairer, for it did give an indication of which side was exerting the greater pressure.

Thus with two trophies safely won, Celtic treated themselves to a close season tour of Denmark and Norway. A plan had been made to go to South Africa that year. Maley had been very keen on that idea now that the Boer War had been over for a good ten years and everything settled back to normality. But he decided against it in view of the excessive distance and the comparative lack of interest in the game among the British ex-patriots who seemed to prefer hockey and cricket, and who didn't even bother to answer his letters!

This time the European tour was in the month of June and included fixtures against the Norwegian and Danish Olympic teams. A strong Celtic team was in fact defeated 4–1 by the Danes, although Maley could always claim that an injury to Patsy Gallacher early on was a significant turning point. Maley himself always would sit proudly in the lounge of the team's hotel, being polite and courteous to everyone, introducing young Danes and Norwegians to Quinn, McMenemy and Young, and being rightly proud of the team that he had played such a large part in creating.

He was always careful that everyone should have the right image of the club, the game of football and the two countries that Celtic represented, Scotland and Ireland. In some ways, this was what Maley was all about. He was of course a great football man, and there were times when it often appeared that he was more interested in money than anything else, but he would, within himself, be far more concerned about the image that his team were giving to the world. He would once or twice be quoted as saying that 'A man must be a Celt on and off the field, otherwise he is of no value to this club'.

1912/13 was, however, a bad season, as Maley tried to blend his old guard with some new ones and did not always succeed. Injuries were a key factor as men like McMenemy, Loney and Quinn were all out for lengthy spells. The prodigy Patsy (as he was now openly called) Gallacher had what might be called a learning experience. He was out injured for a spell after dropping an adze on his foot in his day job at Clydebank shipyard, but he soon recovered. He was obviously very talented, but he still had a great deal to learn to appreciate the problems that were liable to occur if he overdid the trickery. One was that he was likely to be brutally felled by desperate defenders, and the other was that such trickery did not always endear him to his team-mates if positive results in terms of goalscoring were not forthcoming.

Maley, however, took him under his wing. Maley was shrewd enough to realise that in Patsy Gallacher there existed the sort of talent that was seldom seen. It must be nurtured. This might well take time, but it was worth while spending time on this young man, for he had already seen too many 'one season wonders' who had exploded on the scene, then disappeared anonymously.

The problem left-wing position showed signs of being solved when Johnny Browning was introduced. There was something about Browning that Maley did not altogether trust, but he had to admit that there was also something likeable about the gallus youth from Dumbarton with his cheeky attitude. Maley's informants told him that Browning did some wonderful impersonations of him, but Browning was always very polite and respectful to Mr Maley when he was around. There could be little doubt, however, of his playing ability for he was fast, could cross and had a powerful shot. He did, however, have some shady associates off the field and Maley would always keep an eye on him.

Quinn was now quite clearly on the way out, although he did score the only goal of the game at Ibrox on New Year's Day. He had performed in the forward line where knocks and injuries were common for well over a decade, had achieved legendary status in both Scotland and England and was very often referred to quite simply as

'Jimmy'. It was a status afforded to only a very few Celtic players. Dan Doyle had been called in the papers 'Dan', 'Patsy' would soon be a name everyone recognised and of course in latter days there have been a 'Kenny' and a 'Henrik'. The injuries were now beginning to catch up on Jimmy and, as he was now in his mid-thirties, he could not go on much longer.

Similarly, Maley felt that Willie Loney would not last for ever. The Denny man had been the sheet anchor of the great Celtic team of the six Championships in a row, being dubbed 'The Obliterator', 'No Road This Way' and 'The Gobbler' for his ability to crush attacks at birth. He had suffered a mysterious illness the previous season and sustained injuries this season, and it was clear that another great Parkhead career was coming to an end.

But Maley had plans in place for his replacement. They concerned a strapping, muscular Fife miner called Peter Johnstone. He was originally a forward, but was now playing at left half and centre half. Maley was convinced that Peter would in time become a great centre half. He had not yet, however, found a centre forward that would or could replace Jimmy Quinn.

A goalkeeper had emerged, however, in the shape of Charlie Shaw whom Maley had picked up from Queen's Park Rangers after a tip off from his brother Tom. Charlie was destined of course to become one of the real Celtic personalities for the next decade, and Maley would come to see the Twechar man as one of his personal favourites. Maley tended to have good goalkeepers. One thinks of Dan McArthur, Davie Adams, John Thomson and Joe Kennaway, but arguably the best and most popular was Charlie Shaw, the darling of the Brake clubs.

Thus the 1913 season ended with Celtic in transition. The prospect of a totally barren season had been lifted when a makeshift Celtic team luckily beat Rangers in the Charity Cup final in May, even though they had been two goals down in the first ten minutes. Maley, although far from happy at some performances, nevertheless reflected that there had been quite a few plus points. Indeed, Celtic had beaten Rangers twice in the League, and only dismal away form with defeats at Dundee, Raith Rovers, Aberdeen and Motherwell had prevented a stronger League challenge.

The Scottish Cup had brought disappointment at the quarter-final stage when a good Hearts side had beaten Celtic 1-0 in front of a huge crowd at Parkhead. Yet Maley saw the Scottish Cup exit as an opportunity to do a good public relations job for Celtic. Hampden Park was still not totally renovated after the riot of 1909, and this year Maley's lobbying won the nod for Parkhead to stage the Scottish Cup final which everyone expected to be between Hearts and Clyde, but in fact was between Raith Rovers and Falkirk.

Maley himself took charge of operations, painting the goalposts, the dressing rooms and the Balcony Hall of the old pavilion where the Scottish Cup would be presented and generally making sure that everything at Parkhead was in tip-top condition for the big game which would show what great hosts Celtic FC could be.

He awoke on the morning of 12 April to discover that snow had fallen in large quantities over Glasgow. He jumped out of bed, rushed to the ground, discovered a thick layer of snow and by 9 a.m. had assembled a squad of volunteers, including some of his own players, to clear the pitch.

It was April, so the snow was melting anyway, but by midday the pitch was swept and 'garnished' and looked in splendid condition for the game. By early afternoon he was on hand to greet everyone, proud of his pitch, regaling everyone with memories of Celtic's first Scottish Cup final in the snow in 1889, and thoroughly deserving of the description of him in Kirkcaldy's local paper as 'Celtic's energetic secretary'.

Falkirk won the game, and Maley was there to organise the presentation of the cup, making a few jokes about how he wanted his hands on it again, but congratulating (without patronising) Falkirk and Raith Rovers. He handed out the sandwiches, tea and drinks and made a point of talking to everyone, giving the impression to each individual that his was the most interesting conversation he had ever had.

1913 of course marked the silver jubilee of Celtic Football Club. At the AGM on 16 May, Maley was awarded by the directors an honorarium of 300 guineas, a princely sum in 1913, for his contribution to the club. In truth, it was deserved in terms of what he had done, but one might have been justified in asking what had happened to the ideals of the club? 300 guineas would have provided a great deal of food for poor children, and it is to be hoped that Maley (a humane and compassionate man) made his own personal contribution.

He was certainly gracious in his speech in reply. He stated that 'Working for Celtic is a labour of love...the club is part of my existence...success is the one thing worth striving for' and other things which endeared him to the supporters and the directors with whom he shared an amicable and harmonious relationship with seldom a hint of friction.

And no one could deny the phenomenal success of the club. What this club had achieved for its own underprivileged ethnic minority cannot really be gauged, except to say that the Irish in Scotland were now almost totally identified with Celtic Football Club. But there was more than that as well. Protestants had played and continued to play for the club, and there was now a very large group of Scottish Presbyterians (mainly outside Glasgow and West Central Scotland, it had to be admitted) who were willing to call themselves Celtic supporters, won over by the play of the 'Bould' or the 'Mighty' Celts.

An indication of this was the number of 'Celtic' junior and juvenile football teams that appeared throughout Scotland. In some cases, Maley had encouraged them by giving them a set of jerseys or a ball to get them started. He was determined that the name 'Celtic' would always be a good one in the eyes of the Scottish public.

There would of course inevitably be a reaction against the team. But the reaction itself is a compliment to Maley and Celtic. Rangers had emerged as the team most likely to challenge Celtic. Already the two Glasgow giants were called the 'Old Firm', the context being the money that they generated. But Rangers themselves were not yet associated with any form of bigotry. Lamentably, that would arise in its crude form after the First World War. At this stage, Rangers were simply the team most likely to challenge Celtic and therefore those who found Celtic's traditions and symbolism abhorrent or alien tended to filter towards supporting Rangers, as indeed did thousands of people who were quite simply football fans and chose Rangers in the same way that others chose Clyde or Partick Thistle.

Yet, in just twenty-five years, Celtic had become Scotland's (and arguably Britain's) number one team. To say that Maley was entirely responsible for all this is hardly true. Yet one would not be able to point to any other individual and say that 'He did more than Maley'. Brother Walfrid, Glass, Kelly, McMahon, Doyle, Quinn and McMenemy all played a distinguished part in the early years of the Celtic club. The link factor however remained no one other than Willie Maley.

The 1913/14 season saw a return to greatness. It would not be true to say that it was a new Celtic team. Rather, it was an evolution. An interesting mistake is often made by people who should know better when they assert that the great Celtic team of the early twentieth century was Shaw, McNair and Dodds; Young, Loney and Hay et al. This is, of course, not true. Jimmy Hay had been transferred to Newcastle United long before Charlie Shaw made his debut. What is likely to have happened is that grandparents in their old age talked about the teams to youngsters who listened imperfectly. They are two separate, although linked teams.

Goalkeeper Charlie Shaw very soon acquired personality status. Photographs of Charlie make him look older than he actually was, but also show him as a benign, kindly person. Brake clubs were soon named after him. It was often said that no one really knew in 1914 how good a goalkeeper Charlie was, for he was seldom put to the test, although very often there would be 'deafening roars of delight at Shaw's saves'. When after the war, Alan Morton of Rangers scored a goal against him, a song was written about it – a tremendous indirect compliment to Charlie for so few people scored against him!

The centre forward problem caused by the gradual disappearance of Jimmy Quinn was addressed by the drafting in of the Dickensian-sounding Ebenezer Owers who was an honest trier, but no more than that. Later, and more successfully, came Jimmy McColl. Maley had been tireless in his efforts to scour the British Isles, travelling to places like Shelbourne, Tottenham and Liverpool trying to find a replacement for the mighty Quinn, but eventually it was Jimmy McColl, from the Glasgow juniors side St Anthony's, who would fit the bill.

With a team like Celtic had in 1913/14, it was difficult not to score goals, such was the quality of the rest of the forward line that Maley had welded together. Wingers Andy McAtee and Johnny Browning were both traditional Scottish wingers who would charge to the dead-ball line and deliver crosses with pinpoint accuracy. In the middle of the field there was of course Jimmy McMenemy and Patsy Gallacher, and although McMenemy was out for a prolonged spell between 4 October and 27 December with a broken collar-bone sustained in a game against Aberdeen at Parkhead, the result of accidental collision with an Aberdonian called Wyllie, the reserve cover was adequate.

The team had a bad spell in the autumn, which included defeat in the Glasgow Cup to Third Lanark. This was at the time that both McMenemy and Quinn (his career now almost finished) were injured, – 'the Celtic van will be weakened' predicted the *Glasgow Herald* – but Gallacher and McAtee were impressive. McAtee scrambled a late winner against Dundee on 18 October, and was also on the scoresheet the following week against Rangers at Ibrox. The other goal in that 2-0 victory was scored by the young reserve George Whitehead who according to the *Dundee Advertiser* 'is not a Quinn, but of course it is not often we meet a player of the same class as the famous James – but he scored his goal'.

This was surely the mark of greatness in the team and its manager in that they could still win when the odds and the injuries seem to be going against them. Rangers who had won the League Championship for the past three years were competently dispatched once again this time to the tune of 4-0 in the New Year's Day game at Parkhead. Browning scored twice, and Young once, but the pick of the goals was surely that of Jimmy 'Napoleon' McMenemy. He beat five men in a mazy dribble then shot high into the Rangers net, before being engulfed by delighted team-mates. Charlie Shaw added to his fast growing popularity by saving an Alec Bennett penalty. The only blemish after the New Year was an injury-hit defeat by Falkirk. The League was won very comfortably by a six-point margin.

Maley, personally, had an unfortunate experience at St Mirren at the end of January 1914. Johnny McMaster of Celtic and Fred Sowerby of St Mirren were sent off for fighting, and some members of the crowd invaded the field. Maley as linesman acted to try to calm things down, but was jostled in the mêlée and discovered after the game that his pocket had been picked as well! The loss of a wallet was perhaps made up for by Celtic's very comfortable 3-0 victory.

As in 1907 and 1908, the Scottish Cup was added to the League. Passage to the final was unspectacular but competent, and the final was played at Ibrox against Hibs. Before a huge uncompromisingly Irish crowd (from both Scottish cities) who sang anthems like 'God Save Ireland' and 'The Wearing O' The Green', Celtic disappointed in the first game and indeed were lucky to avoid defeat.

For the replay, Maley went for Jimmy McColl as centre forward rather than the unfortunate Ebenezer Owers, and McColl proved his value by scoring twice early on. Johnny Browning added a further two and it was one of Celtic's easier Scottish Cup victories, orchestrated on the field by Maley's diminutive genius from Ireland, Patsy Gallacher.

This was on Thursday 16 April. As Celtic had defeated St Mirren 5-0 on Monday 13 April, all they had to do on Saturday 18 April to win the League was to beat Hibs again. This they did by 3 goals to nil, McMenemy being outstanding once again and vindicating Maley's judgement in moving him to inside left in order to accommodate Patsy Gallacher. But the League was a victory for the defence as well. Only 13 goals were conceded in 38 matches, and a great deal of credit must go to Charlie Shaw whose form was phenomenal.

The 1913/14 season ended with a victory in the Glasgow Charity Cup. A 6-0 tanking of the luckless Third Lanark was almost effort-less, and Maley had cause to be pleased with himself as he made his preparations to go to Central Europe on tour. He was very opti-mistic for the future, for he could see little to stop another great Celtic team from emerging as his previous one had done ten years earlier. Sadly, neither Maley nor anyone else could see what was about to happen in Europe that summer and the devastating conse-quences it would have for all mankind.

Six

WAR CLOUDS

Still on a high after their great 1913/14 season, Maley took Celtic on their now customary summer tour of Europe. Maley enjoyed these things, often thinking that it was a fitting reward for his players. The season over, inevitably discipline was a little laxer, but Maley was always keen that Celtic should continue to be ambassadors for Scotland and the game.

Games were played in Austria-Hungary in the beautiful city of Vienna, in Budapest (where a game against the English Cup winners Burnley had been arranged without Celtic's knowledge!) and of course in Germany, in Berlin and Leipzig. Maley liked Germany, but had been aware of a gradual increase in tension in that country the past few years.

Their attitude to the British Empire was odd. The Kaiser was the grandson of Queen Victoria and the cousin of the present monarch, King George V. It had been no secret that the Kaiser had hated his uncle, King Edward VII ('Fat Old Wales' he had dubbed him when he was the Prince of Wales), but King Edward had been dead for four years now, and it was difficult to analyse the Kaiser's feelings about Great Britain at the moment. He was certainly very unpredictable.

The Germans themselves were even more inscrutable. They were very like the British with whom they had strong ethnic and industrial connections and a similar attitude towards navies and Empire building.

The Germans had always been very hospitable to Celtic on their previous tours. Perhaps it was because Celtic were considered to be the representatives of Scotland and Ireland, rather than England, Maley thought, and the Germans sympathised with what both the Celtic nations had suffered. This was why they liked a football team of that name.

The football had been fairly insignificant. Poor pitches, referees who knew very little about the game, and Celtic, without really trying, usually hammering the opposition, had been the rule of the day. Crowds were enthusiastic, but none too knowledgeable and sometimes not aware of the fine line between supporting your team and sheer downright hooliganism.

Still, it was a good tour, thought Maley, as the team travelled home after the last game on 1 June. He had been struck by the sheer number of young men he had seen in military uniform – and very smart they looked.

He was spending some days on holiday in the lovely Highland village of Tomintoul when he read about the assassination of Archduke Ferdinand in Sarajevo on 28 June. The event did not concern Maley overly much. He had enjoyed a good holiday and was relishing the return of the football season. The players would report for training on 1 August, there would be one or two trial games, usually free to the public before the serious stuff started in the middle of August.

As the hot July continued, many Glaswegians – even some of the poorer ones, Maley reflected with satisfaction – were away 'doon the watter' to places like Dunoon and Rothesay. Richer ones, some with motor cars, toured the Highlands – and the weather was marvellous. The newspapers were full of Ireland again and Maley would admit to himself (although never in public) his annoyance and frustration at the bigoted Orangemen who were fouling up Home Rule. Here was surely a chance for Britain to solve the Irish problem, but they were being stabbed in the back by those who claimed to be 'loyal'.

As July continued however, things became a little more ominous as Germany began to get involved in the dispute between Serbia and the Austro-Hungarian Empire. Maley knew enough about German militarism to be worried, but surely these charming people that Celtic had met so recently were not to plunge Europe into a full-scale war? Even more alarmingly, for a man like Maley, some of the British people, even his own Glasgow Irish, were beginning to talk about the possibility of war – and even to be animated, excited and optimistic about it all.

Maley, of course, was wise enough to know the reason for this. Although perhaps the worst excesses of Victorian slave labour and slum housing were now gradually being addressed, there still remained an astonishing amount of poverty, and with poverty came lack of cultural experience and sheer boredom. Maley thought that whenever the football season arrived again, then perhaps people would stop talking about war.

But sadly, war arrived before football. The Kaiser kept squaring up to the Russians and the French, there was a distinct lack of statesmanship throughout Europe and therefore everyone got themselves backed into a corner and no one would back down and then, unbelievably and tragically, the Kaiser invaded Belgium. Great Britain could not now stand aside, and a terrible war began.

Not that conflict had looked all that terrible in those sunny days of early August. It seemed like an adventure. Britain had not been involved in a major European war since Napoleon 100 years earlier ('Napoleon' was now the nickname of Jimmy McMenemy, Maley recalled) and the spirit of romance, valour and derring-do was in the air. 'All over by Christmas' was the call and young men rushed to the colours lest they miss out on this wonderful opportunity to serve the King and see France.

Maley was now in a quandary. On the one hand, he felt that he had to be patriotic, given his military background and absolute determination that the Irish in Scotland should be seen to play a part in the development and maintenance of the British Empire. On the other, it was hard to harbour war-like feelings against the Germans whom he had met and played football against so recently. He probably rationalised this by saying that the fight was against Ludendorff, Moltke and the Kaiser rather than the German people who were sadly being led astray by such wild men.

Maley's main hope of course was that this 'war' might not became a war at all, that the British Expeditionary Force would indeed deliver a knock out blow before the Germans reached Paris, or that the Kaiser would see reason and repent of his hasty and precipitate action. A deal was a possibility, hoped Maley and many people in Britain, but in the meantime, military involvement must go on.

It would be some time before football was under any kind of threat because of the war, but almost immediately restrictions were imposed. No player, for example, could earn more than £2 and they had to do something 'useful' for the war effort as well. This was not really a problem for Celtic, for Maley was able to use his energy and influence to make sure that his fine players all got jobs in and around Glasgow, so that they could even do a shift on Saturday morning, if required, and turn out for Celtic in the afternoon.

He was not particularly keen on his players joining the colours (a stark contrast to Hearts, for example, who enlisted en masse and are commemorated on a monument outside Haymarket Station), but he did allow the military to use Celtic Park on a matchday to hold recruiting drives. Soldiers would do a display before the start and a loudspeaker appeal was made at half-time, all to encourage men to enlist and not miss the 'carnival of the century' as it was unashamedly called.

The siren voices of military life were not lost on the Celtic crowd. The thought of a smart uniform, clean barracks, good wages, regular food and exercise was appealing to the undernourished and under-privileged. By the time that the football season was properly under-way, the British Army had seen action at places like Mons – an action which the British press portrayed, naturally, as a victory. By the autumn, Paris was saved. Not without cause, 'western civilization' had reason to rejoice, but the more acute observers realised that before Paris could be 'saved', large tracts of Belgium and France must have been 'lost'.

The argument about the continuation of professional football seemed to have been won. Maley and others had pointed out the propaganda effect of football for soldiers on leave, for those employed in munitions industries and as something for the soldiers at the front to discuss (Patsy Gallacher, it was claimed, would in time become the main topic of conversation among Scottish soldiers in Belgium, Mesopotamia, Salonika, Gallipoli and the High Seas). Maley claimed that he sent footballs to soldiers to play with in their off-duty time, and his two sons enlisted, one of them fated to be wounded.

But football in Scotland and England was distinctly emasculated. Internationals could not be played because of the problem involved in men travelling large distances and imposing further strains on wartime transport. This was a blow, and rather surprisingly, the Scottish Cup was also placed into cold storage as well. There was no logical or logistic reason for this, as the distances involved were no more that would have been required for League football. Celtic, for example, managed to take their full team to Aberdeen on 5 December 1914, and Aberdeen them-selves, the most distant team in Scotland, did not at this stage in the war have any great problem in playing their fixtures.

1914/15 was a great season for Celtic. Three League defeats were sustained, one of them on the opening day of the season to Hearts at Tynecastle, one at Ibrox on New Year's Day and one, surprisingly, at Ayr United. It was Hearts who were the main challengers, but although they managed a draw with Celtic at Parkhead in late January, they could not live with the sustained consistency of a fine Celtic side, which now centred around the creative genius of Patsy Gallacher.

Patsy's wiles were by no means the only attraction, however. McColl was an excellent striker, and the left-wing pairing of McMenemy and Browning had no parallel. Patsy's outside right was Andy McAtee, a curious figure who ran with his back hunched and his thick 'billiard table' legs.

The half-back line of Young, Johnstone and McMaster imposed themselves on the midfield so much that the back three of Shaw, McNair and Dodds were seldom required. Johnny McMaster, the lantern-jawed, ungainly left half had now quite clearly filled the role of Jimmy Hay, and the team was complete … and as good in wartime as they had been in peace.

It was a shame that this was not a proper peacetime season, for it meant that this team is not always given by historians the credit that it deserves. Certainly Maley is due a great deal of credit for keeping them together, doing all he could by channels official and unofficial to make sure that they were always available. Regulations meant that group training was difficult, if not impossible, but Maley always made sure that the ground was open so that any player could turn up voluntarily for a session, even if the training session consisted of little other than kicking a ball about on a pitch which was totally dark, save for the inadequate pavilion lights. It says a great deal for the team spirit of Celtic and their desire to work for 'The Boss' that many of them availed themselves of the invitation.

Injuries were only a small problem this season. McColl missed a few games, and Johnstone was out for a spell in the autumn, but by and large the team stayed fit. An exception was the Glasgow Cup game in September against Clyde at Shawfield, when the team were without both Johnstone and McMaster. Maley had to employ Irishman Willie Crone and re-call Alex Gray who worked in the munitions industries while he played McMenemy at centre half and Browning at left half – both hideously out of position. In addition, Charlie Shaw had a poor game (a rare occurrence) and Celtic lost 2-0 to Clyde.

The Glasgow Charity Cup final was played on 8 May 1915 at Ibrox. It was perhaps the closest one could get to a Scottish Cup final in 1915, and the opposition were Rangers, a team who had been seriously weakened by the war demands and had not enjoyed the best of seasons. A large crowd of around 40,000 were there, but by this time strident voices were being heard about whether football should really be played.

It was now clear that the war was going to be a long one, and that an eventual victory was by no means certain. Heavy losses were being sustained, and censorship and the heavily-biased newspaper reporting could not disguise it all. As the crowd made its way to Ibrox, the air was thick with anti–German feeling, for the early editions of the evening papers were carrying stories that the German navy had sunk the *Lusitania* off the coast of Ireland. Many civilians (a lot of them American) and children had perished. This seemed to indicate that all that had been said about the Germans raping nuns and bayoneting children in Belgium was indeed true. Maley was appalled at this hysteria for he found it hard to reconcile the sinking of the *Lusitania* with the Germans he had met, yet it was difficult not to agree with the contention that the war must go on. Half-time saw a recruiting speech, and the sergeant was given a rousing reception.

The game itself was a good one, with Celtic winning 3-2 in spite of being deprived of the services of Patsy Gallacher for a long spell when he was taken off injured. It was significant that Rangers scored their two goals during this time, but an early goal by Joe Dodds, and two late ones by McMenemy and Browning ensured that the Charity Cup joined the Scottish League trophy at Parkhead that summer.

No European tour was possible that summer, something that distressed Maley for he would have liked to have made it an annual event. He had even contemplated playing a few games against Army teams in either England or France, but this was not allowed. All that was allowed was a game in aid of Belgian refugees between Celtic and the Rest of the League. Celtic won it 1-0, something which confirmed the excellence of Celtic, but Maley must have wished that the times were different.

The 1915/16 season was almost a replica of the previous one, with Celtic winning the Scottish League without any real bother, after an uncomfortable spell in the autumn when games were lost to St Mirren, Rangers and Hearts. But Maley delivered his usual pious homilies, 'It is our proud boast that we can accept defeat in the same spirit as that of victory', and rallied the team once again; after 13 November 1915, Celtic did not lose another game until April 1917, except for a Charity game against the Rest of the League.

Just as the 1915/16 season was beginning, the great Alec McNair suffered a grievous blow when his wife died on 21 August, leaving the desolate Alec to bring up a large family on his own. Maley was at his best in such situations, visiting Alec at his Larbert home, comforting him, telling him that his place would be waiting for him when he felt able to resume and even offering money to help pay for a housekeeper to look after the children. Alec recovered from this blow and played for the team for nearly another decade, being such a good player that Maley felt it was worthwhile to go the extra mile for him.

The Glasgow Cup final of 9 October 1915 was held at Hampden, and some sources claim that 70,000 were there, others say the figure was more like 90,000. These figures seem a trifle excessive for war years and may indeed have been deliberately massaged for propaganda purposes to show the troops in the trenches that life was normal at home. Conversely, presumably the Kaiser would read his newspaper and see to his horror that there seemed to be an inexhaustible supply of Scotsmen!

Yet for two of Celtic's players, Joe Dodds and Jimmy McMenemy the war had come tragically close to them. In the ongoing battle at Loos, each of them had recently lost a brother. Maley called the pair of them to his office, expressed his sympathies and told them that the best way to show respect for their brothers' memories was to play the game. It would, in any case, be therapeutic for themselves. The two men, experienced players, looked 'The Boss' in the eye and said they would do their best.

However large the crowd was, they saw a tremendous game of football. Rangers had re-grouped temporarily, had most of their regulars available for once and did well to hold the mighty Celtic team for long spells of the game. But goals by Patsy Gallacher and Johnny Browning were enough to see Celtic home and to delight the men in the trenches when the mail arrived a few days later.

Maley continued to be energetic in his views that football must continue for propaganda and morale reasons. The population were still enthusiastic about the war, and more and more questions were being asked about why 22 fit young men were playing football on a Saturday afternoon instead of being in France. Maley's answer was always that his men were keeping the home fires burning (as the song of the time might have said), engaged in munitions, iron, steel, ship-building and other activities which were so necessary for the war effort.

As Saturdays were the only day allowed for football, problems would arise if games were postponed. Indeed, referees were under pressure in the winter months to play games in manifestly unsuitable conditions, lest information might reach German High Command that it was snowing in Glasgow! On 25 March 1916, however, the referee had no option as Fir Park, Motherwell was carpeted under a heavy fall of snow for the game against Celtic.

Celtic might have won the League that day, and Maley was determined that one way or another, all games should be played lest the League be declared void for the season. Accordingly, the game was rearranged for Saturday 15 April at 6 p.m., a matter of hours after Celtic played Raith Rovers and Motherwell played Ayr United! This arrangement was by no means unique in the circumstances of 1916, and Celtic beat Raith 6-0, the game finishing at about 5 p.m. They then piled into a charabanc (apparently without changing jerseys) to take them the fairly short journey along uncongested roads to Motherwell. There they defeated an exhausted Motherwell (who had already lost to Ayr United) with the same team other than that young Joe Cassidy (summoned post haste from military barracks at Scone) at centre forward took the place of Joe O'Kane.

8,000 people saw this game which finished in crepuscular light with the moon clearly visible. It did in fact give Celtic their thirteenth League championship flag, but it had only been a matter of time anyway. The rest of the season was played out quietly. Games were allowed on Easter Monday, and Celtic played Third Lanark with Joe O'Kane scoring a hat-trick. Attendance was low (about 5,000) because Easter Monday was not a holiday for everyone.

The crowd probably did not know on the Monday afternoon (although they would have been apprised of the facts very soon after) that something serious seemed to have happened in Ireland. There seemed to be some kind of rebellion against the crown with the Post Office seized and large parts of Dublin under rebel control. The rebellion, apparently spearheaded by a Scotsman called Connolly and an Irishman called Pearse, was soon put down and normality was restored to the country of Maley's birth.

Maley was appalled by all this. As an Irishman, and being more aware than most of the tensions in his native country, he knew that things were always likely to boil over, particularly when the Empire was involved in a war that it showed few signs of winning. Maley had often heard the dictum 'England's difficulty is Ireland's opportunity' and it was hardly surprising that the opportunity would be seized, as it had been in 1797 when England had been involved in the war against France.

On the other hand, this was an act of treason in a time of war. It could not be excused on any bogus historical grounds of potato famines, landlords, Cromwell or William of Orange. The culprits must be punished, Maley reckoned, and he knew exactly what his father would have said about them.

Yet Maley was all too aware that his views were by no means shared by the Celtic support. A dignified silence seemed to be the order of the day, and concentration on football. There was still the Charity Cup to play. Rangers were comprehensively thrashed on 6 May, and then the Cup was won in a dazzling display against Partick Thistle on 13 May. Patsy Gallacher, as always, led the circus and he could have beaten the hapless Thistle by more than two goals to nil. Maley, as he often did in these circumstances, gestured to his men to ease off and he was glad to hear the referee's final whistle. There was little point in humiliating fellow professionals, especially when the Thistle team was a makeshift outfit of players, some of whom had just arrived home on leave that morning, others who were clearly past their best and struggling against injuries and yet others who gave every indication of having been picked off the street!

Thus Celtic finished the 1915/16 season having won all three competitions they entered. They were like the teams of 1908 and 1967 in that respect, but the circumstances were so different. The news coming from the front was hardly cheering, even though Ireland had now apparently been settled, at the cost of much blood and (Maley felt secretly) through excessive brutality. Maley knew Ireland well enough to sense that the problem would recur, but for the moment it was not the main concern of the British Empire. Worse was yet to come.

As the football season restarted in August 1916, even British propaganda and control of the newspapers could not hide the undeniable fact that a massive defeat had been sustained in early July at a place called the Somme. In some places, a few hundred yards had been gained; in others there had been no gain at all, and the casualty lists were now reaching horrendous proportions. Any visit to Central Station, Glasgow would see the piteous sight of blinded or limbless soldiers for whom the war was over, now back to lead out what was left of their lives with their families who were grateful that they came back at all. Everyone knew at least someone who would not be coming back.

Ironically, Celtic continued to do well. They had been comparatively unscathed so far thanks to Maley's energetic ability to keep all his men working in jobs on the Home Front. One exception was Peter Johnstone the centre half. Peter was a bit of a loose cannon in that he did not always see eye to eye with Maley. Maley respected his ability and that was why he stayed in the team, but Peter was independent. Coming as he did from Fife, he had started off as a collier, but then he opened a newsagent's shop in Glasgow, and now he decided he wanted some of the action in the war.

Maley could do little to persuade him otherwise, and his last match for the club was in the Glasgow Cup final against Clyde on 7 October 1916. He thus won a medal while he was on leave from the Argyll and Sutherland Highlanders. Some time after that he was transferred to the Seaforth Highlanders. Maley, however much he may privately have deplored the loss of one of his best players, was nevertheless able to use Peter as an example of how Celtic were doing their bit for the war effort.

Another loss this season was Sunny Jim Young, this time to injury. Sunny had been signed by Maley from Bristol Rovers in 1903 and could justifiably claim to have been Maley's 'extension on the field' in that he could read the mind of 'The Boss' and do what 'The Boss' wanted. Young was now the captain of the team and was still going strong at the age of thirty-four, looking good for a few more years yet until he damaged his knee horribly in a game against Hearts on 30 September 1916. He was taken to hospital for an operation and Maley probably knew that Young's career was over.

Maley had always loved Sunny Jim. He would later state:

Celtic have never had a more whole-hearted player. He was a half-back of the rugged type, but there was class in his ruggedness, whilst for stamina he stood in the first rank. His enthusiasm inclined him sometimes to excesses, but a kinder-hearted fellow never wore a Celtic jersey.

Indeed the great Celtic teams of 1904-1910 and from 1914-1917 might not have happened without Sunny. To fill these gaps, Maley deployed a hard-working right half called Jimmy Wilson and also a Lanarkshire man called Willie McStay, therein establishing a family dynasty which would serve Celtic well for almost a century. In addition to that, Celtic lost the services of Patsy Gallacher who was suspended by the Scottish Football Association for six weeks, not for any on-field indiscretion but because he had been fined for 'bad timekeeping' in his job in the shipyards.

Maley was quick to protest about this, for his offence had nothing to do with football. Indeed, it was not the first nor the last occasion when those who had a perceived 'dig' at Celtic seemed to be able to make a few draconian decisions which adversely affected the club. Maley was by no means immune from the 'Celtic paranoia' but he was also able to rationalise it on the grounds that the authorities had to take a high-profile stance on things that could affect the war effort. In fact, Patsy's 'timekeeping' at Celtic Park had not always been of the best, but Maley was pragmatic enough to make excuses for him in this respect, for he was such a great player.

Maley's son Charlie was now in a London hospital suffering from war wounds, from which he recovered. His father was able to visit him once or twice and bring him the continuing good news from Parkhead, something that contrasted with the continuing bad news from Europe.

The Scottish League was won yet again, and once again rather easily, the victory being confirmed on 7 April at Boghead, Dumbarton on a day when the crowd were all enthusiastic about the entry of the USA into the war. The only loss was sustained at Kilmarnock after the League was well won, a feature of Celtic's consistent play being Maley's unfailing ability to spot and bring in youngsters like Adam McLean, and Joe Cassidy (when he was home on leave). The closest challengers were Greenock Morton who were boosted by naval personnel based in the Greenock area, and Rangers were once again out of contention.

Celtic also mopped up the Glasgow Charity Cup for the sixth year in a row beating Rangers 2-0 in the semi-final and Queen's Park 1-0 in the final. A new centre half was introduced for both these games. This was Willie Cringan, who had played for Sunderland before the war, and was still registered with them. In time he would be a fine, if occasionally troublesome servant of the club. How he came to Celtic is a mystery. He was a miner and preferred to work down the mines than in the army – something that he was of course allowed to do under the regulations. But twice Maley had the embarrassing situation of having to explain to the authorities that Cringan was not really a deserter from the army. He did in fact enlist after he had played these two games in the Glasgow Charity Cup, but the army soon decided that he would be a better miner than a soldier. Thus Cringan returned to the pits and was able to play for Celtic, as Maley was easily able to negotiate a deal with Sunderland who were now in abeyance.

The summer of 1917 saw Maley, like the rest of Scotland, becoming more and more anxious about the war. There seemed to be no end to it. The Americans albeit with no experience of European warfare might make a difference, but it would be some time before they could be there in strength. The only answer that the Government seemed to have was to push more and more men into the front line for more carnage and more slaughter. Conscription was now in place, and Maley would be less able to resist the demands of the Army for his star men.

In addition, it was now becoming more and more obvious that food shortages were beginning to hit, especially in large cities like Glasgow. Labour problems, often justified, were also now beginning to come to the fore as people began to look at the shocking housing and hygiene that had existed for more than a century. Men were coming home from their Army barracks and talking about flushing toilets and other unheard of luxuries. Discontent and unhappiness simmered under the surface.

Maley remained a deeply religious man, attending mass and confession regularly and trusting in God to solve all problems. Whatever Maley's politics were, he was no socialist. He still sympathised with the Liberal party, for he was a humane man and always willing in his own words 'to help the lame dog over the stile', although any attempt at the enforced redistribution of wealth appalled him. He believed in monarchy and parliamentary democracy and always staunchly believed that if change were to come – as come it must – it would have to be done through peaceful and lawful methods. He remained the son of a soldier.

From what he could gather of Ireland, the situation seemed to be calmer. From what little he gleaned, he reckoned that the Government were using methods of calming the country which his father would have disapproved of. This included the recruitment of convicts and other ne'er-do-wells to supplement the overstretched army, though it was still a small price to pay for peace. The Empire must not be stabbed in the back while fighting the greater struggle against Germany. Yet what end in sight was there of that?

The only ray of hope seemed to be the United States of America, who had made their stuttering, reluctant steps to join the war. They had loads of wealth and power and would surely tip the balance, eventually, but it would take a long time. Their only experience of war had been against the Red Indians in their so-called 'Wild West' and a few disastrous invasions of Mexico. This was a different war. Could France and Britain last until the Americans could make the vital difference? Then, in early June 1917, came the news that Maley and Celtic had been dreading and fearing. Peter Johnstone had fallen at a place called Arras in France.

Maley was devastated, lapsing into a sort of morose depression that he would do more commonly in future and blaming himself for creating circumstances in which 'big Peter', as he called him, would join up. He went to see Peter's widow, made all the necessary arrangements for her pension and made sure that she lacked for nothing. Yet, little was done at Parkhead to commemorate the heroic death of Peter Johnstone or indeed that of Donnie McLeod, who had played for the team a decade previously and who had been killed at Flanders in October 1917.

Maley suffered a further blow on Friday 9 November 1917, when he received a telegram stating that Father Charles O'Malley had suffered a heart attack and died in Ayr. This was of course Willie's eldest brother, who used the traditional family name O'Malley because he was a priest and did not feel the need to change in order to adapt to British and Scottish society as his father and brothers had done. Charles had been born in the West Indies in 1859 and, being a good eight years older, had never been so close to Willie as Tom, for example, had been.

Charles had trained for the priesthood in Nottingham, and his visits had been fairly infrequent. He had been held up as a great role model for the younger boys to follow, and the family had been very proud of him. He occasionally visited Glasgow to watch the team of Tom and Willie, but he was no great football fan. He was, however, much loved by his parishioners. He was just fifty-eight when he died.

Maley was more upset by this death than he cared to admit, but he played a leading part in the funeral which he attended with his mother and his sons, Charlie and Willie, both in military uniform. The reports of the funeral and the mourners do not mention anything about Mrs William Maley being there. The truth, of course, was that Helen and he had been estranged for many years.

Perhaps Maley's depression about the casualties of the war and the death of his brother affected the players that season, but there were other factors at work as well. The last season of the war saw big changes at Parkhead and a movement of power to the west of the city. Conscription meant the reluctant departure to foreign fields of the likes of McMaster, Dodds, McStay, and McAtee. Their loss was keenly felt, and there was little by the way of reserve strength. An indication of things to come was apparent in the Glasgow Cup when Celtic lost heavily to Rangers, then a string of draws in January meant that ground was lost in the Championship as Rangers, with the benefit of a more settled team, gained a little more consistency than hitherto.

Crucially, Celtic lost 3–1 to Third Lanark on 23 March, and it was a case of an old player coming back to haunt Maley, for the three goals were scored by David McLean. McLean had played for Celtic between 1907 and 1909 and indeed had played a vital part in the forward line in the epic Championship win of 1909. But he had never liked Maley's bullying tactics and being of Presbyterian stock, he resented Maley's emotional blackmail that a percentage of wages should go to some Catholic charity. Maley possibly felt that he did not need to cosset and pamper McLean, for he did have Jimmy Quinn as a centre forward. McLean picked a fight and left, in later life claiming that religious discrimination was the problem.

Objective analysis would have to say that Quinn was the better centre forward, but David McLean actually ended up scoring more goals than McGrory – a record slightly invalidated by the fact that so many were scored in the Second Division for Forfar Athletic. After leaving Celtic in 1909, he went on to play for Preston North End and Sheffield Wednesday, had earned one cap for Scotland in 1912 and played for Third Lanark and Rangers during the war. He would meet Maley yet again.

On that same day that McLean earned his revenge on Maley, Rangers won 2-1 at Airdrie, and then on the last day of the League season, Celtic could only draw with Motherwell at Parkhead, while Rangers scraped through 2-1 against Clyde. This game, played on 13 April, came at the one time in the war when the Germans almost won. The Ludendorf offensive might well have carried the day, until the Allies rallied and fought back. The game itself against Motherwell saw Celtic 'do nothing but shoot' for the last fifteen minutes as they strove to get the one crucial goal that would have denied Rangers the Championship.

The flags were flying at half mast that day for one of Celtic's truly great heroes, Dan Doyle. Dan had died on the Monday before of cancer at the age of fifty-four. Hours before he died, Maley, now totally reconciled with Dan after their arguments in the past, had been in the Glasgow Cancer Hospital to visit him. Dan had at one point rolled back the bedclothes to allow Maley to see his legs and said 'Ah well, they did their little bit for Celtic history!' It is a fine story, rich in Maley's sense of history and theatre, but it suffers a little when Maley tells us that other great Celtic players on their deathbeds apparently did the same as well!

Maley put a brave face on it, but was quite upset at the thought of losing the chance of five championships in a row. He was quite aware that for once Rangers had stolen a march on him by being able to get all their men (and a few from other clubs as well) available at the one time. They had done this by engineering the deployment of men in the shipyards, and by playing 'guest' men from other clubs when and if they happened to be based at the army bases of Largs or Ardrossan. There was a certain amount of consolation however for Maley at the winning of the Glasgow Charity Cup for the seventh season in a row and also an obscure trophy called the War Fund Cup.

It was fair to say that the war was now impinging rather heavily on all aspects of life. Maley, as he sat on Glasgow's trams (once he got over the shock of women conductors and drivers – something that the reactionary in him deplored, although he had to admit that they did a good job) watched Glaswegian humanity in its obvious deprivation and suffering and was coming to the conclusion that if the war did not end soon, the Empire would really have to sue for peace.

Apparently, there was another push on, but Maley was now aware that newspapers in war (and possibly in peace as well) only printed the parts of the truth that they wanted their readers to hear. The sheer number of wounded soldiers in George Square for example and the colossal amount of death notices and obituaries in the *Glasgow Herald* was something that was hard to parallel in human history. Words like 'victory' and 'defeat' were now beginning to mean less and less to Maley.

He could hardly bring himself to agree with agitators like Manny Shinwell and John McLean that the war must end at any cost, but he was now beginning to worry about his men who were still at the front. The death of Peter Johnstone had saddened him, and he was even congratulating himself on keeping the likes of Patsy Gallacher, Charlie Shaw, Jimmy McMenemy and Alec McNair from the fighting. But how long could they avoid the call-up? Maybe they would thank him some day, for too many men were going to the Front and would not come back.

Football was still continuing, although there had been some efforts to stop it altogether for the 1918/19 season. The previous season had seen Dundee, Aberdeen and Raith Rovers excluded from the Scottish League and put into virtual abeyance, such were the logistic problems of transport. In some ways, he was even glad that Rangers had won the 1918 Championship, for it had been the most unreal one so far. Some of the teams that Celtic played against contained men and young boys who had been drafted in from juniors and even school teams. Once or twice, a loudspeaker announcement had been made asking for a volunteer to referee!

Games had been poorly attended (at least away from Glasgow) and there had been several 'last posts' and 'minutes of silence' to commemorate a player or a committee man who had been killed recently. Most grounds had a special enclosure for the 'hospital blue' uniformed with their nurses and volunteers who had pushed the wheelchairs. There had even been some blind men in attendance, listening to a man telling them the progress of the game. It was difficult to concentrate on football, and this was perhaps why the League had been lost, Maley rationalised.

When the season opened again in August, casualties seemed even heavier, but there did seem to be some grounds for thinking that the Germans were about to crack, now that the Americans were there in strength. Celtic opened the season without Jimmy McMenemy. Now aged thirty-eight, Napoleon had been Maley's most consistent player since 1902, and he felt that it was time to step down. He was, in any case, due to be called up, even at his advanced age, in October and he thought that his best years were behind him.

Maley had tried to persuade McMenemy to stay with Celtic until the call-up papers came, but was happy enough to recognise the fine service that McMenemy had given the club and allow him to go temporarily. But McMenemy's call-up never came, being delayed because of a rather serious bout of the 'flu epidemic that was now sweeping Europe and which had an effect on the civilian organizations and the recruiting offices.

The war ended at last on 11 November. Maley could not entirely rejoice, for there had been too much suffering, and there were still other issues to be resolved such as the Irish problem, the Glasgow labour problem and the 'flu epidemic which was beginning to hit the debilitated population hard. The labour problems, in particular, would come to a head in Glasgow in early 1919 with tanks deployed in George Square by a panicky Government who feared Bolshevism and who would not deploy Scottish soldiers from Maryhill Barracks lest their loyalty could not be depended on. The world, Maley felt, would never be the same again.

But there was still football and Celtic. The team had played some mediocre football in the last few weeks of the war, and it was clear that a defeat by Motherwell on 7 December was a clear result of an injury to Patsy Gallacher the week before. Maley then approached McMenemy and asked him if he were available. McMenemy considered this request. He had vowed that he had had enough, but Maley was a mightily persuasive man, and Napoleon reckoned that in the circumstances of 1918/19, it would not matter all that much if he were now on the slow side. He had never been the fastest of players in any case, and as every other team had more than a few has-beens or never-was-ers, why not give it another go? Maley was convinced that the League could be won this year again.

Accordingly, on 14 December (the same day as the so-called 'Khaki' or 'Coupon' Election), Willie McStay took advantage of his early demobilization to turn out for Celtic and he was joined in the team by Napoleon McMenemy to the delight of the fans. The stand rose to a man to greet the return of the two heroes as Celtic went on to defeat Dumbarton 2-0.

Even better news was forthcoming in January with the return of Andy McAtee from the Italian front. The right-wing position had been a problem for some time and Maley had ingeniously plugged the gap temporarily by using a Rangers player called Scott Duncan for two games (this was allowed in the regulations of the time) at the turn of the year. Joe Dodds returned from France at about the same time, and the Celtic team had a settled look, not losing a single League game between 7 December and the end of the season.

Gallacher, of course, remained superb at inside right and with McMenemy back in the other inside position, it was as if the war had never happened, as far as the play of Celtic was concerned. McColl was fed to produce the goods and the only real change in the forward line was Adam McLean for Johnny Browning, whose dissolute lifestyle was obviously disapproved of by Maley.

Willie Cringan had proved an excellent acquisition and he soon became captain, showing leadership qualities that ensured that Celtic won their fifteenth Championship in 1919. It was a close fight too and Celtic had to win their last game at a packed Somerset Park, Ayr to guarantee the title. Maley would have been especially pleased with his men that day, for in every way it was a glorious fightback. Rangers may have won the Championship in 1918, but by 1919 the flag was back where Maley felt it belonged. The future looked bright. If Lloyd George wanted Britain to be a land 'fit for heroes to live in', Maley felt that he had to do the same for his supporters. Celtic should be a team fit for heroes to support.

Yet, it was not all sweetness and light. A Victory Cup had been set up instead of a Scottish Cup that year, and Celtic surprisingly went out to the eventual winners St Mirren. The Glasgow Charity Cup, which had become almost Celtic's own property during the war years, was surrendered to Queen's Park in a singularly dismal performance which had Maley fuming. In particular, Alec McNair had had a poor game against a fine left-winger by the name of Alan Morton. It was clear that there was a long, long trail a-winding into the land of Maley's dreams.

1 *Left:* The famous picture of Maley with his Homburg hat. 2 *Right:* Brother Walfrid of the Marist Brothers. It was he and two others who invited Maley to come along with his brother, Tom, to join the new Celtic club in December 1887. 3 *Below left:* The great James Kelly. He was the founder of the Kelly dynasty who were sadly to lead the club to disaster before the 'coup' of 1894.
4 *Below right:* Willie's brother, Tom Maley, whom he relied on a lot.

5 *Above:* The first-ever Celtic team of 1888. The team are wearing white shirts with green collars and crest – note the knickerbockers and shin guards. Willie Maley is second from the right of the middle row, brother Tom second from left and James Kelly is in the front row with the curious-looking ball at his feet. 6 *Right:* A fine cameo portrait of Willie Maley in about 1892. 7 *Below:* The Celtic team of 1890/91. Celtic are now wearing green and white vertical stripes. Willie Maley is second from the right in the middle row with his brother Tom in civvies beside him. The man in the front row with the cap is the great goal scorer Sandy McMahon.

8 *Top:* Celtic Park in 1900 with the ground specially seated for the Scotland *v.* England international of that year. The crowd are all well dressed and douce. The pavilion is on the left, and on the right is the Grant Stand – which steamed up on cold days! It was replaced by the Main Stand in 1929.

9 *Bottom:* 'Our Bhoys have won the Cup' – pictures of Celtic's first Scottish Cup winners of 1892. Maley is the intense-looking right half of this famous team.

10 *Above:* Celtic in 1896. Maley (extreme right, middle row) on the verge of retiring as a player. Next to him is the great Dan Doyle.

11 *Below:* Celtic in 1898. Maley, with bow tie and cap, is the dapper-looking manager.

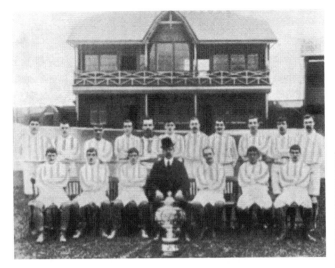

12 *Above:* Celtic in 1901. Maley's hat seems too small for him! Sandy McMahon (fifth from the left in the back row) has clearly been inserted later! The Glasgow Exhibition Trophy may also be a later addition.

13 *Right:* A cartoon of the 1904 Scottish Cup final and the congratulations given to Jimmy Quinn after his hat-trick.

14 Maley wears a boater hat (as do several of the crowd) before this game played on tour in Leipzig, Germany in 1906. Goalkeeper Adams (on Maley's right) wears a green and white jersey and seems also to be sporting some sort of 'abdominal protection'!

15 *Above:* Maley (centre, back row) with the Board of Directors in 1907. His friend James Kelly is second from left in the front row. It was a feature of Maley's management of the club that he seldom fell out with his directors!

16 *Below:* This postcard depicts Celtic's great season of 1907/08. The Charity Cup final of 30 May 1908 is in progress. Observe Hampden's curious stand.

17 Maley's great team of 1908, who won every competition they entered. Notice the goalkeeper Davie Adams (fifth from left in the middle row) has no special jersey. Beside Maley stands the great 'Sunny Jim' Young.

18 1912 was a poorish season for Celtic, the club 'only' winning the Scottish Cup. Maley is on the extreme right of the middle row. Third from right of the front row is Patsy Gallacher. Observe how frail he is and look at his thin legs.

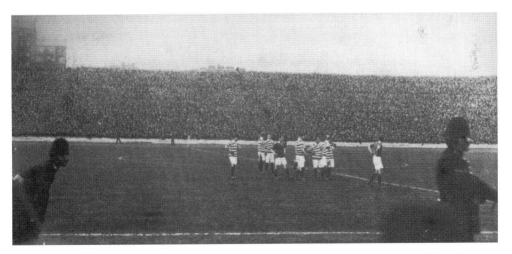

19 Riot is about to break out! It is the replay of the 1909 Scottish Cup final between Celtic and Rangers. The full-time whistle has blown and the players are waiting for extra time, which Maley thought would be a good idea after two games. However, the authorities wanted yet another game to generate even more money.

20 *Above:* Scottish Cup semi-
final 1912 *v.* Hearts at Ibrox.
Patsy Gallacher and Jimmy
Quinn are the Celtic players in
the picture.

21 *Right:* Celtic *v.* Aston Villa at
Parkhead in a friendly in 1912.
This is a rare shot of 'Sunny
Jim' Young, one of Maley's
greatest players and captains.
Sunny was fated to meet his
death in a motorbike accident in
September 1922.

22 A rare picture of the Grant Stand at Celtic Park. Along the front of the upper tier can just be made out 'Barr's Iron Brew'. Celtic are playing against Aberdeen who are wearing their black and gold strips. The players are McMenemy (half hidden) of Celtic, Wilson of Aberdeen, Browning of Celtic and Colman of Aberdeen. This picture was taken on 4 October 1913.

23 The country was already at war in August 1914 when this photograph was taken. Peter Johnstone (third from right in the back row) would not survive the carnage. Maley looks grim, but this was a superb team.

24 Alec McNair.

25 Jimmy Young.

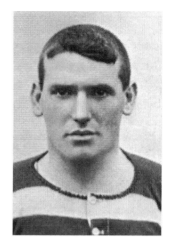

26 Jimmy Quinn.

27 Jimmy McMenemy.

28 A cartoon depicting Maley as 'Mr Moneybags'. He would not be ashamed of this!

29 *Above:* Celtic at the start of season 1920/21. In the middle row, third from left is one of Maley's mistakes. Tom Craig was allowed to depart and eventually ended up a star for Rangers.

30 *Below:* A picture of Celtic in 1921 issued by *All Sports* magazine. Maley is in the front row on the right.

31 Before the Rhine Army *v.* Celtic game in Cologne, Germany on 31 May 1922. Maley is fourth from right of the back row.

32 Celtic in Cologne in 1922 in their charabanc.

33 Celtic on tour in Czechoslovakia in 1922. Maley is in the middle, surprisingly without a hat.

34 Joe Dodds and Alec McNair, Celtic's fine full-back combination.

35 The Scottish Cup winners of 1923 with Maley in the background. The great Patsy Gallacher is second from right in the front row.

36 *Above:* A fine picture of Patsy Gallacher in a game against Airdrie at Parkhead sometime in the early 1920s. The Irish flag is on the flagpole in the centre of what became known as the 'Jungle'.

37 1925 was a famous Scottish Cup victory, being the year of Gallacher's wonder goal, and the year they overtook Queen's Park's record of 10 Scottish Cup wins. They beat Dundee 2-1 in the final.

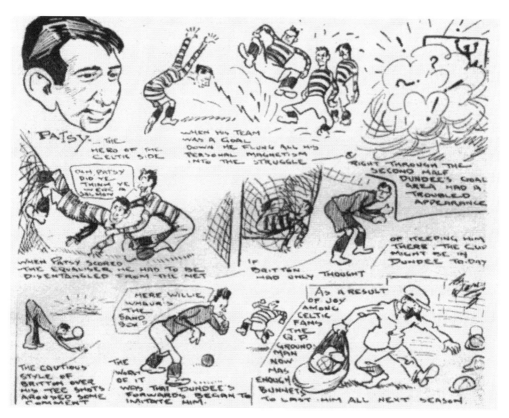

38 A cartoon of the 1925 Scottish Cup final highlighting Patsy Gallacher's famous goal.

39 Car parking and orderly queues at the Scottish Cup final of 1925.

40 *Above:* Crowd control at the Celtic *v.* Dundee Scottish Cup final of 1925. Everybody wears a bonnet.

41 *Below:* Celtic's Scottish League winning team of 1926. Funnily enough, Maley is not in this photograph. He was not usually so bashful.

42 On board S.S. *Caledonia* en route to America in 1931. Maley is on the extreme right of the second row from the front.

43 Maley (seated) with McGrory and Thomson at St. Joseph's College, Dumfries. Maley and McGrory were both practising Roman Catholics, but Thomson belonged to an evangelical sect.

44 A happy party taken at Detroit in 1931. McGrory holds the Scottish Cup, Maley is with the boater hat in the background. His brother Tom is third from the right.

45 *Above:* One of the last photographs of goalkeeper John Thomson, who was killed a few weeks after this picture was taken. Maley looks grim on extreme left of the back row.

46 *Left:* 5 September 1931, Ibrox Stadium. The fatal moment of impact is a split second away as Sam English's knee is about to hit John Thomson's head.

47 Thomson fails to rise following the collision with Sam English.

48 *Top:* Celtic players call for a stretcher for John Thomson. Sam English – himself receiving attention – is also concerned for John.

49 *Middle:* John Thomson is carried off, head swathed in bandages and attended by anxious ambulancemen. He has only hours left to live.

50 *Right:* Celtic with the Scottish Cup of 1933. Maley is on extreme left. Observe his height and imposing presence.

51 *Above left:* Maley (extreme right of middle row) at Lourdes in 1935. His brother Tom (back row next to banner) is already quite ill and will die a few weeks after this photograph was taken.

52 *Above right:* An excellent study of Willie Maley sometime in the 1930s.

53 *Below:* Celtic at Muirton Park, Perth on 24 August 1935. Players are wearing black arm bands and Maley is not there because his brother Tom died that morning.

54 *Above:* Maley (extreme right, front row) with his great team of 1936. He has removed his hat for the occasion, but trainer McMenemy hasn't. Third from left of the front row is the great Jimmy McGrory.

55 *Below:* The Scottish Cup final of 1937 – Maley's last as manager of Celtic. The crowd was a record 147,365. The black and golds of Aberdeen are clearing a Celtic attack.

56 *Top:* These are the excluded from the 1937 Scottish Cup final between Celtic and Aberdeen. Observe the total lack of replica kits and the amount and variety of bonnets. Celtic won 2-1.

57 *Left:* The great team of 1938. Jimmy McMenemy (front right) is the trainer and Maley's right-hand man. Observe the thickly padded shin guards of the players.

58 Maley is a sprightly seventy year old as the team collect the Glasgow Charity Cup at City Chambers in 1938. Willie Lyon is the triumphant captain.

59 Maley (extreme left) with the Board of Directors in 1938. Everything looks fine here, but squalls were soon to develop both within Celtic and in Europe. On the extreme right is Bob Kelly (son of James) who would become an authoritarian chairman after the Second World War.

60 Maley's greatest moment as Willie Lyon collects the Empire Exhibition Trophy of 1938. It is a shame that Maley himself is not in the picture.

61 *Above:* Maley, with soft hat, beside his three greatest players – Jimmy Quinn, Jimmy McGrory and Patsy Gallacher.

62 *Below:* August 1953. The aged Maley now eighty-five (doffing his hat) returns to Parkhead with his old players: Jimmy McMenemy, Willie Loney and Joe Dodds.

Seven

TOMMY, TROUBLE AND THE TWENTIES

The 1920s were the era in which Maley began to lose the place. His basic problem, one felt, stemmed from his background and his inability to cope with the demands of the new age. 'The war changed all that' was a phrase often used of British society with reference to the difficult situation of the clash between Victorian values and the new developments that were now taking place.

Maley certainly represented the Victorian ideal of success, prosperity, hard work and progress. What he had done for Celtic Football Club was obvious and permanent. Now, although he had passed his fiftieth birthday, he still considered himself as in the prime of life and was determined to carry on. The First World War was over, and progress and prosperity beckoned.

But like many a man of the older generation, Maley failed to see or appreciate the vast changes that had occurred since 1914. The war had indeed been won, but at a tremendous cost in manpower, resources, wealth and human suffering. More marked, although perhaps more subtle, was the change in people's attitude. There was now less willingness to accept things as they were. The working man had fought and won. He now demanded a few more crumbs from the victor's cake. When even a few crumbs from the said cake were not forthcoming, the working man no longer acquiesced.

This was seen in the rise of the Labour Party (they would form a government as early as 1924) and the continuing unrest in industry. Glasgow had been at the epicentre of it all during the war and in the immediate aftermath. It did not go away easily, typified perhaps in men like Jimmy Maxton, the ILP firebrand whose constituency and powerbase lay in Bridgeton, a stone's throw from Celtic Park.

If Maley had ever fondly imagined that he would return to being the benign, paternalistic, avuncular figure that he had been to his great teams of the 1900s and the early war years, then he was very far wrong. Professional football, no more or no less than other walks of life, was affected by the phenomenon of the working man occasionally saying 'No' to his bosses. They had said 'Yes' to their bosses in places like the Somme … and they did not want any more of that.

Maley was determined that the war wounded would be welcome at Parkhead. He had designated an enclosure in front of the Grant Stand where disabled soldiers and their attendants would be allowed in free. The blinded were given a seat on a bench and a primitive form of commentary was organised. Andy Aitken, who had played for Newcastle and Scotland before the war, commonly known as the 'daddler', was very impressed with all this and wrote in the *Evening Times*, 'One up for Mr Maley!', implying that Celtic's facilities were better than anyone else's.

The early 1920s, however, were characterised by Maley's inability to cope with the demands of talented football players. Willie Cringan, Johnny Gilchrist, Joe Cassidy and others would fall foul of Maley. Patsy Gallacher might have done likewise had Maley not been shrewd enough and pragmatic enough to go the extra mile to keep that prodigious talent at Celtic Park, but Maley's inability to deal with the new generation was nowhere more marked than with Tommy McInally.

Tommy had come from Barrhead, an orphan boy who never knew his biological father and seems to have been brought up by his aunt, perhaps the mother of Arthur McInally who also played for the club. In the last year of the war, Tommy had played well for the junior team St Anthony's and Maley's spies and contacts had had him well watched. Maley himself saw him play and signed him on, for he was a very talented lad, a good passer, a scorer of goals and a born entertainer.

Maley did like lads who would entertain, but very early on he realised that Tommy McInally was going to be a handful. He was cheerful and happy, but had the stubborn streak that would not accept discipline. He had the need to be the centre of attention, always singing and generally making a noise in the dressing room, telling off-colour jokes and stories that Maley himself could chuckle at privately, but not in public. He would even interrupt team talks. On one occasion, Maley was urging the wing-halves to 'carry the ball'. Tommy said blandly, 'The referee'll gie a foul against us, if they dae that!'

This sort of badinage was alien to Maley. Even Peter Somers of old, who could do brilliant impersonations of Maley at soirées and team gatherings in hotels, knew his place. Yet Maley had always to admit a soft spot for the McInally boy. He knew that his background had lacked a great deal. For a while, Maley tolerated McInally who possessed marvellous football talent and a great love for the club.

Indeed, Tommy was soon dubbed the 'Boy Wonder', such was his dramatic impact in the first post-war season of 1919/20. A hat-trick on his debut against Clydebank, two goals in the next game and another the game after that, soon had the punters believing that the goalscoring exploits of Jimmy Quinn would soon be emulated. Maley certainly thought so, and made the mistake of transferring Jimmy McColl to Stoke at the end of the season.

But the team stuttered after a bright start which had included the winning of the Glasgow Cup, and when Gallacher was injured just before Christmas, form took a severe dip. At the end of January, the team's defeats by Clydebank and Dundee effectively knocked them out of the League race, given Rangers' consistent form. It was Rangers who put Celtic out of the Scottish Cup as well, at the quarter-final stage. McInally was injured and Gallacher only half fit, and Rangers played better on the day.

Thus Rangers won the first round after the war, but there was an even greater embarrassment to Maley caused by the behaviour of his supporters on Monday 26 April, one of Celtic's darker days, given Maley's prolonged and assiduous attempts to portray Celtic as a club free from the scourge of hooliganism. The incident concerned Dundee who had played Rangers two days earlier.

Dundee had lost 6-1 at Ibrox. Their lack of fight had puzzled the scribe of the *Dundee Advertiser* and a few of their players had made unwise statements to the effect that Rangers would be 'worthy champions' and that they were 'better than Celtic'. Clearly, Dundee's Scottish Cup exit at the hands of Celtic earlier in the season still rankled, and it has to be recalled that in the city of Dundee at the time, Celtic, the darlings of Dundee's huge Irish population, were seen as the real rivals of the Dens Parkers. Dundee Hibs (later Dundee United) were still in their infancy. Some of the Celtic crowd saw fit, in these circumstances, to claim that Dundee had not tried too hard against Rangers.

Dundee were booed from the start of the game at Parkhead, and with the score at 1-1, after one or two tackles had gone in, the crowd invaded the field and attacked some Dundee players, particularly McIntosh and the referee Mr McMillan. But for the prompt and strong action of the likes of Alec McNair and Joe Cassidy, who bravely tried to stem the tide of such hooligans, more than two men might have been assaulted. Fortunately, no one was seriously injured, but it was certainly an ugly scene and Maley was appalled.

Surprisingly, however, he did seem to have some control over journalists, for the incident was distinctly downplayed in newspapers with euphemisms like 'boisterous behaviour' and 'unruly elements encroaching' employed to cover up what was a riotous mob who could have seriously hurt some Dundee players.

Maley had even more control of the Scottish League, on whose committee he currently served (he would be president from 1921 until 1924) and the matter was quickly hushed up and relegated to the history books. As Rangers won the League soon after in any case, the game was not replayed and Dundee decided not to pursue the matter. The Scottish League inflicted a token punishment on Celtic of closing the ground from 5 May until 1 September, making them play their first three games of next season away from home.

Immediately after this, Maley fell ill with what looked like pneumonia, but was possibly nothing other than a severe attack of the 'flu bug which had menaced the population since the end of the war. He was being nursed by his aged mother who did her best to protect him from the dire tidings of what had happened on the night of Saturday 1 May 1920. His friend William Wilton, manager of Rangers and a keen sailor, had been drowned in a freak storm near Gourock. Mary Maley had decided that he would not get to hear the news until he was fit and well. But a housekeeper brought him his breakfast one morning and tactlessly told him the news, about which Maley was very upset.

He recovered enough to attend the funeral. On a happier note, Celtic added the Charity Cup to their Glasgow Cup success at the end of the 1919/20 season. Thus it wasn't a season that would be considered to be total failure. Yet the fans were by no means happy with what was happening. The departure of McColl, who had played only nine games that season, was a disappointment, and it was added to by the departure of Jimmy McMenemy on a free transfer. McMenemy had been coaxed back out of retirement in December 1918, but now in summer 1920 he was allowed to go.

With the benefit of retrospect, it seems to have been a bad decision for McMenemy played a vital role in winning the Scottish Cup for Partick Thistle in 1921, but Maley can hardly be criticised for allowing a forty year old to leave the club. But what did concern more and more supporters was the *reason* for Maley's allowing McMenemy to go – his growing obsession with money. The fear was expressed that Patsy Gallacher might be allowed to go. Apparently Stoke City and Dundee Hibs were interested.

The decision that has been much criticised by historians was that of disbanding the reserve team in 1922. To what extent Maley was responsible for this is hard to say, but it would be difficult to escape the conclusion that if he had dug his heels in with the directors and insisted on the retention of the reserve side, he would have won the day. It has been stated that it was this penny pinching which handed supremacy to Rangers (with a few isolated, but spectacular exceptions) for the rest of Maley's career. This is hardly fair, for Celtic could, in theory, at least rely on a vast nursery to provide the players for them, and there was a hard core of West Central Scotland young men currently playing in one or other of the plethora of junior teams who would give their eye teeth to don the green and white jerseys.

There were other, more subtle forces at work as well, but money was indeed never far away from the forefront of Maley's thinking. It was certainly true that he would not pay his players any more than necessary. His argument was that football players, in any case, had a better life and earned more than the average working man. The main motivation to play the game should be love of the game and love of the club. There was, of course, more than a whiff of hypocrisy in all this, for Maley had always made sure that his own nest was well feathered from football and from Celtic.

On the other hand, there was now a far more business-like Rangers set-up in place on the other side of the city. Since the death of Maley's friend William Wilton in May 1920, Rangers had been managed by William Struth, often called the 'Ruthless' in an amateurish play on his name. He had served his apprenticeship with Clyde, and had suffered so much at the hands of the great Celtic teams of the past that he was pledged to do nothing other than take over from them.

To this end, no effort, either financial or anything else, was to be spared. Players would be bought and an early indication of this was the arrival of Alan Morton from Queen's Park. Later players such as Bob McPhail would arrive from Airdrie and it was often said that if a team beat Rangers on a Saturday, by Monday morning there would be a telephone call from Ibrox asking how much they wanted for their star player.

Wealth was already there at Ibrox. The stadium was a fine one and being situated near the shipbuilding yards of the Empire's second city (as Glasgow was called), was ideally located for the population of Govan and Kinning Park. To this was added another dimension, this time a more sinister one. Whether it was Struth himself who deliberately and consciously introduced it is not clear. What is certain is that a trend which had been obvious before the war now became institutionalised and reinforced.

With Celtic being perceived as the 'Catholic' team of West Scotland, it was natural that a reaction would take place and that sooner or later, a 'Protestant' team would arise. There had been a tendency for Rangers to be primarily Protestants before the war, although they had employed a few Catholics as well, notably Willie Kivlichan, who had also played for Celtic. Alec Bennett, a Protestant, who had been one of Maley's great team from 1904–1908 also went to Rangers, perhaps because he felt the Catholic atmosphere at Parkhead a shade oppressive – but there had been no real religious divide until after the war.

Maley himself would always trace the rise of bigotry to Harland and Wolff who opened a shipyard on the Clyde in 1912, and being an Ulster firm, brought many Orange shipyard workers to Glasgow with them. This may be true, and certainly the war itself with its aftermath in Southern Ireland and its absurd myths (for example, that the Orangemen of Northern Ireland were the only men who fought at the Battle of the Somme!) exacerbated the situation. The key factor, however, was that those in charge at Ibrox (and perhaps those in charge at Parkhead as well) realised that there was a huge earner potential if Rangers made it their policy never to sign anyone who was a Roman Catholic.

It must be stated that Rangers fans were not all Orange bigots, for some of them were men genuinely attracted by the excellent fare on offer from men like Tommy Cairns, Sandy Archibald and Alan Morton. There was even a certain morbid fascination and talk about jinxes etc. about why Rangers always seemed capable of winning the Scottish League, but never the Scottish Cup which they had not won since 1903.

Where Maley must be blamed, however, lies in his inability or unwillingness to see the advantages for Celtic in this situation. If Rangers were to refuse to sign a large proportion of the Scottish population on the grounds of their religion, Celtic who were prepared to sign everyone, should have, other things being equal, a stronger team. It is curious that a man who constantly said 'It is not his creed or his nationality that counts but the man himself', failed to take advantage of this situation.

Jock Stein, forty-five years later, was far more aware of all this. He realised that a Roman Catholic player would be his whenever he wished to pluck him, so would concentrate his efforts on signing a Protestant where there might be some competition from Rangers. Thus to name but three, Willie Wallace, Danny McGrain and Kenny Dalglish, Rangers supporters all, became Parkhead legends.

In addition, Stein thus captured the moral high ground of Glasgow. Amazingly, in the swinging sixties, Rangers were still persevering with this absurd policy (and would do so for another twenty years yet), and thus all the trendy lefties, liberals, socialists, hippies and other children of the sixties would have to, if pushed, say that in Glasgow they preferred Celtic. One could not, after all, organise protest marches against racial discrimination in the Southern States of the USA, in South Africa or in Rhodesia, and then condone what Rangers did in Glasgow!

Maley, sadly, did not see the opportunities that presented themselves in this. He did of course sign non-Catholics, but what a team Celtic could have had, for example, if he had got to Bob McPhail of Airdrie before Rangers did, or snatched James Fleming from St Johnstone from under the nose of Struth!

The problem was of course that these players would have cost money. To a point, Maley was correct in stating that he had to beware of finances on the grounds that the hard times of the 1920s affected Celtic supporters more than Rangers fans ... but only to a point. He did on occasion give the impression that he suffered from lack of ambition, something that a Celtic club must never have. In the future, the Kelly dynasty in the 1980s and 1990s were always wanting to do things on the cheap, and they too led the club and their supporters into bad times.

Yet financial parsimony was only one aspect of Maley's character. Another was his sheer obstinacy and stubbornness, that he and only he would know what was best for Celtic and he would decide. There was certainly a lack of any opposition from within the club – the directors were all at this point very much with him, and any player who complained about his lot would be brusquely removed. The supporters were far from happy with what they saw, but they were never organised to protest. They remained loyal, in some cases far too loyal. In any event, there was always the occasional (and sometimes more than occasional) success to rejoice in. There was always, for example, until the mid-1920s, Patsy Gallacher.

It is remarkable to modern eyes that for all his failures from 1920 to 1940 (if you can call 4 League Championships and 6 Scottish Cups in twenty years a failure), Maley was never the object of a 'Maley must go' campaign. There were several reasons for this. One was that he had been the club's only manager. He was so identified with the team that the fortunes of Glasgow Celtic and the fortunes of William Maley were perceived as one and the same thing.

Maley remained rightly associated with his great team of the Edwardian era and the years immediately before the war. Already Celtic youngsters were hearing all about the mighty deeds of Young, Loney and Hay, and the mighty Quinn. There was no reason to doubt that, just as Celtic had been great before under Maley, they would also be great again. Current failures were just temporary blips. Maley the great would soon turn things round.

Another thing was, of course, that Willie Maley was a Glasgow institution, well known and respected throughout the city. Genial and affable, he would talk to everyone, had friends all over Scotland, was a member of the Scottish League Committee and president thereof from 1921 until 1924, had business interests, notably the restaurant in which he had had a partnership since 1920 and which was named somewhat fittingly in view of his perceived meanness 'The Bank'. He was a man of extraordinary energy and did make an effort to live up to the beliefs of his faith. Like the rest of mankind, he sometimes fell short, but he apparently was quite happy with his nickname, originally bestowed upon him in mockery, of the 'Catholic Jew'.

Maley's first joust with Struth's Rangers in season 1920/21 saw him end up decidedly second best, as Rangers won the League by 10 points. Defensively, there could be no doubt that Celtic missed Joe Dodds who had fallen out with Maley and gone to Cowdenbeath for a season (fortunately the 'tiff' was later patched up), and up front there seemed to be a problem in that Gallacher and McInally were too similar both in playing style and temperament, and did not always co-operate too well. March was a bad month with Andy McAtee struggling against injury, two defeats in the League and an unaccountable defeat by Hearts in the Scottish Cup at Parkhead.

There had been some consolation for Celtic, however, in their famous victory over Rangers at Ibrox on New Year's Day (when Joe Cassidy led the way with two goals) and victories in the two Glasgow competitions. The Charity Cup final in particular played on the late date of 14 May was a rewarding one. Not only were Rangers the opponents, but Tommy McInally answered his growing band of critics by scoring both goals in the 2-0 victory, and then started to show off. Earlier that season he had enraged Maley and exasperated the fans by showing off *before* doing the business. Maley had additional reason to be pleased with himself, for he had been able to play Joe Dodds at left-back, peace having broken out between the two of them when Joe returned on 5 May.

Summer 1921 saw a return to the continent of Europe for the first time since before the war. It included a game against Newcastle United which was won, and more sombrely, a tour of some of the battlefields, particularly Ypres where Joe Cassidy had seen action, as indeed had reserves David Pratt and Archie Longmuir. Before a game against a team called Lions de Flandres in a town called Roubaix (which had been occupied by the Germans) a wreath was laid on the war memorial.

The 1921/22 season saw a fascinating finish to the Scottish League campaign, but disappointment in all three Cup competitions. Celtic lost one game at Parkhead all season and that was the Scottish Cup game to Hamilton Accies. It was a curious one as well. Celtic were 3-0 down at half-time and Maley did a curious thing. He came out of the Pavilion at half-time and actually tore into his players *on* the field of play, refusing to allow them the facilities of the dressing room! It had little effect, for Celtic never got back into the game until a Joe Dodds penalty in the 86th minute gave a modicum of respectability.

The booing was intense, and Maley was embarrassed and angry about all this. He knew that it would set the cynics speculating about bribery and associations with bookmakers. Such allegations were not unheard of in the 1920s (indeed they are occasionally current today to explain a strange defeat), but possibly the real reason was the form of Tommy McInally, who was singled out that day for booing by his hitherto adoring fans.

He would play only one more game for the club (ironically once more against Hamilton Accies in a League game which Celtic won handsomely) before his temporary departure from the club at the end of the season. Maley would be quoted as saying that 'McInally is not re-engaged owing to the demands he made, which were peremptorily turned down by the board', and 'McInally attempted to dictate terms to the directors, an ill-advised step which was answered in the only possible way – he was transferred' but there was possibly a lot more to it than that. McInally had pushed Maley too hard, and there was little doubt that his constant clowning had an unsettling effect on the rest of the team. The crowd loved it all, but it occasionally backfired and Maley cannot have been happy at the thought of exiting the Scottish Cup at the quarter-final stage for the third year in a row and thus missing out on the big money.

Certainly once McInally was dropped (although he was nominally injured), the team, which had never really played badly even with the quixotic Tommy, now acquired a consistency and reliability. Joe Cassidy now came into his own and Patsy Gallacher remained superb. A talented player called John McFarlane (soon to be called 'Jean') came in at inside left to allow Cassidy to be in the centre with no other remit than to score goals.

The League Championship went down to the wire, as the modern idiom would have it. Celtic had to travel to Greenock on the last day of the season while Rangers, one point behind, played at Clyde. The stakes were high, for Morton were playing with confidence having defeated Rangers in the Scottish Cup Final a fortnight previously. In a game characterised by serious crowd trouble (a sadly common occurrence in the 1920s given all the disturbed young men which the war had produced), Celtic were 1-0 down to a professional Morton side.

Morton were holding out. Gallacher had picked up a knock and was strangely quiet. He had gone out to the right wing, allowing Andy McAtee to come inside. Cassidy, starved of service, had had to go back to forage for himself. With ten minutes remaining, Johnny Gilchrist sent over a hopeful ball, Morton's goalkeeper fumbled and Andy McAtee was fortuitously on hand to push the ball over the line with his head. It was hardly a clean header, but it was the goal that won the League for Celtic.

Maley had been sitting in the Cappielow stand, directly in front of the Press Box. Some journalists now had a telephone with which they could keep their office informed of what was going on. Maley was thus able to ask the score at the Clyde v. Rangers game. It was a draw, and he knew that if Celtic held out for a draw at Cappielow, the Championship would be won. Fortunately, for the last ten minutes, Gallacher had recovered sufficiently well to play a fuller part in proceedings and held on to the ball to frustrate the Morton team.

Maley would describe the hooliganism at the game and immediately after as 'barbaric', denouncing both his own supporters and those of Morton who had joined in, but in spite of all that, he must have been happy to see the League Championship return for the first time since 1919.

The team celebrated by going back to Europe, mainly to the new country of Czechoslovakia. Controversially, the tour this year included two games in defeated Germany, a move frowned upon by the British establishment whose newspapers were still referring to the German race as 'Hun arch-criminals' 'destroyers of humanity' and other intemperate expressions. Maley, however, deflected the sting off much of the criticism by playing a game against the British Army of the Rhine, as well as a Prussian Select.

Maley argued that he was there to rebuild the friendly relations which had existed before the war and also to cheer up the British soldiers, who were still there lest the Germans tried to rise again. He was much distressed at the impoverished country and the obvious emotional suffering of the people whose losses had been worse than the British side and who had been humiliated into the bargain. It was necessary, he felt, to build the Germans up again lest they begin to listen to some fanatic who might try another war. A great deal of money was raised for German orphanages, and Celtic were frequently described both by the British army and the Germans themselves as 'the greatest football team on earth'.

Maley loved accolades like that. More than anything else he was concerned about Celtic's image. It may have struck him as ironic that here in 1922 with a bloody war having existed in Ireland since the end of the First World War, Celtic, still the Irish team of Scotland, were representing Great Britain in another country that had been devastated by the victorious Empire! He did, however, come to believe more and more that war was no solution to any human problem. He had seen too much suffering at first hand both in his own family and in the sight of wounded ex-servicemen at Parkhead (whom he still allowed in for half price and sometimes for free, in spite of official disapproval) and in the dreadful things that were still happening in the land of his birth.

Yet there did seem to be some progress there as well. In fact, the establishment of the Irish Free State, independent of Westminster but still expressing allegiance to the Crown, and the allowing of the Protestants in the North to stay in Great Britain, would have seemed to Maley as the ideal solution to the problem. Unfortunately, as it seemed to Maley, the hotheads did not see it that way... and a lot would depend on whether the Orange bigots could allow tolerance for the Catholic minority in Ulster.

The 1922/23 season was a regression, brought about by Maley's mishandling of several situations in summer 1922. The team would finish third in the League in 1923, a long way behind Rangers and the impressive Airdrie, now managed by ex-Celtic left-back Willie Orr, one of Maley's great players. Too many sub-standard performances were registered in the first half of the season, and it was clear to most supporters that a mistake had been made in playing terms when Tommy McInally was allowed to go on 4 September 1922 to ply his reluctant trade with Third Lanark. The team also suffered from injuries. In addition, the fact that there was now no reserve team meant that those who were drafted in had to fit in immediately with the new system, while Maley's methods of man-management were now more and more autocratic.

McInally had been for some time the spectre at the feast. At a five-a-side tournament at Lochwinnoch in July 1922, the Celtic five of Dodds, Gilchrist, Cassidy, Gallacher and McLean refused to continue against Tommy McInally who had been allowed to play for Partick Thistle in this tournament, although he was still nominally on the books of Celtic. Dodds alleged a foul had been committed by Tommy and was sent off. The other four joined Dodds by walking off! Maley managed to keep this bizarre incident out of the headlines, but it did indicate how unpopular Tommy was with his fellow players. The supporters certainly thought Tommy's unpopularity may have been to do with his disgraceful performance in the Cup tie against Hamilton and his alleged friendship with bookmakers.

Joe Dodds, now thirty-five, was in any case on his way, this time as player-manager to Queen of the South. He felt that he might have been granted a testimonial match, and thus he left with a bad taste in his mouth, but he had been great servant for Maley and the club. There was no lasting bitterness, for Joe returned to Celtic as a backroom man in 1936 and remained a close friend of Maley until Maley's death. He was much missed by the supporters, who felt that Maley might have done a little more to keep him for another season.

Maley made another big mistake in summer 1922, although it would take several years for his folly to become apparent. Several times, a young reserve half-back called Tom 'Tully' Craig had played in the full team, but Maley had not been all that impressed. In order to acquire a centre forward called Willie Crilly from Alloa to take the place of Tommy McInally, Craig was traded. Crilly's impact on Celtic was absolutely negligible (and he eventually disappeared to the United States, where he played against Celtic in 1931), but Craig played well for Alloa before being transferred to Rangers where he became a great half-back.

Soon after the New Year of 1923, another Celt fell out with Maley and departed. This time, however, there were faults on both sides. Johnnie or 'Jock' Gilchrist was a fine right half and with Cringan and McMaster formed a half-back line which seemed to be a worthy successor to Young, Loney and Hay. He had been capped for Scotland the previous year. But he was not always the best at turning up punctually for training, and Maley held him responsible for the defeat at Ibrox on New Year's Day and the general poor form of the team.

Gilchrist was indeed a likely target. He was once reputed to have told Maley that if Maley wished to talk to him, he would have to be better dressed as Maley was not wearing a jacket at the time. This may have been a myth, but it certainly would have hit home with Maley who was always fastidious about dress. There was little doubt that Gilchrist's 'devil-may-care' attitude was not the right one to adopt before Maley. He was warned several times about failing to appear for training, suspended and finally transferred to Preston North End at the end of January to Maley's ill-disguised relief, as well as joy. Preston had been induced to pay £4,500 for him.

It was probably a good piece of business for the club, and certainly Gilchrist went from bad to worse at Preston and elsewhere as far as attitude was concerned, but the supporters were far from happy at what they saw as asset-stripping. First McInally, then Dodds, now

Gilchrist – the supporters suspected that Maley preferred a team of slaves rather than a talented but rebellious eleven men.

Yet Maley had the last laugh, when the Scottish Cup was lifted on 31 March 1923 for the tenth time, to equal Queen's Park's record. It was the year of Joe Cassidy, who scored at least one goal in every round except one, and it was fitting that it was the heroic Joe who scored the only goal of a dull final against Hibs when he latched on to a long ball from Jean McFarlane. For Maley, it was a rewarding occasion for he now felt that the offloading of Gilchrist and McInally was vindicated, as indeed had been the departure of McColl in 1920. McColl now turned out with Hibs and played against Celtic in the 1923 Scottish Cup final.

This final was of course called the 'All Green' final and the 'Irish' final, and compared frequently with the final of 1914, when the circumstances of the world had been so different. But it might just as justifiably been called the 'Brothers' final. Not only did Celtic have two McStays playing for them, now that Jimmy McStay had been brought in at right half to replace Gilchrist and to join brother Willie, but for the second time two Maleys were the managers in a Scottish Cup final. Alec Maley who had managed Clyde in 1912 was now the manager of Hibs.

For Willie Maley, the Scottish Cup was very important, and he was proud that Celtic had now caught up with Queen's Park's record. Rangers seemed to have a problem with this tournament, which they had not won for twenty years. They had gone out to Ayr United this year, and such repeated failures hurt Rangers for the Scottish Cup was still sometimes considered to be the most important competition in the land.

The problem was that it lulled Maley into a false sense of security in 1923. It allowed him to believe that he had a good team once again, fit to rank alongside 1908 or 1914. This was manifestly not true, but this did not stop him making patronising statements that it was good for the game to see Rangers winning the League or that it was good to see eastern teams (by which he meant Raith Rovers, presumably) doing well, as if the time was fast approaching when

Celtic were to win everything in sight once again. He did not seem to appreciate that Gallacher, brilliant though he was, was only one man and that Patsy, now in his thirties, would not be around for ever. Investment in new talent seemed to be called for, but Maley failed to heed the call.

1923/24 was a disaster of a season, and a self-inflicted disaster. The air of depression that settled over Parkhead that season arrived in September and never really lifted until a crumb of comfort was gained by the winning of the Charity Cup at the end of the season. Maley, himself trying to come to terms with the death of his mother in June of that year at the age of seventy-nine, would claim that the team was 'rebuilding'. This was true to a certain extent for talented youngsters like Peter Wilson, Alex Thomson and Jimmy McGrory were being brought into the team, but the 'rebuilding' was required because of the gradual self-demolition of the past few seasons.

Summer 1923, with the recapture of the Scottish Cup, should have been one of euphoria. Indeed it was among the fans, many of whom did not recall very clearly after nine years the sheer joy that a Scottish Cup success could bring, but the board, in another ill-advised piece of economy, decided to cut wages. There was nothing unusual in all this, for in the 1920s, the country was still recovering from the disastrous war that it had won and pay cuts, lay-offs and redundancies were common. Disaffection and disorder were never too far from the surface, and there was a frightening example of this early in the season. Celtic were playing at Clydebank, and early in the first half the unemployed rushed the exit gate in an attempt to gain entrance. They did so to an extent, necessitating a baton charge by the police, something that Maley, however much he loved law and order, felt was superfluous.

Times were hard indeed, but it did seem odd that parsimony and the pruning of wages were deemed essential in an organization like Celtic which could and did attract large crowds and which had the undivided affection of at least half the nation. Surprisingly the players accepted this for a time, but in September 1923, Willie Cringan as captain and spokesman made a dignified appeal for a bonus system of £2 per win and £1 per draw. This was perfectly valid, but in his statement, Cringan possibly made an unwise reference to the fact that players at Ibrox were rewarded more handsomely than at Parkhead. Maley took offence at this (even though it was true) and in a knee-jerk reaction dropped Cringan from the team, sacked him of the captaincy and transferred him to join Tommy McInally at Third Lanark.

It is a proven fact that whenever there is a dispute at a football club, the team begin to play badly, for there is lacking the vital something that must exist between player and management. It is called trust, or perhaps team spirit and it was one thing that did characterise the great teams that Maley had in the past. Once it has gone, form usually goes as well. One need only look, in recent times, at the 1998/99 season when an absurd dispute about bonuses had such dire consequences for the team. It is one of the main tasks of management to make sure that such disputes do not get out of hand and do not become public.

The team, following Cringan's reluctant departure, now began to play very badly, losing to Dundee, Morton, Clydebank, Falkirk, Raith Rovers, Airdrie and St Mirren as well as a series of draws, particularly goalless draws. It was as if the team were deliberately making a point to Maley and the directors, and cynics were not slow to claim that players were perhaps finding other ways (i.e. bookmakers) of being paid.

A lot of match fixing did indeed take place in the 1920s, but it must be stressed that no evidence was ever found to prove this. More likely is the general feeling of lethargy that pervaded the ground as attendances dropped. Maley reacted as he often did by becoming more depressed, claiming frequently that men like Sunny Jim would not have acted like that – a reference to his great servant captain Jim Young who had been tragically killed in a motor cycle accident a year previously in September 1922.

As often happens when the team is doing badly, the behaviour of the fans similarly deteriorated. One infamous occasion was in Princes Street, Edinburgh in October 1923, when panicky police called in all the reserves to arrest 38 Celtic fans after a 0–0 draw at Hearts. The offences were for nothing more than the disgusting but harmless one of urinating over trees in the Gardens, but the Edinburgh press made much of it the 'intolerable' conduct of the 'Irishmen'.

The team exited lamentably from the Scottish Cup at the first time of asking at Kilmarnock in 1924, and thus were compelled to watch from the sidelines as Rangers won the League again, and Airdrie beat Hibs in the Scottish Cup final. The question remained unanswered as to why a team with as much talent did not do better. Gallacher, who was sometimes moody and at times apparently uninterested, now settled in the licensed trade. McAtee was clearly past his best and Cassidy failed to reproduce his goal-scoring form of the previous year. In defence, Alec McNair who had been around Parkhead for a staggering twenty years was now fallible, if for no other reason than that football is a young man's game, and as Celtic would discover in the 1950s, youngsters, however talented, need time to find their place and to blend with older members of the team. For example, Peter Wilson, the country boy from Beith, was a talented player, but he had the misfortune to join the team towards the end of the season when a particularly bad spell was being endured.

Yet, a straw in the wind appeared at the very end of the season when Maley recalled from Clydebank the youngster called McGrory to blood him in the Charity Cup. The Garngad youngster scored in the semi-final against Queen's Park at centre forward when Cassidy was injured, and then played on the left wing in the final when Cassidy returned. Celtic won the Charity Cup by beating Rangers 2–1, something which did give the Celtic crowd a little to be happy about.

The trouble with McGrory's arrival was that it persuaded Maley that Cassidy was now dispensable. In truth, Joe had had a poor season in 1923/24, but the fans were still shocked to find on the eve of season 1924/25, that the great Joe Cassidy was on his way to Bolton Wanderers. Joe had been no troublemaker, and was retained in great affection by the fans for his two goals against Rangers on New Year's Day 1921 and his goal which won the Scottish Cup final in 1923. He was also a war hero, the owner of the military medal won in the last few days of the war and very much the hero of Parkhead as well. He was not yet twenty-eight when he left Parkhead and he played professional football for another eight years all over the British Isles, although he remained well known as Joe Cassidy of Celtic.

The 1924/25 season was another desperately awful League season, but was redeemed by two brilliant games in the Scottish Cup. Celtic were a mixture of prodigious talent in men like Patsy Gallacher, but also had a few honest triers, as exemplified by left-winger Adam McLean. He was good, but not really anything like as good as Alan Morton of Rangers or Alec Troup of Everton. Connolly was similar, McFarlane at left half was another journeyman and McGrory, although sharp in the centre, clearly needed experience. Questions were now openly beginning to be asked of Patsy Gallacher, who appeared to have been trading on his past reputation for long enough. But Patsy was about to have one final hurrah, and a glorious one it was to be.

Interest settled on the Scottish Cup, once the League was gone. A prolonged struggle took place to get the better of St Mirren, then Celtic found themselves against Rangers in the semi-final. Rangers had already beaten Celtic three times that season, embarrassingly outclassing them on all three occasions. But it was the Scottish Cup, and Rangers were now clearly bothered about their hoodoo in this competition, it being twenty-two years since they had last registered a win. Yet the smart money was certainly on Rangers.

In the dressing room before the game, Maley apparently made the usual statements about the need to play well, behave well and do Celtic credit. He then disappeared to talk to some Rangers directors. It was as if he was losing interest in the game, and certainly he would have had to be very thick-skinned not to become despondent after all the disasters of the past few seasons. He was now more interested, apparently, in his restaurant and other business interests.

But there was Patsy Gallacher. Patsy waited until Maley had gone, made sure the door was closed and then unveiled his plan. It was to play on Rangers' nerves, to talk to direct opponents about jinxes and hoodoos, to unsettle them and to defend for the first fifteen minutes to disorientate them. Whatever else might be said about Maley's tactics, concentration on defence was never normally in his armoury, and Rangers would be lulled into a sense of false security.

Gallacher's tactics worked and to Maley's astonishment, Celtic won a famous victory by 5-0 to earn a Cup Final against Dundee. Maley now instantly became more animated and concentrated himself on the coming struggle. He knew that a win would give Celtic a record eleven victories in the Scottish Cup, and this meant a great deal to him. He appreciated too that Gallacher was the key man, as he had been in the semi-final, and the only instructions that he gave to the rest of the team were to 'Give the ball to Patsy as often as possible'.

However, it looked as though a ghost of Maley's past would be haunting him yet again. David McLean, who had fallen out with him in 1909 and scored a hat-trick for Third Lanark against Celtic in 1918 thereby depriving them of the League, turned up once more. He scored the opener for Dundee. But in the most famous of all of Maley's and Celtic's Scottish Cup victories, Patsy scored with his famous somersault goal with the ball wedged between his legs and then, with just minutes remaining, Maley's young protégé Jimmy McGrory catapulted forward to score the winner with a glorious header. Maley had taken the vulnerable McGrory under his wing when the young man's father had died the previous August. On the day of Mr McGrory senior's funeral, Maley insisted on Jimmy playing at Brockville in the afternoon. Jimmy scored that day and on his own admission never looked back. It was a masterly piece of psychology on the part of Maley, and the sight of McGrory scoring the winning goal in the record-breaking Cup Final must have filled him with particular joy. No wonder he insisted that young McGrory should hold the cup on the team charabanc that night as it wound its way back through the adoring crowds to The Bank restaurant. It was reminiscent of that first Scottish Cup final triumph of 1892 when he, Maley, had been a young player. He hoped that young McGrory would hit the heights, and was not to be disappointed.

There would be no summer tour of Europe, but there was a game in Belfast, against the other Celtic, the Belfast Celtic. Maley could not resist taking the Scottish Cup with him to show off, and as always happened in Ireland, the team were mobbed by thousands of fans at the quay.

Perhaps carried away by the euphoria of summer 1925, perhaps feeling that his paternal skills were now to the fore, or perhaps, more mundanely, influenced by the realisation that the injury-prone Patsy Gallacher could not last for ever, Maley at last bowed to public pressure and recalled Tommy McInally from Cathkin. The negotiations were like pushing against an open door. Tommy was desperate to get back to the club that he loved and Third Lanark, who had seen the downside of Tommy (including watching him being sent off in a game against Celtic) were by no means unhappy to agree a nominal fee.

Instead of tacitly admitting that Tommy should never have been allowed to leave in the first place, or stating that a more flexible approach was required than his rigid, dictatorial stance, Maley was submerged under a welter of his own propaganda. His comment 'I always had a soft spot for the boy and all his foibles' was only half-true, for he hated the 'foibles', although he did occasionally find McInally's sense of humour quite funny. Maley's much-uttered and much-quoted statement that 'We knew he was pining for home, and that when the time was right, he would not say no' was true, but begged the question 'Why was he allowed to go in the first place?'

Perhaps Maley, always a deeply religious man, had been reading his Bible about the prodigal son, and saw himself as the father who prepared the fatted calf for the return of the wayward boy, who had now learned a lesson and would be led, under Maley's guidance into the paths of righteousness.

Certainly, the Celtic-supporting part of Scotland, already uplifted by the great Cup Final of the previous April, were now almost on fire about the news that 'Tommy was back'. There was an immediate spin off in that the first six games of the 1925/26 season yielded 21 goals, with McInally now at inside left supplying the ammunition for young McGrory. Paeans of praise and chants of 'Tommy, Tommy, Tommy McInally' were heard and Maley quite rightly shared in the praise for his imaginative volte-face.

Alec Thomson from Buckhaven was now the inside right and the forward play was a thing to behold in the early matches of that season. Peter Wilson had now fitted in well at right half, teaming up with Jean McFarlane, and hopes were being expressed that this could be one of the greatest Celtic teams ever. Maley was upbeat, ever available to the press and public, and there could be no doubt that the whole Irish community had received a shot in the arm, as it always does when its team is playing well.

Patsy Gallacher had not started the season, however, because of a knee injury and a suspension, and when he did return, it coincided with a bad run of form. He played only four games and was clearly struggling. He did take part in a victory over Rangers in the Glasgow Cup, but the defeat in the final against Clyde was the last game that Patsy played for the club.

The team soon recovered from the glitch in October, and from then on lost only two further League games for the rest of the season. The team was lucky in that they remained comparatively free from injury and the squad was a settled one in every sense of the word. McInally was a joy in his clowning and eccentricities, but also his brilliant passing, reading of the game and goal-scoring. The League was won convincingly by eight points and clinched in a goal-less draw against Kilmarnock on 3 April. This was after an absence of four years and the joy was great.

A disappointment, however, was registered in the Scottish Cup final. Celtic had reached the final with a great deal of comfort, and Maley had no reason to believe that the Scottish Cup would not also be added to the haul. The opponents were St Mirren, whom Celtic had thrashed 6-1 in the League little more than a month earlier. Before a huge crowd of 98,000 Celtic, in all white jerseys, played their worst football for some time and lost 2-0. A goal was lost early, and the team never got back into the game.

The absence of Adam McLean through injury was hardly an excuse, and Maley fumed. Here he had a talented side who might have emulated the feats of 1907, 1908 and 1914 by winning both Scottish trophies, but had thrown it all away through complacency. There was, however, a little comfort to be gained when the Charity Cup was recaptured. The final against Queen's Park was played on 15 May, a matter of days after the collapse of the General Strike. The Celtic crowd were none too happy about how several Queen's Park players, middle-class amateurs had done things like drive buses and trains to cover for strikers, and prolonged barracking took place, to the discomfiture of Maley, no doubt.

Even more remarkable had been the previous week when Celtic beat Third Lanark 2-0 at Parkhead while the strike was still on. Some supporters stayed away as they saw the game as 'strike breaking', others could not reach the ground because of lack of transport, but Maley was determined the game should go on. Few reports exist of this game, for the newspapers were on strike, but we do know that in front of an empty Parkhead, McInally scored against his old teammates and Willie McStay scored a penalty.

The General Strike did, however, have a long-term effect on football. The coal strike would continue for several months after that, and even after the miners were starved back into the pits, old scores were paid back by vindictive mine owners and quite a few men who had taken part in the strike were not given their jobs back. This cult of victimization was carried over into other industries as well, and working-class life in Scotland in the late 1920s and 1930s was as poor and as deprived as it had been at any time since the Industrial Revolution.

Spiralling unemployment and permanently inadequate wages meant that there was little money for football, still the only real mass interest of the working man. To his credit, Maley was aware of this and did try to help with 'unemployed' gates and other things at Parkhead. At away games, aware that many of his supporters had walked because of lack of money (there are well-documented instances of supporters going as far as Dundee), Maley would arrive early, collect as many complimentary tickets from the opposition as he could, buy some more himself and distribute them to the men who had gathered outside in the hope of seeing the last ten minutes of the game once the exit gates had been unlocked.

1926/27 was characterised by the phenomenal goalscoring of Jimmy McGrory with head and foot. Three times he scored 5 goals, and 4 on another 4 occasions. Yet defensive frailties and a few bad days meant that Rangers recaptured the League, something that Celtic could not really complain about since Rangers did beat Celtic twice in that competition.

On Christmas Day 1926, just as Maley was preparing to go to Parkhead to watch Celtic beat Kilmarnock 4-0, he received a phone call from his son Charlie with the sad news that Maley's wife had died in the night in the Royal Samaritan Hospital of a ruptured ovarian abscess which had led to peritonitis. Maley was upset, even though he and his wife had not lived together for many years. He was now living in Hyndland Avenue while she stayed in the house in St James Street South. Relations between the two had been civil but cool, and given Maley's religion, there had been no possibility of a divorce. Yet he remained fond of her and attended the funeral full of regrets. He had loved her once, and she him, but such things happen, he thought to himself. She was only fifty-one and had worked as a maternity nurse.

The good news of that season was that Celtic beat Rangers 1-0 in the Glasgow Cup final of October 1926, and that the Scottish Cup was won again, this time against Second Division East Fife in the final. Patsy Gallacher had now left the club when Falkirk offered £1,500 for him in October. Patsy might have returned to haunt Celtic in the semi-final at Ibrox, but, in spite of a tremendous reception by the Celtic fans, Patsy could not rally the Bairns sufficiently.

Earlier in the competition, Celtic had played at Brechin. A bad mistake by goalkeeper Peter Shevlin in the first minute to allow Brechin's Wattie Gentles to score saw Maley shake his head in the stand. Shevlin would have to be replaced. The next week, Maley took the opportunity to introduce a young lad from Fife called John Thomson. He also made mistakes to start with, but Maley was sufficiently impressed with him to allow him the spot for the rest of the season, including the Scottish Cup final.

Sadly, in a meaningless League fixture at Falkirk (after the semi-final victory) young McGrory, already called the 'goal-scoring machine' fell awkwardly and broke his ribs, meaning that there would be no third Scottish Cup final on the trot for Maley's favourite player. He was hardly missed, for McInally went to the centre and John McMenemy, son of 'Napoleon' was drafted in.

Before the game, a delegation of players approached Maley with a polite request for an extra bonus. Captain Jimmy McStay was the man who delivered the request. Mindful of what had happened to Willie Cringan on a previous occasion, McStay was not unnaturally terrified as he entered the august presence. Maley looked him up and down and said 'What? You want more money for beating a team of miners from Fife? Get out and bring me back that cup!' This was taken as a rejection and McStay returned defeated and dejected, but in fact there was a little extra in the pay packet when the Cup was won for the twelfth time.

In the dressing room, young John McMenemy, a fine player (although nothing like as good as his father) was finding lacing his boots a problem as his hands were shaking so much. It was only his fourth game for the club and he had only been told half an hour previously that he would definitely be in the team. He knew that his father would be watching in the Hampden stand and he was terrified in case his let down the family name.

Maley saw this and came up to him. Putting his arm on his shoulder and speaking so as not to be overheard by the other players in a gentle but firm voice, Maley said 'John, what are you shaking for? It's those miners from Fife who ought to be shaking. It's an honour and a privilege to wear these green and white jerseys. Your father did it often enough. It's your turn now.' Then he repeated what he had said earlier in the week to McStay, 'Get out and bring me back that cup!'

They did just that. Although the Second Division East Fife (from Methil, an area absolutely devastated by the General Strike) fought well and indeed scored the first goal, they were soon overpowered by the mighty Celtic tidal wave. The game was the first in Scotland to be broadcast on the radio, and many ice cream and sweet shops and cafes and restaurants in Fife hit upon the enterprising idea of buying a radio (a huge luxury in 1927) for their customers to listen to while being served tea. The reception was appalling, but the Fifers were able to make out that their gallant men had lost 3-1.

The man of the moment was the irrepressible Tommy McInally. He clowned continually with his Charlie Chaplin impersonations, his ballooning of balls into the crowd, his shaking the hand of the referee and his calling for three cheers for each of his vanquished opponents. What Maley thought of this nonsense is not clear, but it would be hard to be angry with Tommy in these circumstances, for Celtic had now won the Scottish Cup twelve times – twice more than Queen's Park – and Rangers had now gone twenty-four years without winning the trophy.

Rangers would put that right the following season in 1928. In the first Old Firm Scottish Cup final since 1904, Meiklejohn scored the penalty which started the rout of Celtic. It had been the end of a bad two weeks for Celtic. Celtic had matched Rangers throughout the season. Both teams had won their home League match 1-0 against the other, and Celtic had won the Glasgow Cup final in October against Rangers. But then unaccountably, Celtic fell apart on 7 April, losing 3-1 to Motherwell and suffering the loss of William 'Peter' McGonagle with a nasty injury. Two days later on the Holiday Monday they fell to Airdrie by a similar score and now supporters saw this dismal collapse against Rangers in the Scottish Cup final.

The press was understandably full of praise for Rangers' great achievement, but this tended to hide the undeniable trouble behind the scenes at Parkhead. There would be repercussions, for Maley was furious with what he saw as deliberate indiscipline, and there was even the hint of a dressing room rebellion as well.

It had, in the main, been another successful season up to that point. The team had played well and McGrory was still showing the world how to score goals. On 14 January 1928, he had scored eight in a game against Dunfermline Athletic, and seldom did a Saturday pass without him scoring at least one goal. McInally was also in fine form, but it was on McInally that the focus centred – and all for the wrong reasons.

In the first place, he was decidedly overweight, and a far cry from the slim youngster who had beaten the great sprinter W.B. Applegarth in a 100-yards race in 1920. He was now called 'The Glaxo Baby' – an unkind reference to an advertisement for Glaxo baby foods where the baby was a fat rosy-cheeked youngster in stark contrast to the malnutrition of the time. He could still play, and play brilliantly, but the attitude was not right and there were rumours (substantiated ones) that he had a drink problem.

He remained the darling of the fans, but his reputation was a tarnished one. On 15 October at Ibrox, he was sent off for arguing with the referee. This was the direct cause for the 1-0 defeat. Worse came the following week, when Celtic went up to Pittodrie without the suspended McInally and lost in a clear indication of how much Celtic and Maley needed him. On 3 December at Parkhead, to the casual observer, McInally looked the worse for drink, made no effort, (although he did happen to be in the right spot to score Celtic's only goal of the game) and was roundly booed by his own fans who expected better and were now seriously disillusioned. The team lost this game to Motherwell, and Maley, who if substitutes had been allowed in those days would surely have taken him off, suspended him for three weeks.

The team had drawn twice in his absence and Maley decided that he would go the extra mile for the prodigal once again. He went to McInally's home, listened to all the stories about depression, alcohol, inability to cope with the pressures of the team but eventually, almost like a priest, absolved him from past sins and prevailed upon him to turn out for Celtic in the 2 January game against Rangers. Maley's judgement and diplomacy was spot on and 69,000 fans saw a

1-0 win for Celtic. McGrory scored the only goal of the game, but McInally was outstanding.

For a while all went well after this, and Tommy was sober in his lifestyle, disciplined in training and outstanding on the field of play. A slight mystery surrounds what happened in Keith after Celtic beat the local side 6-1 in a Scottish Cup tie and McInally did not arrive back in Glasgow until some three days after the rest of the team. Possibly Maley decided to turn a blind eye to this indiscretion, but then before a game at Motherwell in the Scottish Cup, Tommy's team-mates played a practical joke on him, pretending to be a newspaper reporter on the phone to speak to him. Tommy fell for it, but could not thole the laughter and ridicule of his mates and walked out of the hotel, for ever, apparently.

It was then that Maley made his last big mistake with Tommy. Once more he pleaded with him and once more Tommy returned – but this time his team-mates were not glad to see him back. The team had played well in his absence, winning six games to bring them to the brink of a League and Cup double, and Frank Doyle had been a more than adequate substitute. Maley misjudged the mood of the players, brought back Tommy (as usual, full of regrets and sorry for what he had done) and the team then lost three crucial games – two in the League, and the Scottish Cup final – in eight days.

Perhaps after all, Maley was right. He did have a soft spot for the boy – in this case, far too soft a spot. On this occasion, McInally had gone too far and Maley had been culpable in his indulgence of the Barrhead boy. Maley now came to the conclusion that Tommy would have to go. Tommy was transferred in the close season to Sunderland. This was understandable. What followed was less so.

However, the events of summer 1928 must be seen in the context of what was happening elsewhere. Celtic badly needed a new stand on the London Road side of the ground to replace what had been known as the Grant Stand. Such an enterprise needed money. In times of such economic stringency as the late 1920s, Maley and the Celtic board were against the idea of borrowing. Not enough money, it was felt, was being raised at the gate (not everybody would have agreed with that when they saw that the Scottish Cup Final attracted 118,000 and any Old Firm game could reasonably be expected to attract 50,000 or more) and therefore players would have to be sold.

McInally's transfer had brought in a little income (although that was not the main reason for his departure) but more was required for the stand, which was scheduled to be built in 1929. The obvious person to sell was young McGrory, a priceless talent. The story now takes a bizarre twist. Maley (the father figure) and McGrory (the talented youngster) were both deeply devout men and were due to set off for their summer pilgrimage to Lourdes in France.

En route in London, as if by chance (although Maley's son Charlie told them, as they left Glasgow, that he had received a telegram from him), they met Herbert Chapman, who had been the manager of Huddersfield and had been brought to the mighty and wealthy Arsenal with the express remit of winning the FA Cup for them. There Maley talked with Chapman, Chapman talked with McGrory – but Maley and McGrory pretended to each other that the whole thing did not happen. Chapman offered £8,000 for McGrory, but McGrory, who had no intention of leaving Scotland or Celtic, asked for the ridiculous sum of £2,000 for himself. This was turned down, and Maley and McGrory continued to Lourdes, talking about anything other than the proposed transfer of McGrory to Arsenal.

On the way back, Chapman was once again waiting for them at Waterloo Station. This time the offer was raised to £10,000 (enough to pay for several stands to be built) and McGrory was offered a blank cheque, so desperate was Chapman to land him. Once again, McGrory said no, and no deal was done. The matter was never raised again.

It is difficult to analyse just what exactly Maley was up to in all this. Did he really want money for a stand at the expense of his best player, his own favourite? Did money mean so much to him? Was he so determined to see the ground improved? It is well known that Maley loved it when Celtic Park was used as the venue for Scotland internationals. This had not happened for many years, and Celtic Park would certainly never be considered while it still had the Grant stand. Yet, sell McGrory? Possibly Maley did reckon that another McGrory would come along sooner or later – after all there had been McMahon, Quinn, McColl and Cassidy in the past – and Celtic Park needed to be renovated.

As it happened, Maley was able to sell another player – Adam McLean left to join Tommy McInally in Sunderland. Adam was astounded at this, for he did not want to leave Celtic and was more or less told that he was going. It is said that he had on one occasion asked for a wage rise, but it had been a dignified meeting in which Maley's inevitable 'no' had been polite. His departure was unnecessary in the eyes of the supporters, as enough money was being generated through the turnstiles for the building of the stand (it was opened in August 1929) but the cost to Celtic in playing terms of this asset stripping was dear.

Money was not available to pay for new players and inadequate substitutes were used in the event of injury. Two barren seasons followed in which the initiative was totally surrendered to Rangers without even the semblance of a struggle. Wall Street crashed in 1929, America sneezed and the whole world caught a cold. Unemployment now steepened to enormous levels, and many Scots people decided to try a better life somewhere else. It was to Canada that his Maley's son William junior decided to emigrate in September 1929.

Because of the economic situation, Celtic's gates fell – but the dismal performances on the field did not help either. There were some good players on view, notably McGrory, but there was not a good team. Maley was now over sixty, and was still sometimes giving the impression that Celtic were simply a sideshow in comparison with his Bank restaurant, which was now the epicentre of Glasgow's sporting life, frequented by journalists, bookmakers and members of the Scottish football fraternity.

Yet there were a few good things at Parkhead too. They won the Glasgow Cup in October 1929, players like Wilson, Jimmy McStay and Thomson continued to impress; McGrory, although suffering badly with injury in both seasons, continued to score goals, new players like McGonagle and Scarff developed and all of Scotland continued to be impressed with the clean-living handsome charming young goalkeeper called John Thomson. He was much loved by the girls in particular who, now that Rudolf Valentino the Hollywood star was dead, needed a hero. After a few caps for the Scottish League, all of Scotland was delighted when he made his debut for the full international team in Paris against France in May 1930. He kept a clean sheet as Scotland beat France 2-0.

Eight

1931

The year 1931 is a famous one in the history of Celtic football club. Celtic children are taught to say Thomson, Cook and McGonagle; Wilson, McStay and Geatons; R.Thomson, A.Thomson, McGrory, Scarff and Napier in the same way as the great sides of 1908 and 1967 are drummed into them, and the impression is that this was as great a team as the other two. This is not the case, but they certainly lived through as memorable and as traumatic times as any other Celtic team.

The political scene in Great Britain was bizarre and baffling, as the world economic situation led to the collapse of the Labour government in August and the surrender into a so-called national government with a 'doctor's remedy' to increase unemployment, cut benefits and enlarge the gap between rich and poor. Abroad, the USA was still in the depths of depression, and the world was beginning to view political developments in Germany with increasing interest and alarm.

For Celtic, the League season was a disappointment once again, although they came a little closer to Rangers than had previously been the case. They had beaten them at Parkhead in September 1930, and were very unlucky to go down 1-0 on New Year's Day at Ibrox. With a little more consistency, Celtic might have won the championship rather than losing it by two points. Too many games which should have been won were only draws, and injuries to Peter Wilson in February and March were a bad blow.

Yet there was much for Maley to enthuse over, and he had every reason to think that the long-term future was bright. He reversed his earlier decision of ten years ago, and entered a reserve team in the Alliance League, as it was called. The ground, with its new stand, looked better than it had done for many years, and although attendances were by no means good, they were as good as could be expected in a time of severe recession.

On the field, Peter Wilson and Alec Thomson had justified his faith in them, and Peter Scarff, an inside left who had joined the club from Linwood, was beginning to impress. On the left-wing Charlie Napier, a dapper, elegant dresser off the field and a polished performer on it, was beginning to remind Maley of Patsy Gallacher, and on the right wing was Bertie Thomson, a wild boy who needed a little handling. But, as Maley said to himself, if I could handle McInally, I will also be able to handle this guy. The trouble was, Maley couldn't handle McInally... and was a less than total success with Bertie Thomson.

McGrory, of course, was the personality goal-scorer that the fans loved, and the defence was well bolstered by Jimmy McStay, Peter McGonagle, Charlie Geatons and the Irishman Willie Cook, whom Maley had signed from Port Glasgow juniors in 1930. Behind them was the charismatic John Thomson, already a Scottish international, who was capable of the most amazing saves, and in Maley's view better than great Celtic goalkeepers of the past like Dan McArthur, Davie Adams and Charlie Shaw.

The team picked up the Glasgow Cup in October in spite of Bertie Thomson being sent off in a rough house of a final against Rangers, and challenged more strongly for the League than they had for many years. They reached the final of the Scottish Cup by virtue of a spectacular demolition of Kilmarnock in the semi-final. They had played some fine, even inspiring football on the way to the semi-final, defeating teams like Morton and Aberdeen very comfortably.

Maley was delighted to see Motherwell as the opponents in the final of the Scottish Cup, for he always got on well with their manager, John Hunter who had scored the crucial goals which won the Cup for Dundee in their solitary Scottish Cup success of 1910. He had earned the nickname 'Sailor' because of his curious gait which made him look as if he were a seaman finding it difficult to walk on land. Motherwell's team was fast developing and they had been considered unlucky for a few seasons not to have been among the honours. They had defeated St Mirren in the semi-final, with their left wing partnership of Stevenson and Ferrier looking particularly good.

A six-figure crowd of over 104,000 packed Hampden that bright day of 11 April 1931. At inside right for Motherwell was a Celtic reject in John McMenemy, the son of 'Napoleon', who clearly had a point to prove to Maley, and he had a particularly fine match. With ten minutes to go, Maley was a disillusioned man in the stand. His Celtic team were 2-0 down, to unlucky, deflected goals, but there seemed to be no breaking down the resolute Motherwell defence. Behind the Mount Florida goal, the Motherwell supporters (why couldn't they attend their home games in such numbers?) celebrated noisily with their American style razzamatazz and orchestrated chants of 'Give us an M, Give us an O...' Maley was slightly disturbed to see a few blue colours among them, there to cause mischief with their unpleasant songs about His Holiness The Pope, the Irish race in general and his good self. In Celtic's bad years, they had jeered at him as 'Faily Maley'. But if you were in public life, these things happened, Maley reckoned.

It was perhaps as well that Maley was sitting in the Main Stand, and therefore unable to see the famous Hampden clock above his head which was ticking away and causing such distress to the supporters on the far terracing. The bugles were strangely silent, the flags were drooping disconsolately, the heads were bent as everyone was plunged into melancholic introversion. A few began to argue with their neighbours out of sheer frustration and Maley saw a few of the weaker brethren head up the huge terracing for an early train home.

But suddenly, well within the last ten minutes, a glimmer of hope appeared. The Motherwell defence had been 'prodigal of fouls', according to James Handley, in *The Celtic Story*, and lucky more than once not to concede a penalty. Their spoiling tactics consisted of handling the ball (this would lead to yellow and red cards now!) to give a free kick half-way inside their own half rather than let a move develop. They felt that they could keep the ball away from McGrory better in set piece situations than in open play.

On one such occasion, Charlie Napier took a free kick. 'Cheeky Charlie', 'Happy Feet' 'Clap, Clap Hands Here Come Charlie' as he was called, had a fine football brain. He shaped up as if to drive it, but then lofted it gently over the defensive wall to find McGrory, who made no mistake. Maley was impressed by the attitude of McGrory who shrugged off the congratulations as he ran up the field, pointing obviously to the clock to indicate that the sands of time were sinking fast.

Maley felt in his heart of hearts that this would only be a consolation goal, for Motherwell had regrouped and looked capable of holding out. He looked across at Sailor Hunter. Maley would be glad in a way for his friend, for Sailor did not have a great deal of money to work with at Fir Park and would deserve the success. But Sailor did not look back at Maley. He was intense, watching the play, engrossed in the action apart from the constant looking at his watch which he produced repeatedly from his breast pocket as the minutes ticked away.

Maley himself has to quote the *Glasgow Herald* to describe what happened next. 'My own recollection, blurred by the tremendous excitement of the moment, is too vague to be depended upon' he says, and not for the first time, do we curse the makers of video recorders for not having invented these machines fifty years earlier so that we could dwell on Celtic (and Motherwell)'s most dramatic moment.

What seems to have happened is that well within the last minute Bertie Thomson had the ball on the right wing in front of the Main Stand. (Celtic were attacking the King's Park goal.) The suggestion that he was deliberately holding on to the ball so that he could keep it as a souvenir of a depressing day is ludicrous and disproved by what happened. He avoided the tackle of left-back Hunter and sent over a high-hanging ball, too high for the bullet head of McGrory. Centre half Alan Craig rose to head clear, as he had been doing comfortably all afternoon. But whether flustered by the attentions of McGrory or deceived by the wind, Craig misjudged the flight, the ball hit the side of his head and entered the net for the most famous own goal of all time.

The ground exploded, the Celtic players hugged each other, Alan Craig thumped the ground again and again, and referee Peter Craigmyle, enjoying the theatre of it all, paused so that everyone could look at him and then dramatically pointed upfield, then blew the whistle for full-time. Maley, now a portly gentleman only a few weeks short of his sixty-third birthday, jumped up and down in the stand. Then he remembered himself and his oft-repeated dictum that 'It is our proud boast that we can accept the fruits of victory in the same spirit as the bitterness of defeat', and he turned to commiserate with his friend Sailor Hunter. Sailor was slumped in his seat, staring into space, unable to comprehend it all, a broken man.

The Celtic party treated that Saturday night as if they had already won the Cup. In truth, the advantage lay very much with them, given their Scottish Cup tradition. They had already won the trophy twelve times, and their supporters and players were upbeat and optimistic. In fact, Maley's big job in the days between the final and the Wednesday evening replay was to calm everyone down. The team were going on a tour of the USA and Canada in the summer, and it would be nice to take the Scottish Cup with them. The many Celtic fans 'beyond the wave' would have been delighted to hear of the reprieve, but the job still needed to be done.

The crowd was a little smaller than Saturday, but amazingly for a midweek fixture in the middle of a world recession, only marginally short of six figures and this time full of black faces of miners and overalls of other workers with piece bags on their shoulders, many of whom arrived late for the 5 p.m. kick off. The teatime kick-off allowed schoolboys (and teachers) to attend the game as well.

The final continued its bizarre tradition of crazy goals, but this time it was Motherwell's goalkeeper Alan McClory who had the horrors as Celtic won comfortably 4-2. At one point, Celtic were only 3-2 up with Motherwell battling hard, but McGrory scored the fourth goal when he was on hand for a simple tap in after another McClory mistake.

Later that evening, the phlegmatic Maley, having spoken nicely and graciously to the devastated Sailor Hunter, took the team to his own restaurant 'The Bank' in the centre of Glasgow. It had been a major problem for the blue (!) team bus to get through the Celtic stronghold of the Gorbals that night and had it not been for the eventual arrival of a police escort, accidents might have happened as fans thronged the bus. The exultant crowds stood outside, cheering and chanting, causing another major obstruction until the police managed to bring some semblance of order; the Scottish Cup, bedecked in green, stood in the centre of the table, the directors smiled and the players laughed and joked. Maley smiled tolerantly as some of the wilder ones drank too much – it was perhaps to be understood and forgiven.

John Thomson had brought a charming young lady along with him, introducing her to 'Mr Maley'; Peter Wilson was telling some off-colour jokes, Maley suspected; Bertie Thomson, who had taken over the 'storm petrel' role since Tommy McInally had left, was leading astray his namesake, the kindly Alec; Jimmy McStay was reminiscing to anyone who cared to listen saying '*I captained a team of triers*'; McGrory was talking charmingly to everyone... Maley smiled. The prospect of the American tour (the first ever undertaken, although he himself had been keen on the idea even before the war and in the summer of 1910, he had even sailed across the Atlantic to reconnoitre the possibilities) beckoned, the more immediate prospect of reading tomorrow's newspapers was an even more pleasant one, the food was good, the Cup (Celtic's Cup, he often thought of it as being) was wearing green and white ribbons once again – and it was he, Willie Maley, who had done it all.

He did not say much other than to publicly congratulate his players: 'You boys rose to the occasion and read to the world another lesson that when Celtic want to do it, they will do it.' The tear sprang to his eye, aided perhaps by the champagne, as he recalled it all. That invitation to join Brother Tom at the foundation of this football club all these years ago, the sight of those urchins, barefoot and ragged, in 1892 as the charabanc returned to Celtic Park the first time the Scottish Cup had been won ... the boost and the solace that Celtic had provided for the Irish in Scotland and the increasing number of non-Catholics attracted by their play ... and he, Willie Maley had done it all. Now well into his sixties, would he retire soon? No! It was 'The Celtic', as he called them, that kept him going! A few years later he would write:

> Since I took the Celtic job (as match secretary) in September 1888 at the invitation of Brother Walfrid and John Glass, this club has been my very life and I feel that without it my existence would be empty indeed.

The next home game saw Maley indulge in another bit of theatre. The cup was paraded round the park before the game with Airdrie. With a pipe-band escort Maley himself walked with the Scottish Cup, and then suddenly stopped and invited someone from the crowd to join him and hold the Cup. After a hundred yards or so, he shook hands with the bewildered fan and asked someone else to join him. At half-time, he did the same thing, this time walking in the opposite direction.

In fact, Celtic still had a chance of winning the Scottish League at this point, but Peter Wilson's injury flared up again and Celtic drew at Dens Park, Dundee and then against Queen's Park. Had Wilson been playing, these games might have been won, and Celtic might just have pipped Rangers on goal average. As it was, the supporters had to settle for the Scottish Cup.

The tour of America was an extension of Maley's 'missionary' concept of Celtic. From the early days, they were willing to play in England, Ireland and Europe and now this was a logical step. Teams from Scotland had visited the new world before, but this was something that would change America's outlook on life, Maley believed somewhat unrealistically.

The arrival of Celtic would mean a great deal to all the Scottish and Irish people now resident in the United States. Often the word 'exile' is used loosely to describe Scottish people now resident abroad, but some of these people really were 'exiles'. There were, for example, survivors of the 1916 Easter Rising in Dublin who would never be able to come back to Ireland or any other part of the United Kingdom. There were those who were proscribed from Glasgow society because of their part in the 'Red Clydeside' disturbances of the latter years of the war and immediately afterwards. To them, the visit of Celtic meant absolutely everything.

But most of the Scottish and Irish people in the New World (Scots tended to go to Canada and the Irish to the USA) had gone to America to start a new life, giving up the unequal struggle against economic hardship. Some were descendants of those who had suffered the Potato Famine of 1845 and 1846, others were victims of the Highland Clearances, yet more were of a more recent vintage, having decided that the First World War was a watershed in their lives, and that Great Britain was anything but the 'land fit for heroes to live in' as Lloyd George had ludicrously promised.

America was certainly the land of opportunity. It was often said that if you survived the crossing and the first three days after that, then peace and prosperity beckoned. This was sadly not always so, and the United States in particular were suffering from the same economic depression as Europe. Indeed, it had started there with the Wall Street Crash. But America was a huge country, the so-called the land of the free, the home of film stars and Hollywood, the land of opportunity and freedom of religion. It was romantic, exciting and attractive.

However, football, in the British sense of the word, had as yet failed to take off. Maley firmly believed that it was Celtic's job to take the game to that distant country. Now in 1931, the dream was becoming a reality, and it was all the better because they were taking with them the Scottish Cup!

On 13 May 1931, Celtic set sail from Yorkhill Quay, Glasgow to New York on the SS *Caledonia* with seventeen players, four directors and Maley. Maley in *The Story Of The Celtic* says:

> On the journey across the Atlantic, the directors had a happy thought. Recalling that my brother Tom was so very closely identified with the inception of the club and played such a prominent part in its early struggles, they decided to invite him to join the party, and he crossed in the next steamer which sailed a week later.

That is Maley's version of events. What seems to have happened is that Maley, a very poor sailor, was seasick and confined to his cabin for most of the voyage. When he did come out of his cabin, he was in a foul temper and the players were advised by the directors not to go near him. He vowed that he would go home to Scotland on the next ship as soon as they reached New York, unless his brother Tom could be summoned to help him. The directors, whether wishing to keep him happy or because they felt that Tom would be handy if Willie was indeed to be indisposed in America, complied with the request and wired Tom asking him to join them. Apparently, Maley, on hearing this, immediately cheered up and bore the high seas and the fog of the remaining days of the voyage with fortitude, even appearing sometimes for meals!

When they arrived on 22 May, they were almost immediately in action the following day, defeating the Pennsylvania All Stars 6-1. Wherever they went the reception was overwhelming and Maley himself tells that 'not once, but many times' he saw tears roll down the cheeks of grown men at the sight of their favourite football team and the Scottish Cup. The Scottish Cup, in fact, travelled about in a shopping bag and occasionally in a brown paper bag, and on one occasion would have been lost at a railway station had it not been for the vigilance of a fan!

Thirteen games had been organised between 23 May and 29 June and given all the travelling, not much time was allowed for sightseeing or holidaying as far as the players were concerned. The team actually lost three games, but Maley is quick to make excuses in terms of the hard pitches, poor refereeing, intense heat, primitive conditions and 'receptioning', by which he means presumably over-lavish hospitality to his players the night before!

The worst game seems to have been against a team called Pawtucket Rangers where 'the accommodation would have disgraced a juvenile club'. He is unhappy as he notes that:

> The win-at-all-cost element was met with very often, and I noticed particularly that the defenders were as a rule the most unscrupulous.

The most significant game in the long term was the game at Fall River where the local team won 1-0. It was a better game than most as a spectacle, but the most striking thing was the display of the Canadian goalkeeper James (sic) Kennaway who preferred to be called 'Joe'. He was outstanding, defying the Celtic forwards time and time again. This display would have long-term consequences, and Maley made a remark which became rich in dramatic irony when he said:

> Our people at home fancy John Thomson but they have his equal at Fall River where their goalkeeper saved them time after time by brilliant work.

A different experience was had at a place called Hakaoh, just outside New York. This was the team which represented the New York Jewish community in a way which was eerily reminiscent of how Celtic once represented (and perhaps still did) the Glasgow Catholic community. Maley says 'This team was made up of Jews', but then adds 'not that it would have mattered, of course!' In this battle of ethnic minorities, no quarter was sought or given and the referee seemed to side with the home team.

The game ended 1–1, but McGrory had his jaw broken and had to be taken to hospital while Napier and Scarff were both sent off along with two opposition players in a free-for-all fight. Yet the Hakaoh team after the game made it clear how honoured they were to play against the mighty and famous Celtic team!

Maley had every cause to be pleased with life as he sailed home at the end of June. The crossing was far more tranquil and serene, and he was back to his old self, talking politely and courteously to other passengers, especially elderly and wealthy ladies, and organizing his men to take their part in the nightly entertaining.

Such things, he felt, could not but bond the team together. He was always very keen that his men should 'get on' with each other. He remembered what trouble had been caused by a 'loose cannon' like Tommy McInally, and was determined that it should not happen again. The season which lay ahead was going to be a difficult one. Rangers had now won the League for the past five years and he was aware that another one would equal the record set by his own men twenty years previously. This must not be allowed to happen, he felt, for highly though he regarded Struth, his opposite number, and men like Meiklejohn, McPhail and Morton, they could not in all honesty be compared with his own great side.

He felt that the team that he had at the moment was on the verge of really great things. With McGrory as centre forward anything was possible, and the half-back line of Wilson, McStay and Geatons was approaching the reliability and sheer class of Young, Loney and Hay – and in goal, there was without doubt the greatest 'keeper in the world in young John Thomson.

Maley would watch the athletic and charming John as he played quoits and deck tennis. He would chat with the young women, who were obviously bowled over by his good looks and charm, but there was nothing lecherous or leering about the boy from the mining village of Cardenden in Fife. He would not trust Bertie Thomson or Charlie Napier with the ladies, but John was quite simply every mother's dream for a son. And the bonus was that he was the best goalkeeper in the world – what a future lay ahead for the boy!

When they arrived back at the Broomielaw in early July, a great crowd was awaiting them. Maley, in truth, was more than a little glad to get home for he was no great traveller in spite of all his foreign trips. He would have his few days in the Highlands at Tomintoul, the players could have a couple of weeks with their families and then it was back for training and the full assault on the League championship which must be wrested back this year.

In truth, he saw a spring in the step of all his players, as befitted young men who had won the Scottish Cup and were the envy of a whole nation for their trip to America, something that few people achieved, although many dreamed of. There were still the ravages of unemployment to be seen in Glasgow with all its poverty, slums and general deprivation which shocked Maley. Maley did not entirely take the view that the poor were poor through their own fault, a view he heard disturbingly often, even at Sunday Mass.

The weather was good, however, as the football season reopened. Six games were played in the month of August, and Celtic won five and drew the other – at Pittodrie against Aberdeen when McGrory was out injured. But McGrory returned for the Wednesday evening game against Cowdenbeath and scored four as Celtic ran out 7–0 winners. But Rangers had also started the season well, apart from a defeat by Motherwell. Maybe, Maley thought, it would be Motherwell who would be the team to watch this season. Celtic were due to go there on Halloween, but of more immediate interest was the visit to Ibrox Park on Saturday 5 September.

Although vexed at the dropping of another point to Third Lanark on the previous Wednesday, Maley was confident about the side for the trip to Ibrox. Napier and Cook had been out with injuries and had been replaced by Solis and Morrison at Cathkin but for Ibrox, the squad were all pronounced fit. Both teams, in fact, would be at full strength, although the *Glasgow Herald*, in one of its most infamous mistakes, did state with supreme dramatic irony: 'Many people will learn with regret that English, the Ibrox centre forward is unfit to play.'

Considering that it was now September, it was surprisingly hot and sultry when the bus dropped the team off outside the magnificent entrance of Ibrox. As the players walked onto the park smiling good naturedly at the boos from the Rangers section of the early arrivers, Maley went upstairs for a cup of tea with Bill Struth. They talked about this and that, Struth being interested to hear about America, and discussed and dissected all the other teams in the League (as all managers do when they meet), indulged in a little bitchy gossiping about Motherwell, Dundee and others, slapped each other on the back, laughed hysterically at each other's jokes and even hypocritically wished each other all the best for today's game before disappearing into the dressing room for a last-minute talk.

'Get to the ball smartish, Peter', 'Don't give Morton any leeway, Willie' 'On the ground to the wingers, in the air to Jimmy', 'Watch that sun when you're at that end, John', 'Best of luck' were the sort of things Maley said to his players. He never believed in lengthy team talks, still less did he believe in analysing the strengths and weaknesses of the opposition — that sort of thing was self-defeating, he felt. He was far more interested in what his own men could do — highly paid professionals earning £9 per week did not need detailed instructions. They were fit and raring to go.

He climbed up the stairs to the directors' box, and there he sat down, ignoring the cries of the ignorant rabble in the crowd and even the uncomfortable religious jibes from one or two in the stand, who ought to have known better. If there was any value in Presbyterianism, it must surely include tolerance, but Maley was also uncomfortably aware that Parkhead too did not lack its moronic element.

The first half was dull. Sam English was indeed playing, noted Maley, in spite of the *Glasgow Herald*'s statement to the contrary, but Jimmy McStay was well in control of the centre of the field. 'Nae goals, nae fitba' said Struth to him as they went downstairs, and he had to agree. But it was a hot day, and there was some sort of excuse in that. The pace was slow and lethargic, but Maley knew that all it took was one flash of genius or one mistake by the goalkeeper or defender.

Five minutes into the second half, right-winger Fleming found Rangers centre forward Sam English, who for once had got clear of Jimmy McStay's vice-like grip. He charged in on goal with only John Thomson's red jersey between him and putting Rangers one up. Thomson came out, dived at English's feet and the ball rolled gently past the goal line. The referee, Mr Holburn awarded a goal kick to Celtic, for no foul had been committed by either man.

The Rangers fans behind that goal expressed their anger and disappointment at English, who had not been their greatest hero in the short time that he had been with them. English was limping and Celtic's goalkeeper, John Thomson lay still. English soon recovered and immediately hobbled over to look at Thomson, whose skull had felt the impact of English's knee. English was about to make a joke to McStay and Wilson about how hard Thomson's head must have been, when he saw that Thomson lay still, his face ashen white.

Celtic's trainer and doctor, Willie Kivlichan were soon on the field … and still Thomson did not move. Maley got up from his seat in the stand and walked to the touchline. With Thomson still not moving, Maley walked over to him, sensitive of a chorus of boos, either directed at him or impatient for a resumption of play, from those who believed that Thomson was faking.

As he approached Thomson, he was aware that Meiklejohn, Rangers' captain broke from the cluster of players around Thomson and held up his hands to the crowd gesturing that they should stop, for the player was seriously injured. Once Dr Kivlichan had wrapped a few bandages round Thomson's head, he was carried off, by now making some sort of convulsive jolting movement. 'Concussion' was the word spoken by everyone round about.

Maley, upset at the injury, nevertheless had to direct his attention to the game. Celtic were unlikely to win the game now, and McGonagle the left-back was making to put on the red jersey. Maley acted decisively, and told Geatons the left half to do the job, for

McGonagle would be needed for defensive roles, as a draw was now the limit of Celtic's ambitions.

He then strode back to the stand to watch the rest of the game. It continued as it had been before. It was dull, as Celtic's defenders relentlessly punted the ball up the park and Rangers, themselves handicapped by English now hobbling ineffectively on the wing, were unable to pierce the Celtic defence headed by Charlie Geatons in goal. In fact Geatons was enjoying himself, for he was under no pressure. If he made a mistake, then nobody could really blame him. He was not a goalkeeper.

Ten minutes remained when a Rangers backroom man came up to the stand and gave Maley a message from Dr Kivlichan that John was being taken to the Victoria Hospital 'as a precaution'. Maley was not fooled by this. He suspected that it would be serious, but in the meantime what could he do?

Full-time brought a fair share of boos from disgruntled fans of both teams. Maley shook hands with Struth, then went downstairs to greet his players who had made the best of a bad job. He also had to tell them the news about John. Head injuries were always a matter for concern and concussion could be a very serious. After the players had showered and dressed and were upstairs in the lounge having a cup of tea with their Rangers counterparts, Maley had to field persistent press enquiries as well as more polite concern from the likes of Meiklejohn and English himself who was also moaning about his knee.

Another Rangers backroom man said there was a call for him in Mr Struth's office. Struth himself was there, saying that it was from Kivlichan at the hospital. Struth heard Maley say things like 'Really?', 'Of course' and 'Yes', before he turned and said that he and captain Jimmy McStay had better go to the hospital.

It transpired that Thomson had a depressed fracture of the skull, and that an emergency operation was taking place. Kivlichan knew how serious this was, but all that Maley and McStay and director Tom Colgan could do was wait. A telegram was sent to John's parents in Fife to inform them of the situation. They arrived soon after 9 p.m. and were immediately ushered into Thomson's room.

Shortly before 10 p.m. that night, Maley, McStay and Colgan were summoned into a room by a nurse, there to be told that John Thomson's emergency operation had not been a success and that he had died at 9.25 p.m. News spread through Glasgow like wildfire. By midnight everyone knew, although some dismissed it all merely as gossip. It needed the later editions of the Sunday papers to confirm it. Prayers were said in churches for the young man on the Sunday. It was one of Scottish football's saddest days.

It was also one of the most unusual. Fatal injury in a football match is a very rare phenomenon. The *Glasgow Herald* tries hard to find a parallel but can only talk vaguely about a Dumbartonshire goalkeeper called Wilkinson who died also at Ibrox 'some years ago' and a Hibernian full-back called Main in 1909 who also received fatal injuries. Certainly since 1931, even in world terms, a fatality on a football field has happened extremely seldom. It was a fateful combination of English's knee, the angle at which contact was made and Thomson's hitherto undiagnosed thin skull ('as thin as an eggshell' according to one doctor) which had caused the tragedy.

Maley was ubiquitously energetic in attending to the needs of Thomson's devastated parents. On Tuesday 8 September, a religious service was held at Trinity Church in Claremont Street, Glasgow to commemorate John. Maley and Struth, the respective managers, sat together. There was nothing too remarkable about this, however much the press made of it. What was more significant, in the context of 1931, was that the service was attended by representatives of the Roman Catholic Church and the Church of Scotland. (As it happened, Thomson belonged to neither denomination. He was a member of the Church of Christ, a small evangelical sect.) David Meiklejohn, captain of Rangers, the man who had tried to calm the rabble and who was a practising Christian, read the lesson.

Maley helped to arrange the funeral which was to be held at Bowhill Cemetery, Cardenden on Wednesday 9 September. Even the tragic history of the Fife coalfield with all its pit collapses and untimely deaths through pneumoconiosis and other horrendous illnesses would have been hard put to parallel such an outpouring of grief.

Every football team in Scotland, including teams like Forfar and Queen of the South, with no obvious connection, sent a representative. Thomson was of course the goalkeeper of Scotland, as well as of Celtic. Supporters walked from Glasgow to pay their respects, and players and officials of both Celtic and Rangers attended.

The village of Cardenden itself had never seen anything like it. Miners gave up a day's pay (which they could ill afford) to attend the funeral. Some of the Glasgow supporters camped on the Craigs (as the hills nearby were then called) in the fine weather the night before and the night after the funeral. It was said that 'they walked from Glasgow, but cycled back' for bicycles tended to disappear from garden sheds after the funeral! A grotesque note was struck when the Hearts team bus arrived to drop off the players for the funeral. They then re-embarked and went on to Cowdenbeath where they were playing that night.

Maley himself, visibly distressed at times, played a leading role in the funeral, leading the cortège as John's team-mates took it in turns to carry the coffin from his house to the graveyard. He made a point of talking to and comforting John's brokenhearted mother and father. He welcomed guests as if he himself was the leading mourner. In a sense he was, for he had always been aware of his role as the father figure of all his young players. At the end, he thanked everyone for attending and for 'this glorious demonstration of your love'.

A Fatal Accident Enquiry was held in the middle of October. It came up with the verdict of accidental death, the only verdict that could conceivably have been reached. Maley was of course asked to give evidence. Interestingly enough, several players on either side, including Sam English himself, were never asked to testify, although they were far closer than Maley. By an unfortunate turn of phrase, Maley said 'I hope it was an accident', and hotheads of both sides have taken this remark totally out of context to indicate that Maley was of the opinion that it might not have been an accident.

This is complete nonsense, for the context of the remark was that Maley was in the stand, at least 100 yards away from the collision, and did not have a clear view of what happened. His actual words were:

> I was in the stand, a good distance from the actual occurrence. As to what happened, I cannot say. I saw a clash when the men came together. Both fell, but Thomson could not rise. I hope it was an accident. But I did not see enough to enable me to form an opinion.

Had he said 'I trust it was an accident', it would have sounded almost as bad – the fact was that he did not feel sufficiently confident in his view to state categorically in a Court of Enquiry that he 'knew' it was an accident. It is an interesting example of what can happen when unscrupulous people can put their own pejorative interpretation on totally innocent remarks.

Certainly no one at Parkhead ever seriously believed that it was anything other than an accident, and no one at Ibrox ever thought that Maley or anyone else would be so stupid as to think that. The unfortunate Sam English felt it all his life, although there is no truth in the suggestion that his career was ruined. Certainly, a few idiots shouted 'Murderer' and things like that, particularly at Parkhead on 28 September in the first Old Firm game after the accident. Meiklejohn appealed to the referee about the barracking directed at English, the referee appealed to Maley and the embarrassed Maley made a loudspeaker appeal. It was only partly successful.

Eventually after a few games like this (and not only games involving Celtic), English began to wonder whether Scotland was the right place for him. He neatly sidestepped the worst of the barracking by seeking a transfer to Liverpool, from where his career prospered and he earned caps for Northern Ireland. It was a fine touch from Maley to invite English to be present at the unveiling of the Thomson memorial at Parkhead a few years later.

Maley now had a major job on his hands to lift everyone at Parkhead while coping with his own grief. Maley would always say that it was part of being Celtic, which was a very remarkable and unusual institution. As a Celtic video puts it, 'Celtic, like the race that bears their name, must suffer the extremes in grief and joy'. Maley would keep a stiff upper lip and accept that life must go on.

Yet, he was not as insouciant as he appeared. He was deeply affected by it all, and his melancholy would have grave consequences for the club in other respects as well. For the moment, all he could do was to grin and make the most of it. The week after the accident saw Celtic due to play Queen's Park at Celtic Park. Maley may have toyed with the idea of asking for a postponement (which would surely have been granted by the Scottish League, who had already postponed the midweek clash against Airdrie), but he felt that it would be better to pay tribute to John and then move on.

Maley, even in these circumstances, could not resist a little touch of theatre. A lone piper was in attendance. Queen's Park walked out, then the Celtic team slowly walked out – without a goalkeeper. They then turned to the west goal at the Railway End of the ground and looked towards the empty goal as a lone piper played a lament 'The Last Post' and 'Lead Kindly Light'. Then after a short silence, the reserve goalkeeper John Falconer walked out to take his place and the game commenced, with both sides doing well in a 2-2 draw. At half-time the lone piper reappeared to play 'The Floo'ers O' The Forest'.

Maley set about erecting a monument to John at Parkhead and he also had the necessary task of finding a deputy, for John Falconer was good, but not as good as Thomson. Coen had a game or two, then someone suggested to Maley that Joe Kennaway of Fall River, whom they had met in the summer, might be good. Kennaway had talked a lot to the Celtic party after the game and said that he would like to play in Scotland. With imagination and initiative, Maley sent off a telegram. Kennaway accepted and played his first game for Celtic against Motherwell at Fir Park on 31 October.

1931, that remarkable year for Celtic and Maley, came to its sombre end as Hamilton beat a demotivated and demoralised Celtic team 3-0 on Hogmanay. One of the unanswerable questions of that year remains 'Would Maley have sold Thomson?'. The answer may well be 'Yes', if we remember his attempt to sell McGrory to Arsenal.

There were certainly rumours that Arsenal were interested. Maley did, in fact, sell the right-back Willie Cook to Everton in 1932, and there is no reason to suppose that he would have rejected a bid for Thomson, for he might have felt that goalkeepers are easily replaced. Whether Thomson would have gone is a different matter.

It was often said that a large part of Maley died with Thomson. In some ways, Thomson was exactly the kind of player that Maley wanted. Talented, skilful, charming, handsome and clean-living – Thomson was all these things, and clearly the Scottish selectors thought so, for he was the current Scotland goalkeeper. But what Maley liked was that Thomson, the boy from the Fife mining village who belonged to an obscure Protestant religious sect, had earned all that he had earned through his association with Celtic, the so-called team of the Irish Catholics! Thomson could not have done it without Celtic or without Maley … but now he had been so cruelly taken away. Maley would take some time to recover.

Nine

THE BROODING
DICTATOR 1932–35

The 1931/32 season which had started so optimistically for Celtic, spluttered impotently to a depressing conclusion. In one sense, Maley would have been happy, for Rangers did not equal the six titles in a row which had been achieved by his own great side in the Edwardian era. The 1932 championship was won by Motherwell, and deservedly so, by 5 points from Rangers. Maley was one of the first to send his congratulations to Sailor Hunter and his men. The Motherwell side which had come so close to beating Celtic in last season's epic Scottish Cup final (which now seemed so long ago) at last had some recompense.

Celtic's woes consisted of a great deal more than the John Thomson tragedy. Injuries were prevalent, in particular to McGrory who was out after the New Year's Day game against Rangers (in which he scored the only goal in a 2-1 defeat) until he was unwisely brought back for the Scottish Cup tie at Fir Park, Motherwell in mid-February. His injury was aggravated, and the team lost dismally 0-2. It was one of Maley's less happy decisions, for it deprived Celtic of McGrory's services for virtually the rest of the season.

It was sadly a pattern that was beginning to develop. As had happened after the untimely deaths of Peter Johnstone and Sunny Jim Young, Maley lapsed into a kind of melancholic depression from which neither he himself nor anyone else could shake him. His judgement went as well, as can be seen from the eccentric and quixotic team selections that appeared from time to time. The reserve team had been resurrected for two years now, but Maley's ability to judge a player seemed to have deserted him.

Economically, things were bad as well. The unemployment situation was no better under Ramsay McDonald's National Government, and supporters simply did not have the money to spend – or rather, they did not feel that they wished to allocate any part of their inadequate income on a football match to see a team who were making little progress. Crowds of less than 10,000 were commonplace at Parkhead, especially in the second half of the season when it was obvious that the team were heading nowhere.

In addition, there was a problem with Peter Scarff. Peter was a fine, hardworking inside left whom Maley had recruited from a Linwood juvenile team in 1928. He was hailed as the successor to McMenemy and McInally, both of whom had graced the inside left position. He certainly showed fine touches, although he was not yet in all conscience as good as these two. Nevertheless, he was still young, in his early twenties, and it appeared that he had a long future ahead of him.

But in a few games towards the end of 1931, he had seemed breathless and on one occasion he collapsed after a training session. Another time, he coughed up blood (an ominous sign) at half-time, and after the game against Leith Athletic on 19 December (which Celtic had coasted 6-0), he said he was going home to bed because he felt tired.

He did not reappear for training, and Maley became concerned. His symptoms were the classic ones of that scourge of the 1930s – tuberculosis or consumption as it was called, meaning basically the eating away of the lung. Maley tried to console himself as he went to Mass that Christmas by saying to himself that great advances had been made in recent years in the treatment of tuberculosis (if that was what it was) and that, in any case, the disease only attacked the underfed, not the fit, professional footballer.

Early in the New Year, Maley's worst forebodings were confirmed, and Peter Scarff was admitted to the Bridge of Weir sanatorium suffering from pulmonary tuberculosis. Maley visited him assiduously and prayed to St Jude, St Anthony and other saints. For a while Maley was encouraged by what he saw in the sanatorium. Fresh air was what was required and Scarff slept some nights in a room with a roof, but only three walls so that he could breathe better. Some improvement was seen, and Maley was very encouraged by news of other patients, some of whom had recovered sufficiently to go home and lead normal lives, even if only for a short time. Maley told Scarff that he would soon be back at Parkhead – 'My heavens' (a favourite phrase of his) 'we are needing you back!'

On one occasion, Maley took some friends of his and some Celtic players including the charismatic McGrory to the sanatorium to give a concert for the patients. Maley himself sang and did recitations, and spent long hours chatting with the patients and the nurses, occasionally on a Sunday afternoon, when visiting Peter, organizing a Domino League. It was another of his kindly traits. He did not lack patience with people who were genuinely ill, and seemed able to empathise with them. He was in addition a lonely man now, having stayed on his own for some time, and he probably enjoyed company.

There was another uncomfortable reminder (as if he needed one) of mortality in the death, in February 1932, of his old friend and team-mate James Kelly who was of course a director of the club. James and he had been friends since they met in 1888 and Kelly's death at the age of sixty-two was a shock to Maley. In the early days, there had been no greater worker and friend for the Celtic than James Kelly, and of course Kelly in his capacity as chairman and then director had backed Maley to the hilt. Maley was glad to see that the Kelly family would continue to administer Celtic, for young Robert seemed very keen to take on his father's mantle. It was a pity about the young man's arm disability which had prevented him becoming a player like his father.

1932/33 was a Jekyll and Hyde season. League form was only sporadically good. A League challenge might have been made after a fine spell in November and December but poor and inconsistent form in the latter half of the season let Celtic down. As it was, the Championship reverted to Rangers once again.

The supporters were shocked and disappointed when Maley sold the Irish right-back Willie Cook to Everton between Christmas and New Year. It was precisely the wrong decision in playing terms and sent out the wrong signals of lack of ambition to both supporters and opponents. As in the aftermath of the sale of Crerand in 1963, Dalglish in 1977 and Nicholas in 1983, form suffered and, just as importantly, the supporters became disheartened.

Maley would frequently make bleating statements in public about lack of money, even on occasion castigating his supporters for not turning up in sufficient numbers. Only to a point can we sympathise with this. It was of course true that the 1930s were the middle of a recession, but this affected everyone and Celtic with their impressive stadium and huge (potential) support seemed able to ride out the world financial crisis better than most.

Maley's obsession with money (a gradual thing which crept up on him and only slowly metamorphisised his personality) prevented him from seeing one basic thing. It was something that he had seen very well in the 1890s, but seemed to be blind to now. Celtic Football Club were more than a football club in that they represented an ethnic minority – a fairly large ethnic minority, it has to be said, but traditionally a disadvantaged one. A football club could do little to deal with the basic causes of all this. That would have to be left to politicians. What the team could do, however, was to improve morale, to give its supporters something to be proud of, to show them that failure need not be the inevitable consequence of being an ethnic minority. Willie Maley had done this in the 1900s and 1910s. He was lamentably failing to do so now.

He also retreated into a defensive shell of the 'world is against me' kind of paranoia which is always to a large extent self-fulfilling. He would complain for example that at a pre-season five-a-side tournament, everyone would cheer for Partick Thistle or Third Lanark or Kilmarnock – and either boo or simply ignore Celtic. Once again, we can agree with him to an extent. People, with only a passing interest in football would indeed be happy to see Clyde beating Celtic, but they would feel similarly if Clyde beat Rangers. It was the fact that Celtic were large and successful. It was that which people did not like, it was not necessarily because they were Irish or Catholic.

Prejudice against Roman Catholics did certainly exist in Scotland in the 1930s and occasionally we read disturbing reports about how the Church of Scotland seemed to sanction and justify it, talking about 'the Irish problem'. But moaning about things like persecution and discrimination does not tend to help the problem and if anything makes it worse. Maley should really have been big enough and intellectually honest enough to see this.

In any case, Celtic did have a huge support of their own. It had been very much to the credit of Maley that he had tapped the goodwill of the community and harnessed it to football, but it did need to be retained. Complaining about lack of money on the one hand and religious prejudice on the other was not the best way of dealing with the problem. In Maley's case it intensified the problem, for he was an influential person and his statements were taken more seriously than they might otherwise have been.

A certain amount of respectability was restored to a somewhat depressing picture by the capture of the 1933 Scottish Cup. This was Celtic's fourteenth winning of the trophy, and Maley had in one way or another been involved in every one of them. It did cheer him up and also cheered up the huge support who had attend faithfully the Scottish Cup final, however reluctant they had been about other games.

Willie Cook's place had been taken by Bobby Hogg, a seventeen year old from Larkhall Royal Albert. Although he was thrown into the side before he was really ready for it, the youngster, after a few unhappy experiences, became very dependable and steady. Peter Scarff had not returned, and Maley possibly knew that although there was now and again a chink of optimism in his condition, the chances of him ever playing football again were exceedingly slim.

The forward line had now evolved so that Charlie Napier played at inside left and on the left wing appeared Hugh O'Donnell, a man who had the advantage, as far as the supporters were concerned, in sharing the same name as a famous medieval Irish rebel! He and his brother Frank had joined the club from Wellesley Juniors, the same team as the late John Thomson.

McGrory continued to be the man of the moment. If he wasn't a national hero before, he would become one on 1 April 1933 in the Scotland *v.* England game, the day that the Hampden Roar was born, when he picked up a great ball from Rangers' Bob McPhail to score a wonderful goal. Because of the position in which he played and because of his unflinching courage in the face of danger, he was prone to frequent injury, and when he was out of the team, it showed. But, as Maley often thought, there could seldom ever be a more archetypal Celt than James McGrory.

McGrory's poor, underprivileged background in the Garngad meant that he was exactly what Celtic were about. He understood the moods, the frustrations and the joys of the supporters – indeed, he was a supporter himself – and he was a perfect role model. Never in trouble on the field even in the face of intense provocation, McGrory represented all that Celtic should be. His scoring record was phenomenal. Maley may have had some kind of guilty conscience about his attempt to sell him to Arsenal in 1928. He certainly never tried the same again, for he knew that McGrory was Celtic through and through.

The Scottish Cup campaign of 1933 began at Dunfermline, a very poor Second Division team in those days. McGrory scored a hattrick (the supporters had a song which was based on a hymn 'Tell me the old, old story, A hat-trick for McGrory') and young Hugh O'Donnell did likewise. Falkirk and then Partick Thistle provided stiff opposition, but McGrory came to the rescue in both games with fine, opportunist goals.

The quarter-final put Celtic to Cliftonhill to play Albion Rovers. It was here that Maley had another opportunity to be charming and gracious to important people, which was something he relished. Sir Harry Lauder was the guest of honour at this game, and was introduced to both sets of players before sitting in the small stand next to Maley. Both men were seen in prolonged and earnest conversation about the game.

Maley might have been embarrassed about his team for they under-performed and were glad of a few saves from reserve goalkeeper John Wallace to earn a goalless draw. The replay was won comfortably, however, and then Celtic had two epic semi-finals in front of large crowds of 87,000 and 63,000 to get the better of Hearts. The first game was 0-0 and finished with mutterings about it being a fix so as to get another big gate in the replay.

Such a charge was frequently made in those days, and cannot be proved or disproved, but Celtic's apparently depleted coffers were certainly given a boost by the replay, which Celtic won 2-1. Goals came from McGrory (of course) and the man that many fans (and possibly Maley himself) considered to be Celtic's best player in that era – Alec Thomson. He had matured over the years and delighted in being called 'McGrory's fetch and carry man'. On this occasion, however, it was he who scored the goal.

For the second time in three years, Celtic and Motherwell faced each other in the final of the Scottish Cup, and 102,000 fans attended, once again making it difficult to take seriously Maley's moans about lack of money for the club. The huge crowd this time saw a very disappointing game, in contrast to the epics of two years previously. The weather was dull, and so was the football, although Celtic's Peter Wilson and Charlie Geatons were outstanding in midfield.

Early in the second half came the only goal of the game, and it was a McGrory tap-in after a Motherwell defender had failed to clear an innocuous cross. It was a goal that became known as McGrory's 'saftest o' the familie' after the famous Harry Lauder music-hall song of the time. But it was enough to land the Scottish Cup, for the Celtic defence with Jimmy McStay's commanding call of 'Face the ball, Celts' very much in evidence, was enough to hold out against any potential Motherwell counter-attack.

Maley was happy once again, yet the celebrations were far more muted than they had been two years ago. Maley had still not got over the death of John Thomson, perhaps he never would, and there was the ongoing agony of Peter Scarff. Peter had listened to the final on the radio at the sanatorium, and Maley made sure that the Scottish Cup was brought to him the following day, something that impressed the other patients and the nurses. But Maley was now painfully aware that although Peter was not necessarily in constant discomfort, he would never play again. His voice was weak, his chest spluttered audibly, and although he made a brave effort to be sociable, Peter was on the downward slope.

Maley himself was now sixty-five, an age when quite a lot of men would have contemplated retirement. But he was still physically fit, as one would have expected of a man with a long tradition of looking after himself. His habits continued to be frugal, he did his fair share of physical exercise and his religious faith sustained him – to an extent. Perhaps he may have considered retirement or resignation, but Celtic was too much part of him, and he did not trust anyone else to be in charge of this great club. As long as Celtic kept on winning things, at least occasionally, no one would try to sack him.

Scarff died in December 1933. The distraught Maley, in the finest of Celtic traditions, draped the green and white jersey on his coffin at Kilbarchan cemetery. He had now seen too many players, younger than himself, who had died prematurely, and it was hardly surprising that he began to feel very sad. He became even more distanced from the players, except his favourites like McGrory and McStay. He would often come to Parkhead, leave the training to someone like Jimmy McMenemy who joined the club in an official capacity as trainer in 1934, shut himself in his office and work away at writing letters with only the briefest and curtest of nods to anyone he met.

There was certainly enough to depress him on the field of play, for the 1933/34 and 1934/35 seasons were barren ones, with Scottish Cup defeats at the quarter-final stage and League positions of third and second. Some progress was made in 1935, but not enough. Maley took to complaining about the attitude of players comparing them with the old days, and even saying that the atmosphere in the ground was not as pleasant nor supportive as it once had been.

This was true. The support dropped alarmingly, and those who did attend regularly made their feelings known in no uncertain terms about how unhappy they were with the poor fare on offer, and the lack of any real challenge to Rangers. Many great players aged simultaneously. Bertie Thomson left the club in August 1933, first to Blackpool, then to Motherwell. This was no real surprise, for Maley and he had never seen eye to eye. After a 4-1 defeat at the hands of Queen's Park in September 1932, Bertie was suspended for drunkenness and lack of effort and was out of the team for a long time, before being brought back in time for the Scottish-Cup run. Maley had been prepared to go the extra mile for the likes of McInally in the past, but he was less prepared to do so for a man of lesser ability on the field and with greater capacity to get into trouble off it.

Yet Bertie Thomson was much loved by the fans. On 8 December 1934, when he was playing for Motherwell against Celtic, a bizarre incident took place. As the teams came onto the field, some supporters ran on and presented him with a horseshoe in green and white colours, wishing him all the best. And this was when he was playing for the opposition! Maley was apparently furious, but the point was being made that Maley had let him go too early. However, Bertie's dissolute lifestyle led to an early death in 1937.

Alec Thomson and Peter Wilson, both of whom were suffering from loss of form and being sucked in by the all-enveloping melancholy of Celtic Park, left in 1934, although both had a certain amount of football left in them, one felt. The same year of 1934 saw the departure of Jimmy McStay, a man who had given everything for Celtic and Maley. Jimmy, now approaching his fortieth birthday, went to Hamilton Accies.

1935 was another bad year for the club, and serious questions were now being asked about whether it was wise that the ageing Maley should continue in such exalted and unchallenged power. Certainly the directors did not yet think fit to retire him or even to suggest, ever so gently, that it might be an idea at least to relax the reins of power, if not hand them over entirely to someone else. But the fans continued to grumble, not without cause, about the lack of success.

Further departures took place in the shape of the two O'Donnell brothers. They were hardworking, industrious players but Frank (the inside left), in particular, disappointed the fans. Hugh was fast and could cross a ball but, like everyone else in that Celtic team that lacked someone to buck them up, he was prone to off days. The general depression of the supporters led to Frank in particular being booed, not necessarily because he was the only one playing badly (although he was certainly on the slow side – so much so that he was the easy target), for even legends like McGrory were not immune from such treatment!

Frank, like most football players, was basically a sensitive soul and he found little support from Maley on this issue. If he talked to Maley at all, Maley would merely shrug his shoulders and say that the fans paid their money, so it was up to him not to give them cause to boo and catcall.

At the end of the unsuccessful 1934/35 season, Preston North End approached Maley with a view to signing Hugh O'Donnell. Maley, to the chagrin of the support, agreed and then offered Frank as well for a total cost of £5,000. The departure of the brothers immediately led to an advance in their careers, and Frank would eventually be capped for Scotland!

But if the supporters were unhappy about the O'Donnells' departure, things were made one hundred times worse when Charlie Napier left the club a month later. If arguments could rage about the value or otherwise of the two O'Donnells, no one could dispute the value of Charlie Napier. He had been capped for Scotland three times, and there had been days in the past few seasons when the play of Napier was all that Celtic fans could be happy about.

In an era which desperately needed a hero, and in a culture which similarly desperately needed one, 'Cheeky Charlie' was the closest that one could get. Always immaculately dressed off the field and a class act on it, 'Happy Feet' (as he came to be known), showed all the signs of becoming another Patsy Gallacher, so total was his control of a football, passing it, dribbling with it, supplying McGrory with low crosses and high crosses and scoring not a few goals himself.

He did make one mistake though, and that was in thinking that he could hold a pistol to Maley's head. He refused to sign to renew his contract in 1935 unless he was granted a benefit. He was possibly being a little presumptuous in this respect, but banked on the fact that he was so loved by the Celtic fans that Maley would be emotionally blackmailed into complying with this request. This cut no ice with Maley at all, who was fed up with fans booing his players and by implication criticising his good self.

Maley refused, and a month later in stepped Derby County with an offer of £5,000 that Maley had no intention of turning down. It was as well that this happened during the close season, otherwise there would have been quite a great deal of discontent, including boycotts, demonstrations etc. As it was, there still existed a great deal of unhappiness as the 1935/36 season began. But the old man was not finished yet. Behind the scenes, a great deal had been happening in terms of the development of the young players, and Maley was about to fight back from the dreadful years of the early 1930s.

They were dreadful years in other areas of the world as well. Japan had invaded Manchuria and the League of Nations, believed to be the body that would stop any further wars, were powerless to act. Mussolini was threatening Ethiopia and, worst of all, Hitler was in total control in Germany.

Yet the worst of the recession in Britain was past. Unemployment was dropping, but was still too high. Maley continued to be distressed at the number of these poor dispirited fellows standing outside Parkhead on match days, unable to afford even the reduced charges. He had on occasion told some of his gate checkers to allow them in for nothing, but he could not do that too obviously. For one thing, it was illegal and for another he did not want Celtic to get the reputation of being an easy touch for scroungers!

Ten

MALEY'S
GLORIOUS SUNSET

There had, in fact, been quite a few improvements in season
1934/35, but the lack of any obvious tangible success, even in the
two Glasgow tournaments, tended to obscure this fact. A great step
forward had been made in October 1934 with the appointment of
Jimmy McMenemy as coach/trainer and there were those who
argued that the manager of Celtic in the late 1930s was in fact
Jimmy McMenemy.

This is less than fair to Maley, and nothing like the truth. Although
McMenemy acted as a link between the players and the authoritarian and seemingly unapproachable Maley, it was still Maley who ran
the show, picking the team, deciding which players were needing to
be brought along gently, who needed sterner treatment and occasionally (and therefore more effectively) making a surprise appear-
ance at training or in the dressing room to make a valid point. His
knowledge of football and its tactics remained second to none.

There was indeed a certain spring to Maley's step once again, for
he had got over the deep depression that had followed the deaths of
Thomson and Scarff. He smarted from the criticism that came his

way for the poor results of 1934 and 1935 and for his selling of star players, but he took heart from the fine team that he saw developing around him from 1935 onwards, the fruits of his reinstating of a reserve team. He certainly did not in any way regret the sale of those players who had gone to England. The O'Donnells were competent, but no more than that and although Napier was a fine player, Maley had never been a fan of him as a person, disliking his 'flash Harry' charm and occasionally extravagant dress sense.

In general terms, Maley felt that the worst of the economic recession had passed. With a bit of luck, attendances would begin to rise. Unemployment started to drop, and a slow prosperity slowly began to trickle down to everyone. Yet, it was obvious that there was a very grim reason for the turnaround in economic affairs.

But did the country have the guts for that? Frankly, the answer was 'no', for it was less than twenty years since the First World War and all its horrendous casualties were so fresh in people's memories. Could anyone countenance that happening again? And this time it might be far worse, for there was the threat of bombing from the air. There had been a little of that in the First World War from Zeppelins. Now Hitler was making much more sophisticated machines than that.

In the meantime, the Government decided to be prepared. Factories that had been closed suddenly opened up again to make parts for aeroplanes, tanks and mechanised transport. In Glasgow, shipbuilding received a shot in the arm. Steel returned to Motherwell. In Dundee, jute was needed once more for sandbags, and although it would take time for full employment to be restored, things were certainly moving in the right direction.

They were moving in the right direction at Parkhead as well in 1935/36 season, for after an opening-day defeat at Aberdeen (which had been a bogey ground for Celtic for the past ten years or so) the team settled and did not lose again in the League until December. Maley, however, suffered a blow and a huge personal loss on 24 August when his brother Tom died in the early hours of the morning.

Tom, who was seventy, had been in poor health for some time. The two brothers had of course played a significant role in Celtic's birth, and although Tom, the wilder of the two men, had had a chequered career which had included being sacked as manager of Manchester City for illegal payments to players, he had always kept coming back to Celtic. Willie leaned on him a great deal, as had been proved in 1931 when he needed his brother in the USA with him to help him on the tour. Maley had funeral arrangements to see to, so most unusually missed a Celtic game – the trip to Muirton Park, Perth. He appeared at Buchanan Street station to tell them the bad news and also to encourage them to 'pull out a little extra today' for Tom. He was also at the station in his black tie and wearing a black arm band to welcome them back that evening after a 3-2 win.

A bonus in the early part of the season was the sheer quality of the play. For the first time since Andy McAtee and Johnny Browning, the team had two excellent wingers in Jimmy Delaney and Frank Murphy. Delaney had been signed in 1933 from Stoneyburn Juniors, and he was now considered ready for first-team football. He was a fast, speedy winger with the ability to cut inside and supply excellent crosses to the ever-ready McGrory, who had now been with the club for over a decade; hardly a week passed without him seeming to break some kind of record.

It was a shame that Frank Murphy played on the left wing at the same time as Delaney played on the right, for the charisma of Delaney tended to overshadow the fine performances of Murphy on the left. Having served his apprenticeship in the impeccably Celtic areas of Coatbridge, Croy and St Roch's, Murphy had played a few games last year, but really broke into the team in September 1935, his first game being the 2-1 win over Rangers at Ibrox. Murphy was light, nippy and clever and, like Delaney, supplied the sort of service which McGrory required.

Murphy would frequently admit to being scared of Maley. Murphy was by nature a very shy man, and Maley often picked on him in a way that smacked of bullying, even to the extent of paying Murphy less than the others. Yet Maley was, in public at least, never anything less than totally appreciative of the value of Frank Murphy.

The wing-halves were the old warhorse Chick Geatons and a new player called George Paterson. They were privileged in that they had two wingers to supply, and a favourite trick of both was to swing a long ball across the park to the winger in the other half of the field. Thus Paterson (the left half) would frequently supply Delaney, and Geatons would feed Murphy.

Maley had surprised a few people by going to Queen's Park for a new centre half to plug the gap which had been left by the departure of Jimmy McStay. Celtic needed a commander, an authoritarian figure on the field and they found one in Willie Lyon. Cynics said that Maley had gone to Queen's Park because they were amateurs and that Lyon would therefore be cheap. This was true, but Maley was still able to judge a player, and Lyon, who later became a major and won the Military Cross in the Second World War, was exactly what was needed. Not only could he play, but he was a fine captain as well. He would soon show fine leadership qualities.

Jock Morrison replaced Peter McGonagle in the autumn of 1935 and he was another fine, if unspectacular player. He had been with Celtic since 1929, and had always been a willing reserve and a fine squad man. Although he was unable to replace McGonagle until 1935, he nevertheless stuck around, listening, learning and waiting. Eventually, he broke into the team and became one of the best left-backs that Celtic had ever had.

The inside men had also both been maturing for a while and from 1935 onwards came to their ripening. They were Willie Buchan, an excellent inside right from the Grangemouth area and the streetwise Glaswegian Johnny Crum. Both of these men were fine players and fitted in perfectly to a team that was already brimming with talent.

McGrory was absolutely phenomenal that season. In only three League games did he fail to score, and it was obvious that when he was not playing, the team did not do quite so well. For example, on 14 December, Celtic unaccountably lost to Dunfermline Athletic at East

End Park. The reason was that McGrory had picked up a knock and the rejigged forward line failed to function properly without him.

It was in the course of that season that he became the record goalscorer. He achieved this accolade twice in fact! He scored on 19 October at Airdrie to beat Steve Bloomer's record of 352, but then it was discovered that Hughie Ferguson had apparently scored 362, depending on which newspaper report one read. But on 21 December when Aberdeen came to Parkhead, he scored a hat-trick in a 5-3 victory which beat that one as well!

Most of his 50 League goals scored that year were simple tap-ins, brought about by his having the old centre forward's ability simply to be in the right place at the right time. Others were less straightforward. For example, the goal that he scored at Arbroath in April was much talked about, for it showed his sheer courage as well as his other skills. A hard ball was driven across the face of the goal by Frank Murphy. It was partially cleared and was bobbing about at knee height. McGrory dived forward and at about a foot off the ground bulleted home a great header.

As happens in the best of seasons, the team hit a poor patch. Celtic had beaten Rangers 2-1 at Ibrox in September (Kennaway saving a penalty), but Rangers gained revenge twice, once by beating them in the final of the Glasgow Cup and then again on New Year's Day at Parkhead when the Light Blues edged home by the odd goal in seven when Kennaway was out injured and the deputy goalkeeper James Foley had an unlucky day.

This was not a disaster, and soon the team recovered for a spell, but then in early February they went down to Hearts at Tynecastle, and the following week they amazed the footballing world and horrified their fans by losing to St Johnstone in a Scottish Cup tie at Parkhead.

St Johnstone could not believe it, and neither could Maley. He could find no reason for this unaccountable loss until he realised that McGrory had not received sufficient service. Buchan had scored Celtic's solitary goal against St Johnstone, and several others had tried to do likewise. He had already spoken to a few players about this, notably George Paterson, but he now decided that a team talk was in order.

Unlike Stein, who held team talks almost every day, this was an unusual procedure for Maley, at least for Maley in his maturer years. First of all, he asked if everyone was happy. No one said anything, for they all lacked courage as he glowered at them all. He then told them that they were a good side, singling out a few players and praising their commitment and contribution to this hitherto successful season. He said that although the Cup had now gone, the League was still within their grasp for they were still ahead of Rangers. Did they want to throw all this away?

He said that he was never one for long tactical discussions about the opposition. He felt that this if anything tended to be counter-productive for it might indicate that the opposition were better than they really were. What he was interested in was what Celtic could do. He then said that football was a very simple game, and that if they managed to get the ball to the feet or the head of Jimmy McGrory, McGrory would do the rest. It was as simple as that. Football, he said frequently, was a simple game – get the ball into the penalty area and score! Whereupon, he turned round and walked out of the room.

The players quite clearly took Maley at his word, and McGrory, although now at the veteran stage and the only current member of the Celtic team who had won a League Championship medal (in 1926), managed to evade centre halves and put the finishing touches to the thrusts of Buchan and Crum and the inch-perfect crosses of Delaney and Murphy.

On 14 March in a game against Motherwell, McGrory managed to score a hat-trick in three minutes! He scored, then Motherwell took their centre, lost possession immediately to George Paterson from where a move began and McGrory netted. The same thing happened immediately afterwards, and after McGrory scored his hat-trick, Motherwell's centre forward at the restart tapped the ball to his inside right who booted the ball up the field, lest McGrory score yet again!

But wait a bit, don't be so fast,
We've left the star turn till the last
There in the midst o a'his glory
Goal a minute James McGrory!

The following Saturday saw a win against Dundee at Dens Park in which Delaney scored the other goal in addition to feeding McGrory. Hibs were then thrashed 4-1.

No one could ever explain why McGrory was not chosen for Scotland at Wembley that year, the place unaccountably going to one David McCulloch who played for Brentford! But Celtic kept pressing on regardless towards the title, and a key day seems to have been 11 April, the day of McGrory's famous diving header at Arbroath, for Rangers went down to Hamilton Accies that day.

Celtic then won a tight game against Clyde at Parkhead on the Holiday Monday, which meant that two points would more or less settle the title for the first time since 1926. Maley rubbed his hands at the prospect of the big gate to see Ayr United on 18 April, and he was not disappointed as over 40,000 were at Parkhead that day. Celtic won 6-0 and somewhat predictably McGrory scored a hat-trick! McGrory picked up a knee injury, and missed a penalty which on his own admission 'nearly hit the corner flag'. In theory Rangers could still catch Celtic on goal average, but it was a forlorn hope.

Thus on the last day of the season, 25 April, Maley celebrated his sixty-eighth birthday with a 3-1 win over Partick Thistle at Firhill and their eighteenth League Championship. This was at least the third occasion that the League Championship had been secured on his birthday! He had much to be proud of in his new team, not least because two of the goals that day had been scored by McGrory's deputy Willie Fagan. Next season promised to be even better, he felt, but the main thing was that he, in the very best of Celtic traditions, had fought back from adversity. Celtic were now at last back where they should be. His prudent housekeeping and shrewd purchases had confounded his critics, to whom he was now prepared, as always, to be gracious.

There was even more for him to be happy about at the end of the season when Celtic brought to an end a long dismal run in the Glasgow competitions by beating Rangers 4–2 in a fine display of football. It almost goes without saying that McGrory scored a goal but the other three were scored by young Jimmy Delaney. The understandably proud young man came in with his face wreathed in smiles, only to be met by a scowling Maley who made as if to go past him without saying anything. Delaney, courageous in the circumstances, said something along the lines of 'How did you like that, Boss?' Maley snarled 'Don't let it go to your head!' Delaney was hurt by such boorish and apparently ungracious behaviour, but he also made sure that he took the old man's advice. Maley, for his part, was delighted for young Delaney, but did not like to show his feelings.

This was 1936, and two world events cast their shadow over Maley. One was the concatenation of circumstances which affected the British Crown. Maley, always a supporter of royalty, was genuinely distressed at the death of King George V at the start of the year and harboured doubts about the playboy Prince of Wales becoming King Edward VIII. But he was the King, and that was that. The King was dead, long live the King.

It was curious that Maley, a staunch Catholic, should be so concerned about royalty, the one body which officially prevented Catholics from joining it. But perhaps he inherited this from his father who, of course, had served the crown. But being a Catholic, Maley also disapproved strongly of divorce and remarriage and when in the late summer, stories began to circulate about the King and an American woman called Wallis Simpson, who had been twice divorced, Maley became very distressed indeed. When the King abdicated in December, Maley was totally bewildered and upset, and it may be that it actually affected his judgement.

The other world event was altogether more serious, and it was the Spanish Civil War. Maley saw quite clearly that the Celtic supporting community would be in a quandary about all this. Normally, the Irish in Scotland had no major political problem. They simply voted Labour, a mildly left-wing party which the Church hierarchy had no real quarrel with, however rare it might be in European terms for a Catholic community to vote for the left.

But the Spanish Civil War, which would last without mercy or pity and with great loss of blood for three years, tended to make people choose one side or the other. The Republican government was the legitimate authority and enjoyed the blessing and the support of the British Labour party, but the Nationalist rebels under General Franco numbered the Catholic Church among its allies. It was complicated enough, but became more so when the Republicans attracted the support of Communist Russia and the Nationalists were helped by Hitler!

Maley himself probably preferred Franco, but he knew that most of the Catholic community, which he still claimed on occasion to represent, would have preferred the Republicans. What he could have done of course would have been to bury his head in the sand, as the British government was doing at this time, talk about 'Non-Intervention' and neutrality and hope the problem would go away.

But it would not go away, however much the British government and people hoped that it would. Quite a few people saw that the Spanish Civil War was little other than a dress rehearsal for the big show that was soon to enfold, and Maley was upset to see posters outside Parkhead on match days encouraging young men to join the International Brigades to fight on the Republican side. It would also have been interesting to find out what Maley's reaction was when, a matter of days after the Scottish Cup final of 1937, the Germans with the connivance of Franco obliterated the inoffensive town of Guérnica in the strongly Catholic Basque district of Spain.

Maley was, of course, astute enough to know that war was coming, and for this reason perhaps he threw himself more and more into football and Celtic. At the same time, he found it more and more difficult to relate to people and in particular his own players to whom he gave a whole batch of unjustifiable and bewildering diktats.

No player was allowed to own a motor car, for example, and he also said that 'Football must not be played during the close season'. He was, of course, unable to enforce either command, both of which were ignored. Maley clearly had not heard of the dictum that it is ridiculous to forbid something that one can't enforce. But Maley now, having enrolled Joe Dodds to help McMenemy with the training and coaching, withdrew more and more into himself. Young reserves never actually saw him, other than the distant figure with his ubiquitous homburg hat and top coat sitting in the stand watching the weekly first team *v.* second team game.

The same team as had won the League in 1936 took the field for 1936/37. As with the previous season, they were remarkably free from injuries and the team stayed settled, but this time an element of inconsistency crept into the play in January and the result was that Rangers won the League yet again and Aberdeen were second. But Celtic and Maley still had their moment of glory.

It centred on the Scottish Cup final. Many things conspired to bring about the record attendance of over 147,000 – it was Aberdeen's first-ever Scottish Cup final and a chance to unleash the massive, if dormant, north-eastern support on a major occasion. However, it also said something about Celtic's huge following which, although frustrated by a few indifferent performances in the League race, remained loyal to the cause.

But there was more to it than that. The week before, 149,000 fans had been at Hampden to see the Scotland *v.* England game, and it revealed the gargantuan hold that football had on the Scottish public, far more than any place else in the world. The appetite was whetted all the more because this was clearly a community under threat, a world living on borrowed time. They had obviously decided to enjoy their football while they could. Maley himself was apparently taken aback by the huge crowds at both games, worrying when he saw the swaying at the top of the terracings.

The Celtic support were in fine fettle, in huge numbers and on top of their form as far as singing and cheering went. This was only a few years after Maley had repeatedly complained about the lack of spirit both in the players and in the support. Maley had resurrected Celtic. Some might argue that it had been he who had caused the problem in the first place, but whatever the reason, he had certainly brought them back.

Yet it nearly didn't happen for Celtic. January had been the month in which the League challenge fizzled out and at the end of that month, Celtic had been very lucky not to concede a penalty to Stenhousemuir at Ochilview. This might well have put them out, for Celtic were struggling to draw at the time. That same day, however, saw Celtic earn another break when Rangers went down to Queen of the South at Dumfries.

The replay saw no real problem, but in the quarter-final at Parkhead, against the old foe Motherwell, a 4-4 draw was the result – and it too could have gone against Celtic. Willie Lyon scored a penalty when the team were 4-2 down, and Willie Buchan scrambled a late equaliser. The replay was similarly tight, but Celtic scraped through 2-1.

The semi-final saw Celtic beat in front of 76,000 fans the same day that Aberdeen reached their first-ever final by beating Morton. Aberdeen usually did well against Celtic, something that brought a happy smile to the face of Paddy Travers, a former Celt who possibly felt that he might have had a better deal from Maley. A more objective assessment would have to conclude that Maley made the right decision in December 1911, when he dropped Paddy Travers in favour of giving a debut to Patsy Gallacher!

But Travers had a keen football brain, and whenever the subject of Maley's retirement came up (he was now nearly sixty-nine) Travers was frequently mentioned as the potential 'heir apparent'. Indeed, when he left Aberdeen in the middle of the following season, it was falsely reported in some newspapers that he had gone to Celtic to replace Maley. In fact, he went to another Glasgow team, Celtic's near neighbours Clyde!

Maley was bidding to win his fifteenth Scottish Cup and as well as the continuing speculation about his future, there was also the talk that this might be the last Scottish Cup final for Jimmy McGrory. McGrory had played in five Scottish Cup finals, and had won three, scoring a goal on each victorious occasion. Now well into his thirties, he was increasingly injury prone and visibly slowing down.

McGrory's career also seemed to be living on borrowed time. It would be nice if he managed to score again.

Maley was very impressed by the huge crowd. A couple of years later, when he was writing his *The Story of The Celtic*, he said:

> When I mention that the final of 1936/37 was attended by the magnificent number of 144,303 spectators [in fact there were a few more than that], I recall the struggles of our early days – days when nothing but great enthusiasm and dogged determination kept the flag flying. While paying willing and due tribute to our opponents on the many occasions on which records were established, I maintain that the Celtic club has made a tremendous contribution to the game in Scotland, and I claim that the position it occupies, quite apart from its many great achievements, entitles it to the respect, even admiration, of every true sportsman.

What he said was true, and it was also true to claim that even the attendance the week before at the international had a great deal to do with Celtic. Not only did Jimmy Delaney play (as well as the ex-Celt Frank O'Donnell), but it is also true in general terms that the game in Scotland would never have taken off to reach such meteoric heights, had it not been for the success of Celtic. Not only did they attract their own support, who might have been lost to the game otherwise, but they did set the standard for the other clubs, notably Rangers, to reach and attempt to surpass.

The 1937 Cup Final itself, commonly referred to as 'The Sardine Final' because of the vast tightly-packed crowd, was close, but Celtic emerged victorious. It might have been nice if McGrory had scored, but in fact Celtic's goalscorers were Crum and Buchan. McGrory was instrumental in both goals – heading on a Paterson free-kick which was blocked, but Crum nipped in to score in the resultant scramble, and then flicking on a nice ball for Buchan to score the winner halfway through the second half.

The black and gold of Aberdeen attacked vigorously and many thought that they deserved a draw and a replay, but all too soon for the Aberdonians, Paddy Travers stood up, smiled and said 'Congratulations, Mr Maley', not yet able to call him 'Willie', for he was still in awe of him.

The Cup was duly presented in the lounge at Hampden (as happened in these days), photographs were taken in front of the deserted terraces, and then it was off to 'The Bank' restaurant through the cheering crowds for a celebration. Young players were given a glass of milk (!) to celebrate, but more senior players celebrated with more gusto. Maley himself, a moderate drinker, would take a sherry and even perhaps permitted himself a smile, something that some of his players seldom saw. He had taken the liberty of inviting a couple of guests – Mr and Mrs Thomson from Cardenden, the parents of John.

There was one bizarre game at the end of the season. The last meaningless League game was played at Fir Park, Motherwell on a Friday night before Celtic were due to travel on the overnight sleeper to see the English Cup Final at Wembley between Sunderland and Preston North End. Motherwell won 8-0. Granted Morrison was out and Buchan had to take over in goal after Kennaway was injured, but explanations for the enormity of the defeat range from excessive celebration of last week's Scottish Cup win through bets with bookies to a deliberate attempt to humiliate Maley, who, in spite of the past week's success, was anything but popular with certain players!

But the team duly performed when things became serious again and following another win in the Glasgow Charity Cup in an excellent final where the team came from behind to beat Queen's Park, Maley prepared for the next season. He was well aware that this would be the fiftieth anniversary of the club who had played their first game in 1888, although most historians now date their founding to November 1887 when the decision was taken. By the end of the season, Maley would be seventy, and surely he could then retire. Or would he? He really was enjoying himself, and if he finished the season with a fistful of silver, it would be virtually impossible for the directors to put pressure on him to leave.

He was also aware that it was thirty years since the great 'clean sweep' year of 1908 when all four trophies were annexed. It would be nice to do this again, mused Maley and he certainly felt that he had the players to do that. He had always laid great stress on his captain, and had always got on well with the three Jimmies, Hay, Young and McStay, who had skippered the side. Now he had another great captain, Willie Lyon, a man not from the Celtic tradition – in fact he was an Englishman from Lancashire – but an absolute lion-heart in action, and an inspirational role model for all young players.

There was another reason why he wanted to do well this season. He was aware that he couldn't have too many more years as manager, but the sands of time were also possibly running out for peace.

Maley was also working very hard on a new book, *The Story Of The Celtic*, which he hoped to have ready for the Golden Jubilee. He had already serialised his history of Celtic in the *Weekly News* and he felt that a book might be a more permanent memento of the glorious history of the club. Naturally the aspects of history that showed him in a bad light would be eschewed, but the book remains an invaluable source of material for the early years.

War was clearly coming, but in the meantime, football was still to be enjoyed. Maley was not so lucky with injuries this year and the start was inconsistent. By the end of September, his dream of a clean sweep was in ruins, for Rangers had beaten Celtic in the Glasgow Cup. In that autumn he also lost two players. One was Jimmy McGrory, who played his last game in October and became Kilmarnock's manager in December. There is a certain feeling that Maley was not happy with McGrory for this, and there were to be unhappy repercussions for Maley.

Losing the ageing McGrory was a disappointment; selling Willie Buchan to Blackpool for the vast amount of £10,000 was sheer greed. Maley simply did not seem to like Buchan. It cannot really have been for anything that he had done on the field, for Buchan was a model professional. It seems like one of Maley's irrational whims, particularly when he saw that Buchan could be replaced by men like Malcolm MacDonald or John Divers. Besides, as ever obsessed with money (something that his accountancy background all these years ago had inculcated into him) the thought of £10,000, a record for a Scottish player to an English club simply could not be resisted. Buchan claims that he was summoned to 'The Bank' that Monday morning in November 1937 and told that the transfer had been arranged. He could of course have refused, but there seemed little point in arguing with Maley. Buchan had done his bit for Celtic, and England was a new opportunity. In any case, he preferred to play his football in a less dictatorial climate.

The knives might have been out for Maley after this unnecessary piece of asset stripping, and words like 'senile' and 'geriatric' were much used, but Maley confounded them all yet again. The team, without Buchan or McGrory, went on a run of 13 League games without being defeated, including a 3-0 thrashing of Rangers at Parkhead on New Year's Day, twice registering scores of 6-1, and on Christmas Day hammering Kilmarnock (of whom Jimmy McGrory had been manager for little more than a week) 8-0. McGrory was perturbed at Maley's aggressive and gloating attitude towards him, which was in so much contrast to the rousing reception that McGrory received from the Parkhead crowd as he took his seat in the stand.

Yet McGrory had his revenge. In early March, his determined Kilmarnock side (who would reach the final that season) put Celtic out of the Scottish Cup at Parkhead by winning 2-1. One could say that Kilmarnock were distinctly lucky and certainly get the benefit of a few dodgy refereeing decisions, but that was no excuse for Maley's behaviour to the man who still idolised him. Maley refused to shake McGrory's hand and when McGrory knocked on his door to say goodbye as the team bus was about to leave, Maley deliberately busied himself in paperwork to avoid speaking to him, not even looking him in the eye.

Maley was upset that the Scottish Cup had been lost, for he had desperately wanted to win it in the Golden Jubilee season, but there was still the League. Celtic were in pole position, but stumbled badly with two draws in March and a defeat at Falkirk in early April immediately after the Cup debacle.

But this was a talented team, and Maley rallied them so that they beat Motherwell 4-1, a great goal being scored by Joe Carruth whom Maley had brought in for the injured Delaney. It was the same day that Scotland (without any Celtic players) beat England 1-0 at Wembley, and then Celtic beat Dundee home and away, with Delaney back and on song on both occasions.

Love Street, Paisley was the scene for Celtic's clinching of the League Championship, although the collapse of Rangers meant that this year the closest challengers were Hearts whom Celtic had beaten both home and away. The game against St Mirren was won comfortably 3-1 on 23 April, and thus Maley celebrated his seventieth birthday on Monday 25 April with Celtic as League champions for the nineteenth time. He possibly would have preferred to have won the Cup, but he was aware that the League meant that Celtic were the best team in Scotland.

If anyone had the slightest doubt about that, it was dispelled on 14 May when Celtic lifted the Glasgow Charity Cup for the third year in a row beating Rangers 2-0 in a very one-sided final. Goals had been scored by Jimmy Delaney, now recognised as a truly remarkable player and a tall, young man called John Divers who had been lurking in the Reserves since 1932, but whom Maley had brought in as inside left. Once again, the Midas touch seemed to be in evidence, for Divers had had an outstanding season, and Maley had every right to be happy about his team who were champions of Scotland. Very soon, he would be able to claim that they were the best in Britain as well.

Summer 1938 saw a huge piece of British propaganda in Glasgow. It was called the Empire Exhibition, and Glaswegians loved it. It was a spectacular exhibition in Bellahouston Park with the Tait Tower and all sorts of other things. Perhaps the Glasgow Garden Festival of 1988 was the closest thing to approach it in modern times for its scale and magnificence. It was decided that the Empire Exhibition would include a football tournament as well for the best teams in Britain. All games would be played at Ibrox Stadium which was just across the road from Bellahouston Park, and four teams from

Scotland and four teams from England would be invited to play. Thus Celtic, Rangers, Aberdeen and Hearts were invited to join Brentford, Sunderland, Everton and Chelsea.

Maley was very interested in this tournament. Maley had often seen Celtic in British rather than Scottish terms, and from the earliest of times had been interested in friendlies against English and Irish teams. He would probably have loved to have seen a British League perhaps and certainly a British Cup, but was aware that there was not a great deal of enthusiasm for the travelling that would be involved. In addition, top English clubs were very happy to play Celtic and Rangers, but revealed a lot less interest in travelling to play Motherwell, Dundee or Aberdeen.

This tournament was therefore the closest that he was ever likely to get to his ideal of a British Cup. Anything involving a European dimension was obviously out of the question until air travel became a regular occurrence, so it would probably be fair to describe the Empire Exhibition Trophy of 1938 as the unofficial club Championship of the World, although it must be pointed out that the top four teams in England in 1938 according to the League table were Arsenal, Wolves, Preston and Charlton, none of whom competed for the Empire Exhibition Trophy.

Indeed, the tournament did not rate top billing in the English press, for they were far more concerned with their international game against Germany (where the tight-lipped English men, acting on craven orders from the Foreign Office, gave the Heil Hitler salute), the World Cup to be held in France later that summer and of course the arrival of Don Bradman and the Australians for another Ashes competition.

Glasgow, however, was all agog for the competition. Celtic's first game in the knock-out competition was against Sunderland on Wednesday 25 May. It was a good game, but ended 0-0 after extra time, and Delaney was injured. This necessitated the drafting in of Matt Lynch for the replay held the following night, but the youngster played well in a 3-1 victory in the traditional Scottish conditions of pouring rain. Sunderland had gone ahead, but a fine second-half performance against the tiring Englishmen saw Celtic through. The goals came from Divers (twice) and Crum, but the man of the match was Frank Murphy on the left wing, whose speed and crosses were a constant bother to Sunderland.

Surprisingly, Rangers went down to Everton at Ibrox, but Scottish teams won the other two ties, Aberdeen beating an ill-motivated and under-prepared Chelsea, and Hearts beating Brentford. Celtic thus played Hearts in the semi-final on Thursday 3 June, and, still missing the injured Delaney, had a struggle. Hearts fought hard and had it not been for Joe Kennaway and Willie Lyon in the centre of the defence they might well have won. As it was, Johnny Crum scored the only goal of the game with a tap-in from close range after some good build-up work by MacDonald and Divers. This was half way through the second half, and Celtic, with Lyon outstanding, were then professional enough to withstand the late Hearts pressure.

Thus, it was Everton in the final on 10 Thursday June. 'Fetch a polis man, Everton's getting murdered!' was the war cry that night, but it was far from that. Willie Cook who had left Celtic to join Everton in 1932 was there, and so too were famous men like Tommy Lawton and Joe Mercer. Lawton, however, was well policed by Lyon, once again the best man on the field, and Celtic's goal came in extra time when Divers released Crum. Crum scored, and then ran round the back of the goal to do an impromptu Highland Fling.

Maley may well have laughed at this exuberance, and when he looked down to the field from his seat in the stand to watch Willie Lyon receive the trophy from the Earl of Elgin, he may well have looked, as a newspaper man put it 'like the cat which had just got all the cream'. He normally disapproved of excessive showing of emotion, but this was a special occasion for him, as in less than a week's time, the club were about to have their Golden Jubilee dinner. In the circumstances, it was difficult to see such an event as being anything other than a prolonged encomium of the life and times of Willie Maley.

Indeed, it would have been the ideal time for the septuagenarian Maley to announce his retiral. Certainly many people were hoping so. The directors, who like everyone else were in awe of the great man, would have welcomed such a decision and without a shadow of a doubt quite a few of his players would have been glad to see the back of this remote and authoritarian figure who, for all his legendary and almost cult status in Scottish football, seemed to have lost the knack of talking to his men. Most communications were through the underlings Dodds or McMenemy. Any direct meeting with him was usually bad news.

Yet Maley's finger was still on the pulse. He knew absolutely everything that went on, for he retained his network of spies inside and outside the club, and his knowledge of human nature could not be surpassed. More than one player has said that they would always go to Parkhead on the same tram as Maley, but choose to sit on the other deck so as not to have to face him. They would then go on one more stop so that they did not have to walk the short distance to the ground in his company, such was the fear that he inspired. But Maley knew that they did this, and perhaps in his own quiet way, chuckled to himself. The best managers are not always the most popular, he mused to himself, and he knew (for they met regularly) that his opposite number at Rangers, Bill Struth, was similarly feared and hated. 'Oderint, dum metuant' – 'Let them hate, provided that they fear' might well have been his motto.

Maley himself may well have dabbled with the thought of retirement. There would have been a tremendous symmetry of the fifty years where he was in at the beginning and was now leaving at the end. He had almost finished his book *The Story of The Celtic* and he was ideally placed to have been the elder statesman on Celtic and indeed Scottish football, respected and admired. He might even, he mused, have become a director of Celtic Football Club, but sadly that invitation did not arrive.

Two things perhaps motivated him to keep going. One was the realisation that football and Celtic were his life. He had few other interests. He went to the cinema, as did most people in Glasgow in the 1930s, and being the man that he was, was usually offered the best seats in the house for nothing; he used to play the occasional game of golf, and he was very much involved in his church, being a frequent attender at mass and confession. Yet there would be nothing to fill his days in retirement. He was still in perfect health, as befitted a man who had been a sportsman and retained his fitness. He was certainly not ready to curl up and wait for death.

The other thing, of course, was that 1938 had been such a highly successful season. As manager of officially the best team in Scotland, unofficially the best team in Britain and therefore probably the best team in the world, this was no time to give up. He had tasted success. He enjoyed it, and he also remembered the bad days of not all that long ago when he had been plunged into the depths of melancholia and depression. Football, with all its vicissitudes and turns of fortune, remained his life, and Celtic, the team that he created almost on his own, still needed him, especially in view of the lack of obvious successor.

He had often considered this problem of who his successor might be. McMenemy was too nice, a great tactician but not by nature a hard man, like he himself was; Dodds likewise; McGrory too young and too recent; McStay a possibility, but perhaps not mentally attuned for the massive job of Celtic; Paddy Travers also a possibility, but had no great record of success. He was at Aberdeen for thirteen years, and yes, he had had a certain amount of success against Celtic at Pittodrie... but he still hadn't won anything for the Black and Golds. No, it had to be himself, he reckoned.

The Jubilee Dinner at the Grosvenor Hotel in Glasgow on Wednesday 16 June 1938, less than a week after the lifting of the Empire Exhibition Trophy was Maley at his theatrical best. Deliberately arriving slighty late so as to have everyone look at him as he made his way to the top table (but not so late as to miss anything), the august figure, still walking briskly, albeit with a slight stoop, took his place to cheers from the company. He smiled graciously at everyone before grace was said and the meal commenced.

His wayward genius Tommy McInally approached him at one point. With his impish grin still visible on his now sadly bloated and dissolute face, Tommy said 'Afore we go ony further, Boss, am I getting a bonus for coming here?' Maley, in spite of himself had to smile. Tommy, he thought, would never be short of a word or two.

He sat, listening benignly to the nice things said about him and the club by representatives of Rangers, Queen's Park and others. He then accepted a cheque from the chairman Mr Tom White for 2,500 guineas – a phenomenal amount in 1938. This was an honorarium of 50 guineas for every year he had spent with the club, and although no one could deny that it was just a small reward for what he had done for Celtic and the Irish community since he had been invited to come along with his brother Tom in December 1887, it was widely taken as a hint that it might be a good time to go. It was certainly a fine 'golden handshake' which would see him comfortably off for the rest of his life.

When he rose to reply, it was confidently expected that he would make the appropriate statement of retiral, but he failed to do so, pledging himself instead to continue to fight for the club and for what was best for them and the game. He spoke charmingly making the company laugh sycophantically with his light-hearted references to the past and the great players that it had been his privilege to work with. He talked with sadness about those who were 'no longer with us' (in that fine euphemism) singling out John Thomson, Barney Battles, Dan Doyle, Sunny Jim, Peter Scarff, his own brother Tom and Bertie Thomson who had died just a year previously.

He then praised Steve Callaghan, Celtic's chief scout who had been instrumental in landing so much talent in recent years, and listed the 'firsts' that Celtic had achieved. They were the first to visit the continent of Europe, the first to win two League games in one day, the first to build a double decker stand, the first to have a sports and athletics competition, the first to install telegraphic facilities for the press and then (jokingly) the first to have a strike, a riot and a number of fires!

His voice broke in emotion as he said:

No manager has been given a greater liberty than I. I am proud to say that I have never betrayed that trust. My love for Celtic has been a craze, there would have been no Celtic without the struggles of Brother Walfrid and John Glass. Since I took this job fifty years ago at their invitation, the club has been my very life and I really feel that without it my existence would be empty indeed...

He continued in this vein. Sometimes the tears were theatrical, other times they were perhaps genuine. He eventually sat down to a huge round of applause. Following many other votes of thanks, the formal part of the evening came to an end. Maley then spent the rest of the evening talking to all the ladies, whom he charmed, then all his friends and even to some of his players. It was nice to see Tommy McInally and Patsy Gallacher, and mighty men like Willie Loney, Alec McNair, Jimmy Quinn, Jimmy Hay and many others.

He was last off the premises, leaving his taxi waiting until a few recalcitrants had been ushered out of the bar. It was June, so it was not even dark at midnight and Maley remained an obvious and striking figure in the crepuscular atmosphere. The evening was a commemoration of the first glorious fifty years of Glasgow Celtic. It was also a commemoration of Willie Maley. Perhaps this was fitting, for the two concepts of Maley and Celtic had almost been indistinguishable.

Eleven

DEPARTURE

It would, of course, have been a lot better if Maley had retired that night in June 1938. He would have gone out at the top, and Celtic would have faced the future under fresher and (it would have to be said) better leadership. His last eighteen months at the Parkhead helm were unhappy ones, and for almost the first time in his life, he seemed to be suffering from prolonged ill health.

It was often said that Maley's obsession with money was an unhealthy one. He was personally very acquisitive (although the story that he kept all the takings from one particular turnstile for every home game lacks any solid evidence to back it up, however widely it was believed). He was equally unwilling to disburse the club's money. McGrory tells the story, for example, of how Maley managed to get off with paying him £8 per week, while the rest of the players earned £9. Frank Murphy tells a similar tale and a constant gripe from Celtic players generally was that they earned less than their counterparts at Ibrox.

This is not to say that Maley was an ungenerous man. He always claimed that he would help 'the lame dog over the stile' and, to a certain extent, it remained true that Celtic did give a certain amount to charitable causes under Maley's managership. The club had, however, come a long way from the laudable original intention of providing food for poor Catholic children, and it was Maley more than anyone else who provided the necessary good stewardship to make Celtic the phenomenal success on the football field that they became. Those who seek success on the field must realise that it must be paid for, one way or other. Maley perhaps realised that more that anyone.

There was something very appropriate, therefore, in the downfall of Maley, brought about as it was by two separate and apparently unrelated disputes about money. In one dispute, Maley was wanting more money for himself; in the other he was refusing, on behalf of the club, to pay to players what they felt they deserved.

The honorarium of 2,500 guineas given by the directors to Maley was generous and handsome. It was also meant to be seen as a 'golden handshake' and that Maley would take the hint and retire. This he refused to do – a colossal misjudgement as it turned out – and the directors now decided to be awkward by refusing to pay the income tax on this honorarium. This was hardly unreasonable, as Maley was still being paid by the club over and above this honorarium. Maley would have to pay the income tax himself. It was not a huge amount, and Maley still came out of the deal very well, but this perceived injustice lingered around him for the rest of his days at Celtic Park.

A feature of Maley's remarkable tenure of fifty years at the club hitherto was the almost total lack of friction between himself and the directors. They seemed to be at one on most things, sharing for example a fundamental desire to see the club do well on the field and also sharing a love of good football, as well as a desire to see the club on a permanently sound financial footing. No doubt there must have been a few spats, but they had all been kept 'in house' as it were, and no one was allowed to exploit things. Maley, of course, was given a free hand to run the footballing side of the business in the way that he wanted, and it often seemed to the outsider that his voice did not go unheard in other aspects of the organization as well.

But now this support had gone. There had been a few hints that not everything was as it should have been since 1932 when Maley's friend James Kelly died. The directors were in a quandary because they could hardly be seen to sack Maley in view of what he had achieved in 1938. Yet they cannot have believed that it was wise to leave a seventy year old in charge of such a huge organization. Possibly they should have tackled the problem head on in 1938 and brought in McStay or McGrory (both believed by the fans to be learning the trade at Alloa and Kilmarnock respectively) while giving Maley some secretarial or public relations post or even (the best solution) invited him to join them on the board.

Then another dispute arose with the players. One of the directors had led some players to understand that bonuses would be paid for the Empire Exhibition Trophy. There would be nothing unreasonable about that. The players, no less than the manager, had brought glory to the club and deserved some sort of financial reward for this.

Captain Willie Lyon was chosen to approach Maley to sort out this financial matter. Maley was never good at negotiating, seeing everything as a threat and a challenge to him. Willie Cringan, Charlie Napier and Tommy McInally had all been lost to the club for asking for more money. This time Maley, proving that old adage that stubbornness comes with old age, was even more determined not to be dictated to, and said 'no', but advised Lyon to take the matter up with the director who had made the ill-advised remark. That director would doubtless pay for it himself, Maley added.

Whether there was anything in that last remark to tie in with the income tax on the honorarium will never be known, but the result was that for 1938/39 season, Maley found himself isolated. The directors would not pay his income tax on the honorarium as he wanted, and Maley himself would not give the players the money they wanted. The result was that everybody suffered.

In a pay dispute, such are the tensions and the feelings involved, the form of a football team invariably suffers. It is the function of good management not to allow these things to happen. They should all be dealt with behind closed doors, and should be dealt with speedily so that the affair is strangled at birth. The issue of bonus payments for the Empire Exhibition Trophy was small and trivial (and the club could certainly have been magnanimous enough to pay out in order to keep the loyalty of so many fine players) and need not have escalated to the extent that it did.

Ironically, on the wider stage of world affairs, a much more important matter was being settled (temporarily) by yielding. Europe was once again on the brink of war. As the football season started in August 1938, Hitler was demanding part of Czechoslovakia, the Sudetenland where lived so many German speakers. Britain and France, weighing up all the possibilities, decided for the time being at least to appease Germany, on the grounds that a war (by all predictions far worse than the First World War had been) was too horrible to contemplate – for the moment. It could be swept under the carpet – and this was what happened at Munich in September 1938.

But when Mr Chamberlain came home with 'peace in our time' on 1 October 1938, Celtic were in the throes of inconsistency, scoring loads of goals, including a fine 6-2 win over Rangers on 10 September, but having lost to Aberdeen and Hamilton. Then the Glasgow Cup was won (a fine cartoon in a newspaper showed Willie Lyon putting the cup into a sack and saying 'Well, Hitler's not going to get that one!') on 15 October and hopes began to be expressed that this might yet be another good Celtic season, whatever the problems might be inside Parkhead and in the power centres of Europe.

But then Maley took ill, a strange undefined illness but possibly depression. Jimmy McMenemy the trainer and Joe Dodds the reserve-team coach were in charge of the teams, and at the same time injuries struck. Form plummeted, and in five games between Christmas Eve and 7 January, Celtic earned only one point. MacDonald, Paterson, Crum, Divers and Lyon all missed games at various times, and by the time that Maley returned (his illness would continue fitfully after that), any chance of the Scottish League was lost.

Maley was probably depressed for several reasons. In the first place he did genuinely worry about the prospect of another war, remembering so well the previous one in which he had lost men like Donnie McLeod and Peter Johnstone. He was also worn down by the unhappy atmosphere at Celtic Park, and the awareness that he was no longer completely in command of the situation. But most of all, he was simply too old for this kind of onerous job, and this was nature's way of telling him to give up.

But he would not go. He came back and saw Celtic on a Scottish Cup run which lasted as long as the quarter-final. According to the press 80,840 spectators (a somewhat suspiciously high figure for a Wednesday afternoon) saw Celtic beat Hearts in a replay at Parkhead in late February before Celtic went down to the strong going Motherwell at Fir Park in early March.

Injuries continued to dog the club and morale was not high. The worst injury came on 1 April 1939 when Jimmy Delaney, after a clash with Arbroath's Atilio Becci, broke his arm. No one knew it at the time, but it would put Delaney out of the game for a very long spell. Becci, in spite of his Italian descent and the fact that his parents were interned, fought in the British Army during the Second World War and, being a Celtic supporter, kept worrying about the great damage that he had done to his hero Jimmy Delaney.

The season thus ended in depression and in total contrast to the previous year. Maley may well have felt that he really should go now, but determination kept him there. In any case, things were definitely happening on the world stage, for Hitler had now annexed Czechoslovakia and was making unambiguous statements about Poland. It was no longer a question of whether there was going to be a war or not, it was a question of when.

A similar question, it might have been said, hung over Willie Maley and his tenure of the Parkhead chair. Yet it was not just a question of Maley obstinately clinging to power. The directors showed a similar lack of initiative by their craven refusal to do anything about it. A more imaginative board would have paid the income tax on Maley's honorarium and offered him a seat on the board, perhaps even allowing him to revert to his original role of match secretary while appointing McStay or McGrory or even McMenemy or Dodds to the managerial post.

There is no easy answer to why they did not do this. Perhaps they felt that they could not cope with Maley at board level for he would certainly be obstinate and truculent; perhaps they did not feel it right that someone who had for long been an employee, however distinguished and illustrious, could be seen suddenly to become an employer. Perhaps, there had been other things going on behind the scenes which meant that it was better to preserve the status quo.

There was certainly a certain disapproval of 'The Bank' restaurant, where illegal bookmakers and others of criminal tendencies met. The directors did not like the idea that players, particularly the young ones, met in such an environment. Yet they baulked at removing Maley. Perhaps, like everyone else in summer 1939, their minds were transfixed on things other than football.

Unlike in 1914, when everything happened suddenly (Celtic had been on tour in Europe which included Germany a couple of months before the invasion of Belgium), 1939 was full of foreboding with an ominous atmosphere. There was not, except in a very few cases, any great enthusiasm for military travels and adventures. Advice was given in the press about how to cook with less than the normal ingredients, air-raid shelters and gas masks were openly discussed and marriages were arranged in a hurry while there was still time. The defeat of Republican Spain in April 1939 had shown the world the power of Fascism. Too late were people beginning to realise that Spain's struggle and that of Czechoslovakia had indeed been Britain's as well.

A few youngsters might have relished the idea of wearing uniforms and learning how to use guns, but those who had been involved in the last war (it was only twenty years ago) and had seen the horrendous casualties were less keen. Maley kept on recalling Donnie McLeod and Peter Johnstone and shuddered at the thought that this might happen to Crum, Divers or Delaney.

Yet curiously enough, as often happens, national emergencies see a decline in depressive illnesses and Maley in some ways shook off his lethargy and listlessness of last season, and in spite of his seventy-one years, appeared regularly at Celtic Park during the summer of 1939, talking once again amiably to all who cared to talk to him, although avoiding contentious issues like retirement and directors.

The football season started as always in early August. Celtic opened their League campaign at Pittodrie and lost 3-1 to the Black and Golds. Yet Maley always enjoyed his trips to Aberdeen. To a very large extent Celtic had been unsuccessful in the Granite City since the First World War, but Aberdeen was a city that he liked. Devoid as it was of any sort of religious bigotry, Aberdeen had often seemed a place for Maley to live in his later years. Certainly, if one ignored the occasional mindless comment from young fish porters, he was always accepted there. Celtic were welcome, and so was he.

There was a tendency for Celtic to make a weekend of it when they went to Aberdeen. Maley enjoyed that and in particular relished the opportunity to have a walk through the streets on the Saturday morning without necessarily been recognised. It was nice to see a city which was by no means as obsessed with football as others were. Celtic had actually lost to Aberdeen at home as well before 1 September. Maley knew as he put on his radio that Friday morning that it had happened. The serious tones of the announcers, even before the 7 a.m. news, told him that. It was hardly a surprise in any case, although Maley, like many others, did nourish a small hope that Mussolini or His Holiness the Pope might just dissuade Hitler from doing what he seemed set to do.

How this would affect football, Maley did not know. It might even be closed down totally. Maley hoped not, for he recalled the First World War and the number of letters that soldiers had sent asking how Patsy Gallacher was playing. He smiled to himself at the recollection as his tram with its grim-faced passengers lurched its way along London Road that fine Friday morning.

War of course had not yet been declared and Great Britian would of course present an ultimatum. The games scheduled for Saturday 2

September would still go ahead, although what would happen after that was anybody's guess. Celtic had Clyde at Parkhead that day, and Maley received a telegram that day from the Scottish League confirming that the games would go ahead and that it was felt appropriate that the National Anthem should be played over the loudspeaker.

This presented Maley with a dilemma. He himself was of course a royalist sympathiser and would have been an unqualified supporter if only Roman Catholics were still not prevented by the archaic Bill of Rights from marrying into that institution. He could therefore to a certain extent understand why his supporters often booed when 'God Save The King' was played on big occasions. He had been somewhat embarrassed by this behaviour at the Empire Exhibition Trophy final of 1938.

Yet this was a national emergency, one which affected Catholics and Protestants alike, Irish and Scottish, Fenians and Orangemen. The National Anthem should be played, he felt, for the British Crown was the rallying point for the English-speaking world against Germany. He was afraid nonetheless that this occasion might be spoiled by those who wished to further the cause of the Irish Free State. Worse still, he felt that any such disturbance might be seized by Nazi propagandists as evidence that Great Britain was less than 100 per cent behind the idea of war.

He need not have worried. The mood was far too sombre. The 20,000 who arrived stood mainly in silence, apart from an insignificant minority. The game proceeded and Celtic won 1-0, thanks to a goal from John Divers. As the game finished, a great cheer and clapping broke out around the ground, not in appreciation of a great game of football (it hadn't been) but due to the realization that this might be the last game of football for some time at Celtic Park or any other ground.

War was of course declared the following day, and very soon emergency regulations had their effect on football. In what was clearly a knee-jerk hysterical reaction, football, cinemas and theatres were all to be closed down indefinitely, such was the fear of air-raids brought home by the German bombing of Guernica in Spain in 1937.

After a few protests and a sensible rethink, such measures were deemed too draconian, and football was begun again although on a limited basis. The Scottish League and Cup were suspended and attendances were severely restricted. Full-time football was not allowed, and players' wages were set at £2 so that, as in the First World War, they would have to work at something else as well.

For a while Maley was happy with this, for the Glasgow Cup and Charity Cup would continue and the Scottish League would be replaced by a Western Regional Division. In addition, the restriction of £2 per week meant that he would never again be dictated to by players wanting more money. But there was another factor which pleased him, the more that he thought of it.

His age was no longer a problem. He remembered the last war when seventy and even eighty-year-olds were given jobs, sometimes in vital industries, such had been the shortage of manpower. The same was going to have to happen again, for there would be no messing about with conscription this time. It would be introduced very soon. No one could then really point accusingly to Maley at the age of seventy-one for running a football team. It would not even be unusual.

Besides, weren't the seasons during the First World War among the best in Celtic's history? Did Sunny Jim and Patsy Gallacher not provide the necessary relief for soldiers on leave or those who worked in the munitions industry? Yes, there would be restrictions, but they would be the same restrictions as affected other teams. Celtic and Maley could indeed come out of this war smelling of roses.

If Maley did feel like this, it was a dreadful piece of self delusion. Nothing could hide the fact that the team were playing dreadfully, the players had no confidence in him and that in any case he was now even more cantankerous and difficult than ever. By Christmas 1939, Celtic had won only two games in the Western Division and were consequently floundering in the lower reaches – something that even in the very unreal situation of wartime was totally unacceptable for a Celtic team.

The war was now openly referred to as the 'phoney war'. Little seemed to be happening on the Western Front. Poland had of course been subjugated and divided up between the Germany and Russia without Britain or France firing a single shot in its defence. There had been some naval action in the South Atlantic involving the Admiral Graf Spee. Apart from that important but minor success, there did not seem to be very much involving the British Army.

On the home front, there was much activity of soldiers in uniform, men being recruited, barrage balloons in evidence, hysterical appeals about the black out to diminish the effect of air raids and the censorship. The first Christmas of the war was a bad one with a lot of snow, and the joke was that although the censors tried to hide it, people couldn't help noticing!

Celtic meanwhile were showing no signs of any improvement. It is superficial to say that as this was a war situation, Celtic's poor form did not matter. It certainly did to their still vast support. It was probably after the game at Parkhead on 30 December that the directors decided that strong action was now called for. The game was against Motherwell and ended up in a 2-2 draw. It had been not a bad game with Celtic scoring good goals through Carruth and Divers, but the play of the home team (still without the badly injured Jimmy Delaney) had caused the fans some distress and not for the first time that season, boos, catcalls and the slow handclap had been heard.

Enough was enough, Maley was summoned into the directors' room and told that his services were no longer required. How he reacted to this news is not recorded, but it can be assumed that the directors were embarrassed but sadly convinced that the deed had to be done. People who didn't 'like the way that it was done' are less than fair to the board. In truth, there is no easy way to sack a man, especially in this case where they had bent over backwards to be nice to him and offered him the chance eighteen months previously to offer his resignation or to retire gracefully.

The news was made public on New Year's Day and he would depart from the club he loved a month later on 1 February 1940. At the end of the season he would write:

Personally I can never forget the 1939/40 season. It has been to me the end of my football career and has robbed me of the very tang of life. Football has been my thoughts morning, noon and night for all the fifty-two years I have been in it, and it has been hard to drop out of my regular ways.

The news was presented to the Celtic fans at a time when they had other things on their mind, otherwise it might have been interesting to see what the reaction would have been. The weather continued to be very bad, although superhuman efforts were made to ensure that football continued for security reasons so that the Nazis would not know how bad the weather was in Scotland! There is the true story which was only made public after the war about how Rex Kingsley did a commentary on a game he did not see. This was in fog-bound Edinburgh. The game had to go on, and the BBC had to imply that the conditions were good. Two boys stood behind each goal and ran to the commentator's seat in the stand with a note of who scored a goal while Kingsley made everything else up!

This was on New Year's Day 1940 and the *Glasgow Herald* of that day clearly does not know the news about Maley's demission. It talks at length about the Old Firm tussle that day due to be played at Ibrox where wartime regulations will provide a bigger crowd than would have been allowed at Parkhead, but does not mention Maley's position at all. However, the 2 January 1940 edition says that before the game, (an honourable 1–1 draw) Maley had told everyone that he was going to retire 'in the next few weeks'. The writer of the *Glasgow Herald* then mentions a few of his achievements and states hyperbolically that 'Maley's story is really the story of Scottish football'.

In the next few days, Maley's departure is not mentioned, and by the middle of February with Jimmy McStay in place, a new and disastrous age of Celtic history was about to begin. We can but guess at how Maley reacted to all this. The popular belief was that he sulked and secretly rejoiced at the lack of Celtic success on the field, but as to how true this is, we do not know. Certainly it would be a good ten years before he ever appeared at Celtic Park again.

But Maley had one big moment on 28 February 1940 when he was introduced to the King and Queen in his capacity as sports adviser to the War Relief Fund of the City of Glasgow. Their majesties met Maley at the Glasgow Green air-raid patrol station. Maley, of course, cannot resist boasting about all this in an article to the *Evening Times* a few days later and he includes such sycophantic drivel as:

> As I watched the royal couple, I was struck by the genuine pleasure it seemed to give them to those of their subjects privileged to shake hands with them. It was not just a case of talk and walk on. The King especially seemed to wish to convey to everyone he spoke to the idea that he or she was as important as anyone present.

Maley particularly impressed the Queen because they had a common acquintance in Tom Hanick who was the Provost of Forfar. She spoke in a kind, soft voice apparently and made everyone feel at home.

No doubt this occasion, for a while, took the edge off the pain at losing the Celtic job. It was also true that Maley received an invitation to attend a game at Ibrox any time he wished. He accepted this invitation on many occasions, was happy to be seen in the directors' box, talking sagely to all his contacts from Rangers and other clubs about football, which was increasingly becoming an irrelevance to the desperate struggle that was ensuing about the future of western civilization.

Yet it is hard to believe the popular myth that Maley sat at Ibrox, fuming and fulminating at those who ran Celtic, cheering every Rangers goal (Rangers won virtually everything during the war years) and smirking 'I told you so' at every Celtic reverse. It was he who said 'Once a Celt, always a Celt', and it is extremely hard to believe that this did not apply to himself. Moreover, would he have been happy at the anti-Catholic hate hurled from all sides by people who clearly did not appreciate that in a war being fought to preserve virtues of tolerance and decency, some sort of acceptance had to be extended to those of a different faith?

It is probably true that the war made everyone forget about Maley. He simply was not anything like the main topic of conversation, even when Scottish football was being discussed. People were far too involved in the replacement of Chamberlain by Churchill, the fall of France, the Battle of Britain and the Blitz to get too involved in Willie Maley. By the time that the tide turned after El Alamein, Anzio and D-Day and people began to get interested in more leisurely pursuits like football, Maley was even further away from the scene, and men would return from the front in 1945 and 1946 wondering if he was still alive.

He was of course still alive, and would remain so until 1958.

Twelve

RETIREMENT
AND DEATH

Little is known of Maley's subsequent life, which was very low profile indeed. He might have chosen to write his memoirs had he not
already done so in the *Weekly News* in 1936 and his *The Story of The
Celtic* which appeared in 1939. He was possibly too old to become a
journalist, but there would have been nothing to stop him writing a
weekly column for one of the many football newspapers and jour-
nals in circulation in the late 1940s. He did occasionally make a contribution, but there was nothing regular.

   Such had been the intensity of his feud with the Celtic directorate
since January 1940 that he was not seen back at Celtic Park until 10
August 1953 when Celtic played a Bohemians Select side for the 'Willie
Maley Testimonial Fund' in aid of the Grampian sanatorium in
Kingussie. He was enthusiastically greeted back to the ground that he
loved and, now aged eighty-five, walked to the centre of the field with
his former players Joe Dodds, Jimmy McMenemy and Willie Loney to
the prolonged applause of the fans who still loved him. Thereafter, peace
having been made, he was back at Parkhead as often as his declining
health would permit. He loved the club and the ground so much.

He would rejoice in the successes of the club under his great goalscorer Jimmy McGrory with whom he also had fallen out in 1938 but had since built bridges. The League and Cup double were won by Celtic in 1954 (for the first time since Maley's great team of 1914) and Maley was delighted for the club to whom the testimonial game in 1953 had reconciled him. In fact, there had been a rapprochement before that, for Bob Kelly who was now in charge of the club was keen to bridge the gap between the club and his father's old friend. Patsy Gallacher's death and funeral in June 1953 had provided that opportunity.

Maley had been distraught at the death of his greatest ever player. Tommy Gallacher (Patsy's son) had been summoned home from South Africa as his father's condition deteriorated. Tommy played for Dundee and was on a close season tour. Tommy arrived at his father's house and as he turned the key in the door, was aware of someone sobbing. This was Willie Maley, distressed at the suffering of his beloved Patsy.

It was Maley's sad duty to attend funerals galore throughout the 1950s, including those of Joe Cassidy, Patsy Gallacher, Willie Loney, Tommy McInally and many others. His friend Jim Black of Forfar Athletic (to whom he used to confide all his secrets and compare notes on the running of a small and a large club – they were remarkably similar, they decided!) died in 1951, and in 1956 his old rival Bill Struth of Rangers passed away. Struth and Maley had never been close friends in the way that William Wilton and he had been, but they were associates and respected each other, both of them aware that Celtic needed Rangers and vice versa, and neither of them keen to minimise differences for fear of killing the goose that laid the golden egg.

On Wednesday 2 April 1958, in the middle of Holy Week, Willie Maley died in a nursing home at 32, Mansion House Road, Glasgow at 8.30 a.m. The death certificate says that his normal address was 17, Hyndland Avenue where he had lived since the 1920s and that he was Company Managing Director (of The Bank Restaurant Ltd). He was aged eighty-nine and died of arteriosclerosis and senility. The death was registered by his son Charles Maley.

Cyril Horne in the *Glasgow Herald* the following day says:

Celtic FC was his life. Many of the players who served under him had mixed feelings about the discipline Mr Maley exerted, but I do not know one who at the end of his career did not concede that he had been correct. He was not merely, however, a man of stern discipline and distinctive judgement in football matters. There was no greater sentimentalist, no kinder man. The good deeds that he did were known only to a few outwith the recipients and then almost always because they in their appreciation referred to them in later years. It is unlikely that Celtic Football Club will ever have a greater Celt.

His funeral was held on Good Friday morning (4 April – a day of snowstorms and cold weather) in St Peter's Church, Hyndland and he was later buried 'fortified by the Holy Rites' in Cathcart Cemetery. The crowd of mourners was huge and Cyril Horne amused himself by picking a Scotland team from among the mourners. He came up with Harkness (Hearts); Campbell (Queen's Park) and Hilley (Celtic); Wilson (Celtic), Meiklejohn (Rangers) and Geatons (Celtic); Connolly (Celtic), McMenemy (Celtic), McGrory (Celtic), McPhail (Rangers) and McLean (Celtic).

The following day, a minute's silence was observed and black arm bands worn, both at Pittodrie where Celtic went on to beat Aberdeen 1-0 and at Parkhead where Clyde beat Motherwell 3-2 in the Scottish Cup semi-final. For days afterwards, the press was full of tributes to the great man. Everyone seemed to be agreed on one thing, that Celtic would never have been anything without him. He was indeed the man who put the 'tick' in Celtic.

Any analysis of his 'contribution to Celtic' is almost a contradiction. For so many years he was Celtic. Certainly there would have been a Celtic without him, but it is hard to imagine such an outfit, without Maley, having anything like the success that they had with him. Had he gone to Sheffield United or Manchester City in the 1890s when opportunities had presented themselves, the Celtic team might well have fallen away to mediocrity, and the support, without the necessary success to stimulate them, might have turned to other activities, sporting or otherwise.

Therefore Rangers would not have risen to such heights either. Therefore the game in Scotland would not have been so popular and so much of Scottish cultural history of the twentieth century would have been lost. The integration of the Irish into Scotland over the last 150 years has not been easy. Yet it has been easier than it might have been when one considers the hideous problems that have faced ethnic minorities in other countries. Perhaps it has been a good thing that the ethnic minority have had their football team to focus on, that men like Maley did act as role models for their behaviour rather than wilder political animals who might well have led them astray. Perhaps the single-minded determination of Willie Maley and his obsessive focus on sport and football in particular was the one key factor which integrated the Irish.

He was a politician as well. He never took any great part in party politics, although he certainly held his opinions on everything, but he was fascinated by the politics of Scottish football. He always had his allies, notably Jimmy Philip of Aberdeen and Jimmy Black of Forfar, and usually Willie Struth and other members of the Rangers establishment. For such a high profile person, 'The Big Fella' or 'The Boss' as he was known as by his players and others, seemed to have had very few enemies.

No one ever seemed to bear any lasting animosity towards him. In his capacity as manager of Celtic Football Club, he had to be strict to the players and parsimonious with the purse strings, sometimes excessively so, with occasional disastrous results for the club. Players whom he did not like tended to be very suspicious of him, but there were very few who did not make things up to him once he left the club. Maley himself says that:

I have known of only one Celtic player who failed to retain his love for the club which had made him, and was not always glad to heart to hear of its success and to come back to the old spot and renew his acquaintance with players and officials.

Comparisons between himself and Jock Stein, Celtic's other great manager may be considered otiose, for they lived in different times and in different circumstances. Yet there are similarities – the main one being that they were both great managers of Celtic Football Club! Another one was the sheer bulk and presence of both men – something that is very necessary in arguments!

Maley had his favourites. Like Jock Stein, he loved goalscorers and was excellent at spotting and encouraging them – Sandy McMahon, Jimmy Quinn, Jimmy McColl, Joe Cassidy and, of course, Jimmy McGrory. It was often said about Jock Stein that he did not understand goalkeepers. This was not true of Maley, who nurtured Davie Adams, Charlie Shaw, John Thomson and Joe Kennaway. Midfielders abounded under Maley – Sunny Jim, Jimmy Hay, Peter Wilson, Alex Thomson and defenders like Willie Loney, the McStay brothers and Willie Lyon were as good as one could get. And then his two great dribblers and entertainers – Patsy Gallacher and Tommy McInally – what can be said about them?

He did have the ability to inspire loyalty. One thinks of Alec McNair and Jimmy McMenemy who stayed with him for twenty years in the case of McNair and seventeen in the case of McMenemy. McNair in particular, had no great emotional tie with Celtic before he met Maley (being from Stenhousemuir), but he found the chemistry to work for him and earn names like 'The Icicle' for his calm, defensive work. McMenemy was also a great help to Maley when he returned as trainer in the late 1930s.

Maley's faults lay in his occasional stubbornness (as happens with all dictators when few people challenge them) and his propensity to lapse into melancholic, self-pitying depression. Usually it was some event that brought this on – often the untimely death of a player like Peter Johnstone, Sunny Jim, John Thomson or Peter Scarff – or in the case of 1938 an argument with directors, and when this happened the team always suffered. Such was the hold that he had over them. This was why he was called Mr Celtic.

Without Maley, there would today be no Celtic. How nice it is that one of the present supporters songs seems to capture that:

Willie Maley was his name
He brought some great names to the game
When he was boss at Celtic Park,
Taught them how to play football
Made them greatest of them all
Gallacher and Quinn have made their mark

Oh, they gave us Jimmy McGrory and Paul McStay
Johnstone, Tully, Murdoch, Auld and Hay,
And most of football's greats have passed through Parkhead's gates
To play the game in the Glasgow Celtic way.

It is a fine appreciation of a man who has now been dead for nearly fifty years, but is still remembered as the man who made Celtic what they are today. Without Maley and his continuing legacy, there would have been no Jock Stein, no Billy McNeill, no European Cup and no Henrik Larsson. He was indeed the man who put the 'tick' in Celtic:

Whaur wid the Celtic be
Withoot Wullie Malee?
He's always there to split and share
The passions o' us a'
He's the man who tells them a'
The best wey to play the ba'
Yes, he's the man wha'pits the tick in Celtic!

Index

Printed in Great Britain
by Amazon

13772317R00142